Kajsa

Augusta's Granddaughter

Kajsa had lost her adoptive mother at an early age and was at the mercy of the men who should have protected her.

Judit Martin

AUTHOR'S NOTES

Well into the first years of the twentieth century Swedes spoke in a manner which sounds awkward to to the ears of English speakers. Instead of addressing each other in the second person ("Are you tired, Carl?" or "It's time for you to get up, Carl,") they used the third person ("Is Carl [or he] tired?" or "It's time for Carl [or him] to get up,") when speaking directly to each other. In the middle of the century the use of the Swedish equivalent of 'you' in its more formal plural form began to take over when one spoke with strangers and acquaintances, while 'you' in its more informal singular form was reserved for family and friends. Finally, by the end of the 1960s, there was a campaign to encourage people to use the informal singular 'you' with everyone. For the sake of authenticity and atmosphere, I have written as people spoke at the time in which the story takes place.

A note on satchels: Poor people carried such things as clothes, rations, goods to sell, supplies, and sometimes even small children, in satchels, hung over the shoulder or slung across the back.

She also carried her own newborn child, Signe, in the same satchel after she gave birth to her. Kajsa also carried her things in a satchel when she left her adopted home. She carried her things in her satchel when she left her job as a maid and went to Stockholm after becoming pregnant.

Her son, Bror, also carried things his mother gave him in a satchel. Poor people didn't have suitcases or trunks in those days.

Many thanks to: Hanna Martin, Bill Mitchell, and Don Thomas for reading the text and making helpful suggestions.
Cover text by: Maja Ridell
Cover design by: M. A. Cook Design
Front cover photo by: Judit Martin
Back cover author photo by: Barbara Brady Conn
Proof readers/editors: Deb Schense, Mary Sharp, and David Wright.

Also by Judit Martin is "Augusta's Daughter," the prequel to "Kajsa."

ISBN-13: 978-1572161184 ISBN: 1572161183
Library of Congress Control Number: 2016961860
©2017 Judit Martin   Printed in the USA

To CS

Tack för hjälpen!

ABOUT THE AUTHOR

Judit Martin, whose ancestors were early English and Scottish immigrants, grew up in Franklin, Michigan. After high school in nearby Birmingham, she attended Beloit College in Beloit, Wisconsin, and in 1961 graduated from Washington State University in Pullman, Washington, with a degree in English and a teaching certificate. She taught for several years before setting out to fulfill her childhood dream of spending two years travelling in Europe. Captivated by the experience, she extended her stay with a job teaching English in a Turkish girls' school in Izmir, Turkey, followed by a job at the American School in London. When she finally came to Sweden in 1969 she fell in love with the countryside, with its remnants of the old peasant culture, and settled there.

As a single mother, she raised her two Swedish-born daughters out in the country near the mining village of Zinkgruvan, where she still lives in her slightly primitive old house. For many years she worked as a weather observer for the Swedish weather bureau, going outside every three hours, day and night, to observe and report the weather, a job which left her much free time in which to write. She has had several short stories published in Scottish literary magazines and two documentary books published in Swedish. "Augusta's Daughter" is her first published novel. "Although I have dual citizenship," Judit says, "after over forty years in Sweden, I don't feel like an American, nor am I a Swede. I am just myself, which suits me perfectly."

OTHER TITLES BY JUDIT MARTIN:

"Augusta's Daughter" (first novel in this series)
"Swedish Portraits" (five short stories)
"The Bridge" (a short story)
"Every Three Hours" (documentary)
"Var Tredje Timme" (documentary in Swedish)
"Minnen från vår barndoms Zinkgruvan" (documentary in Swedish)

CONTENTS

INTRODUCTION

Kajsa's story is aimed primarily toward Swedish Americans, many of whom know only that their ancestors emigrated to "the land in the west" because they were either poor, with no chance of rising above their poverty, or oppressed, or seeking religious freedom and breathing space from the strict centuries-old social codes which ruled their lives. These people wanted the freedom to live their lives as they saw fit, without the state, the church, or their neighbors interfering. But "poverty," "oppression," "religious freedom," and "social codes" are simply words we use to describe something without actually describing it, assuming that we all know what these words entail. And if asked to define them, we would define them according to our own American background and experience and values. But to a Swedish peasant 150 years ago, those words had their own Swedish meanings.

Although Kajsa is a figment of my imagination, her story could very well be true. Her life, as I have portrayed it, was similar to that of thousands of peasant women of that time. To our modern-day eyes, some of the events in her life can seem rather extreme and beyond belief, not to mention grim, but in each case there is documented evidence that such things were actually quite common. Life was not just as we see it portrayed in paintings of peasants in folk costumes dancing around a Midsummer pole or making hay. There was also a back side to those pictures called everyday life. This is Kajsa's everyday life in the latter half of the 1800s.

NOTE:

Pronunciation of Kajsa: "kaj" rhymes with "fly"

Kajsa's Ancestry

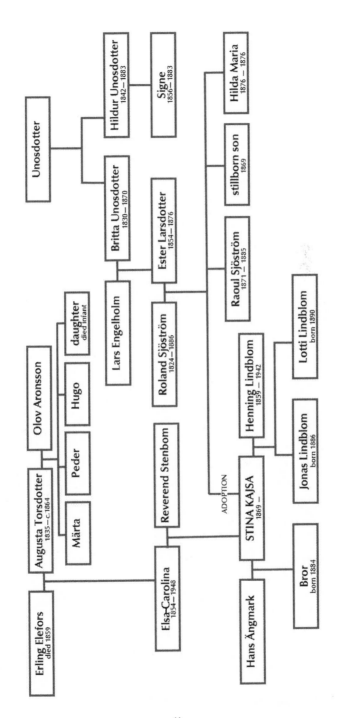

CARRIE

America, Christmas 1949

It was with a sigh of relief that I closed the door to my classroom after having wished the last group of pupils a Merry Christmas. I had only been teaching for a year and a half and already I was asking myself if that was all there was to life. Day in and day out. Year after year. A myriad of young faces passing before me. When school finished in June, Ralph and I were going to get married, and from there onward my future was laid out like a long straight road before me: two more years of teaching, then at home with two children until they were grown, whereupon I would return to teaching for the duration. Ralph was well on his way to becoming a college professor and we had plans of living in the stimulating environment of a small college town. Even though the prospect of such a life left me feeling a little empty, it was better than any of the other alternatives I could imagine. And perhaps it could have worked, had I not spent the summer after graduation in Sweden with my great grandmother Elsa-Carolina. But those few months irrevocably changed my life. Sweden was the first place I had ever felt at home. I returned to America a different person, only to find that there was no one with whom I could share my experience, no one who could even begin to understand how I felt. Not even Ralph. In the months that followed I did my best to acclimate myself to the life which lay ahead of me, but I never quite succeeded. I felt like a stranger in a strange land. I longed for something else, but I didn't know what. For the moment, Christmas vacation was sufficient.

When I got home I kicked off my snowy boots, dumped my books and ungraded papers onto the kitchen table, and began to sort through the pile of Christmas cards that had come with the day's mail. Hidden amongst them was one with a foreign stamp. Without even looking at it I knew it was from Katja, my Swedish half-cousin several times removed. We had been corresponding since my return to America and I had quickly understood that we shared more than just our joint great grandmother Elsa-Carolina. Several years before we had known of each other's existence, Katja had spent a year in the States studying English and thus understood my feelings about both countries. Having become my close friend and confidant during my Swedish summer, she alone knew of my growing misgivings about the future looming before me.

Hurriedly I looked through the other cards, saving hers for last.

1

Hopefully it included a letter. Before opening it, I made myself a cup of tea and started a fire in the fireplace, then sat down with my stockinged feet propped up on the fender. Finally, I slipped the tip of Elsa-Carolina's letter opener under the flap of the envelope and slit it open in a single stroke. When I pulled out the card I realized my hands were shaking. A little gnome in a red cap pulling a sled stared up at me from under the words *GOD JUL.*[1] To my disappointment, there was no letter, just a short message written on the card itself. I began to read it half-heartedly.

My Dear Cousin Carrie,

Perhaps it is time to act on that feeling that you belong here in Sweden rather than in middle class America. There is a job teaching English waiting here for you next autumn, if you want it. But you must decide by the first of March. I do hope you will cease your longing and come home to us.

Love,

Cousin Katja
P.S. Here's to a Happy New Life!

I could hardly believe what I had just read. I closed the card and stuck it back in its envelope, as if it were an ordinary Christmas card like all the others. I must have read it wrong. I finished my tea as if nothing had happened. Then, taking a deep breath, I picked up the envelope again. My hands shook even more than before as I pulled out the card and opened it. The message was as I had read it the first time.

Without even stopping to consider Ralph, I picked up the phone and wired Katja: "I'll take it! Coming in June." All of a sudden I felt free, like a bird that has just learned to fly. That simple message, enclosed in an innocent-looking envelope, completely changed the course of my life.

As soon as school was out in June I packed the things I wanted to keep in a large steamer trunk to take with me, got rid of the rest, and gave up my rented house. Ralph could not understand why I was breaking

---

1. Merry Christmas.

our engagement, nor could I explain it to him. My parents just shook their heads. How could I throw Ralph and my whole future to the wind? Clearly I was being thoughtless and irresponsible. They all assumed this was a last fling, that I would be back in a year and my life would proceed according to plan. Even then I knew they were wrong.

I arrived in Sweden in the middle of June and moved into Katja's spare bedroom for the time being. My summer project was to learn Swedish as quickly as possible. It was difficult for Katja and me to speak Swedish together, because we had too much to talk about that went far beyond my limited vocabulary and grammar. But her grandmother, Kajsa, proved to be the perfect teacher. Her English was limited, forcing me to learn by association, in the same way that a small child learns its mother tongue. Consequently, my summer days were spent helping Kajsa with her many daily tasks while we carried on a simple conversation which grew more and more complex as time passed. To my surprise, I found that she was almost a carbon copy of her mother, my great grandmother Elsa-Carolina, whom she had never met until they were both old women.

One sunny August day when we were sitting outside drinking our *elva kaffe*,[2] Kajsa suddenly put her hand on my arm, causing me to look at her questioningly.

"Katja tell me you write what my mother say about her life. That is so?"

I nodded.

"If I tell you mine and my family's life, you could write it down, too?" she asked hesitantly. "For my one grandchild Katja."

"Oh, yes, of course!" I told her, immediately excited by the thought. "And she can pass it down to her children and grandchildren."

"No, Katja wants no children."

"But maybe she will change her mind."

"You do not know Katja if you think that," she concluded, shaking her finger. "No, just for Katja. She is much interested in the old life. When she's a small child she ask me about my growing up. I always say I will tell her when she is older, but now she is older but too busy to

_____

2. Eleven o'clock coffee, a tradition in Sweden.

hear. But me and Katja we are close friends and she wants to know my life. There was much happening to me under the time I was growing up that I do not tell to my mother when she come here because it would make her sad. But it is part of me and Katja should know."

And thus it was that, throughout her remaining years, Kajsa filled me with random stories about the people and events that had filled her long and rich life, while I copied down her words in Swedish. As we progressed, she read through what I had written, red pencil in hand, to see that I had gotten both facts and grammar right. It wasn't until many years later, after I had turned Elsa-Carolina's story into a book, that I realized that Kajsa's story also needed to reach people beyond her immediate family, for it, too, is a story that belongs to others with a Swedish immigrant background. Looking back at it through the eyes of time, like Elsa-Carolina's story, parts of it seem brutal, almost unbelievable. But life was hard, and often unjust, in those days. And it was especially so for those who were poor. And for women.

ESTER

Björkdalen Gård,[3] Sweden, September 1948
Although the days were still warm, the birch leaves had begun to surrender to the chilly nights, their summer green giving way to autumn's golden yellow. As always, the wind played with them, but now the slightest twist sent them spinning to a certain death on the ground below. Kajsa watched through the kitchen window, while rocking slowly back and forth in the same rocking chair in which she had been rocked as a baby. The room was quiet, save for the Mora clock[4] standing in the corner, its ticking faithfully measuring the passing of the hours, the days, the years. Now and then she stopped rocking long enough to take a sip from the coffee cup standing on the little round table beside her chair. After the death of her husband Henning, she had begun taking her *elva kaffe* by the window to avoid being faced with his empty chair on the opposite side of the kitchen table. With time it had become a habit. She had felt less lonely gazing out at the fields and forest, following the changing seasons—until the past summer, when people she had never known existed entered her kitchen and her life. Suddenly, events, that neither she nor Henning had ever been able to understand, fell into place. How she wished he could have been there to finally see how it all fit together. During those few short summer months, surrounded by so much and so many, Kajsa's loneliness had disappeared. For the first time in her almost eighty years, she felt whole. Then came the end of summer, leaving her kitchen with nothing but the ghosts of those recent months and an even greater loneliness than before.

Björkdalen, Spring 1869
At last the long winter gave way to spring. Almost overnight wildflowers along the wagon roads and edges of fields pushed to the surface, drawn by the warmth of the sun, and burst into bloom. On the trees above them buds swelled, then unrolled their wrinkled leaves like butterflies emerging from cocoons. Everyone gave thanks. And tried to forget. But, although the famine of 1868–69 had finally released its death grip on the countryside, it lived on as a nightmare in the memory of those

---

3. Farm.

4. A traditional type of grandfather clock made in the town of Mora.

5

impoverished peasants who had survived it. For the thousands who had not survived, the process of dying had been the long, drawn-out torture of slow starvation, while others looked on helplessly. No family had escaped the touch of death's cold, indifferent fingers. It had been the worst famine in Sweden's history; worse even than the catastrophic famine of 1783–84.

Death had also paid a call at Björkdalen Gård, but by now his visit was all but forgotten. At least by Ester Larsdotter. She had other things to think about. Her gaze followed the patches of sunlight flickering across the well-worn wooden floor as they chased the shadows of the gently twisting birch leaves beyond the open window. Just before reaching the chair where she sat nursing the child they stopped, as if forbidden to go further. She watched them, as a cat watches sunbeams, daring them to touch her toes. It was a game with which she had entertained herself as a child. But she was no longer a child; she was a mother with a child to care for. Reluctantly she gave in, ashamed of her childishness and, stretching out her legs, let the sun crawl up her body until it brushed the tiny hand lying on her naked breast. Her eyes closed and she lost herself in the rhythm of the child's mouth sucking milk from her body into its own. It seemed like a miracle; that spring had actually come, that she was alive, and that she had a baby. Half a year ago she would never have believed it possible.

Roland Sjöström and his young wife Ester Larsdotter had fared better during the famine than the numerous landless peasants scattered throughout the countryside. As the fifth generation of Sjöströms to own Björkdalen Gård, Roland had absorbed the art of farming by osmosis as he was growing up. From his grandfather he had learned to read the signs of coming weather conditions by observing the local plants and animals, a knowledge that had served to warn him that hard times were on the way. Thus he had taken precautions to insure that they had more than enough flour, potatoes, lingonberries,[5] salted herring, cheese, and smoked sausages locked away in the storage buildings, as well as plenty of hay, straw, and dried leaves for the livestock in the barn. As so often happened, the parish's emergency supplies had already been depleted by the middle of the winter. However, it was well-known that the beggars who knocked on Sjöström's door never came away with empty sacks, even if they received nothing more than

---

5. Similar to cranberries, plentiful in the forest and easily stored for winter.

dried bread[6] and a bit of cheese, for he found it necessary to uphold the respect of the community. But the winter of 1868–69 proved to be unusually long and hard. Eventually, when it became obvious that spring was not on its way, Sjöström realized that, if he weren't careful, his household was going to pay for his generosity. At all costs, he must keep his small supply of seed potatoes and grain intact. Without them he would have nothing to plant for the coming year.

It was during this merciless winter that Ester gave birth to Sjöström's son. Her greatest fear had not been that of giving birth; it was the fear that she would be delivered of a girl-child. Sjöström wanted an heir. A girl-child was unacceptable. The previous year his first wife had died in childbed after having given birth to a premature boy-child. Thus it was that he had set his hopes on his neighbor's daughter Ester.

Although the tradition of arranged marriages had begun to die out amongst the peasants, it still thrived amongst the landowning farmers. Ester had not wanted to marry Roland Sjöström. Even though it was common for older men to take young wives still in their child-bearing years, to her he was an unattractive old widower more than twice her age, with thinning hair and a fat belly. But as long as she was unmarried, it was her father who made all the decisions concerning her life. Women did not have the intelligence to think for themselves. Quite simply, a man was a woman's head.

Ester's father, Lars Engelholm, owned Lunna Gård, the farm adjoining Sjöströms, as Björkdalen was referred to locally. As neighbors, her father and Sjöström got along without conflicts. The only thorn in their neighborliness was a bit of land lying between them. It belonged to Björkdalen Gård, but could only be accessed from Lunna Gård. For all practical purposes, it was useless to Roland Sjöström, even though the soil was rich. For years Engelholm had hankered after it, but Sjöström had refused to sell it. Then came the autumn when the two men shared sleeping quarters at the Michelsmäss market in September.[7] At the end of the first day they celebrated their successful business ventures by uncorking a bottle of *brännvin*[8] and passing it back and forth. When they were both sufficiently tipsy, Sjöström came up with a solution to

---

6. Bread was only baked a couple of times a year, after which it was dried and stored, to later be dunked in one's coffee. People only ate fresh bread on special occasions, such as Christmas.

7. Even after 1864, when commerce in the countryside became legal, people continued to purchase their necessities at the spring and autumn open markets.

8. A very widely consumed vodka-like alcoholic drink, distilled from grain or potatoes, dating back to the 1500s.

the age-old land problem.

"If Engelholm were to give me his youngest daughter in marriage, we'd become as one large family. Then there'd be no more worryin' over that piece a' land that's always been a sore point 'tween us. It'd be Engelholm's ta use as he sees fit for the rest a' his life," he suggested, while wiping the *brännvin* from his moustache.

Lars Engelholm regarded his neighbor somewhat suspiciously.

" 'Tis Ester he means?" he replied guardedly. Of his five children, only Lilly and Ester were still at home, the older three, all boys, having emigrated to America.

Sjöström nodded.

Engelholm thought for a minute, then took another swig from the bottle standing on the table between them.

"Why not take Lilly," he offered. "Ester she's barely nineteen. B'sides, I have been plannin' ta keep her home as *hemmadotter.*[9] Britta and I we're gettin' on in years and we'll eventually need her ta care for us."

"It's just an idea. 'Tis Ester I fancy, not Lilly. But give it some thought."

Engelholm thought about it. The piece of land in question would certainly be a benefit to him, but at the same time, he preferred to keep Ester at home. She was more conscientious than her older sister, more reliable.

Sjöström, on the other hand, wanted a wife; or more exactly, he needed a son to take over the farm and carry on the Sjöström name. Of course, he could look around at the other available women, but it was Ester he wanted. He had known her since she was a baby. Even when he was a grown man and she but a child he had been attracted to her, an attraction fed by her stand-offishness towards him. And she was known to be both clever and obedient. Lilly, on the other hand, possessed neither of these qualities. She was nonchalant, unreliable, and physically unattractive. Of course, he could spill his seed in her and hopefully get a son, but any woman would do in that case. No, he had his mind set on Ester and he wasn't going to settle for second best. And he knew that Engelholm coveted that bit of land. Such a marriage could give each of them something they wanted.

Without mentioning it to his wife, Lars Engelholm thought over the proposal for several days. The only thing against it was having to keep Lilly as a *hemmadotter* instead of Ester. Gaining access to that piece of

---

9. A daughter who, rather than marrying, stayed at home and cared for her aging parents.

land was very appealing. He would be stupid to let the opportunity pass.

Having made up his mind, he set out one evening for the little inn outside the village where Sjöström spent his evenings drinking since his wife's death. The cold autumn wind caused him to shiver as he picked his way through the muddy ruts in the wagon track in the moonlight. By the time he reached the inn he was more than ready for a warming shot or two of *brännvin*. Pulling open the heavy wooden door, he stepped over the worn-down doorsill into the dark smoke-filled room. The pungent smell of sweat, alcohol, and urine was overwhelming, made worse by the stink coming from the few fish oil lamps. The weak light they gave off was hardly worth their unpleasantness. Peering around the room he could make out two strangers sitting on the built-in bed along the back wall, obviously travelers who were stopping there for the night. Otherwise, the dozen or so men were local peasants, all of whom were already drunk. Some were straddling the wooden benches with their backs against the timber wall, talking loudly to themselves or those around them. Others sat with their heads hanging heavily over the roughly planed tables, silently clutching *brännvin* bottles. Two of them, who could never agree on anything, were already arguing, soon to come to blows.

No one so much as lifted a cap or attempted to stand up respectfully when Engelholm came in, nor was he greeted by the proprietress, Madame Moa. It was a poor man's inn and not frequented by those belonging to the better social classes. Nor were his kind welcome there. The landless peasants, who lived in half-rotten thatched cottages with many mouths to feed, had more than enough of their overlords during the day. They had no desire to look at them while they drank to forget them. This was their inn and they felt no need to show respect for intruders.

Roland Sjöström sat in the far corner, hunched over a beer mug and an empty *brännvin* glass. He didn't give a damn whether he was welcome or not. To him, these peasants were no better than the animals in his barn. He didn't need to feel welcome. He came to the inn simply to sit in a corner and drink, where no one paid any attention to him. Since his wife had died his cook and kitchen maid had taken to hovering around him, making sure that he had everything he needed. It was stifling. The atmosphere of indifference he felt from those in the inn was a relief.

Lars Engelholm made his way across the hard-packed earthen floor to Sjöström's table, careful not to slip on the gobs of spit and spilled beer.

"Sjöström?" he said, hoping not to anger him by interrupting his solitude. "Mind if I sit down?"

With a shrug of his shoulders, Sjöström motioned to him to take the empty chair.

"What brings Engelholm here?" he wondered dimly.

"If Sjöström's offer still holds, I'm here to take him up on it."

"Is Engelholm saying he's willin' to trade Ester for the land?"

" 'Tis so."

"Moa!" Sjöström shouted, waking up from his stupor. "Bring a bottle of the best homebrew in the house an' another glass."

Madame Moa gave him a toss of her head, indicating that he could serve himself. But when he took a few copper coins from his pocket and slapped them onto the table top noisily she relented. For her, money was worth more than her pride. She set the bottle and glass on the table, then scooped the coins into her hand. Just as she turned to go, Sjöström grabbed her and pulled her down on his lap.

"Ack! Dirty ol' billy goat! Le' me go!" she cried, beating on his arms.

"Gladly!" he laughed, shoving her away. "Why'd I want ol' worn-out Moa when I can have a young virgin like Ester Larsdotter!"

He filled the two glasses with *brännvin.*

"Let's shake hands an' seal the arrangement!" he declared.

With some effort he pulled himself to his feet. Engelholm did likewise and they shook hands across the table.

Sjöström nodded towards their glasses.

"*Skål*[10] for our future relations!" he declared.

"*Skål!*" Engelholm echoed.

It didn't take them long to finish off the rest of the bottle. By the time they got up to leave they were both light-hearted and unsteady on their feet; so unsteady that they were forced to make their way towards home arm in arm to keep from stumbling in the ruts. When they came to where their paths parted, they promised each other to inform their respective households of their agreement the first thing in the morning. Upon hearing that she was to become the *hemmadotter,* Lilly protested loudly and in an angry manner unfitting of a young woman of her social standing. Ester, on the other hand, was stunned. "I do not like Herr Sjöström. He is as old as Father," was all she managed to say.

"Age matters not," Engelholm replied. "He is a highly respected man in the village. Ester should feel honored that he wants her."

"He is just wanting a son," she was tempted to add, but thought

---

10. Cheers!

better of it out of respect for her father. Sjöström might be highly respected by those who knew him from a distance, but those who had closer contact with him were aware of the fact that he had another side, a side which he only showed to those who were powerless against him. As a child she had been afraid of him. He reminded her of a bear. Once she had reached conformation age he had begun cornering her at village gatherings, squeezing her breasts with his coarse farmer's hands or pressing her against a wall with his huge body. To her fear was added disgust. She had tried to tell her mother of his behavior, but had found it embarrassing, for one did not talk about such things. Britta had understood, but had had no sympathy.

" 'Tis a woman's lot in life!" she declared straightening her back with a haughty jerk.

And now once again Ester appealed to her mother to intervene, but Britta refused.

"That's how life is," was all she said curtly and turned away from her daughter.

Ester felt abandoned. How could her mother stand there and let her father trade her to Roland Sjöström for a bit of land! It wasn't the fact that her father chose a husband for her; she had always known that it was up to him to do so. It was the fact that he had chosen Roland Sjöström. Given her choice, she would rather remain an unmarried *hemmadotter* at Lunna Gård. But she had not been given the choice. As a woman, she had no rights. She found it natural that she was forced to obey her father, but the thought of Sjöström taking over that role filled her with dread.

In spite of her reluctance, Ester Larsdotter and Roland Sjöström became engaged almost immediately once the agreement had been reached. Because children were vital in rural society, engaged couples often had sexual relations to determine whether or not they could produce offspring before making their final commitment. But Ester refused to give in to Roland Sjöström's physical advances. She found him repugnant. Her excuse for pushing him away was that she wanted to wear the parish's bridal crown on her wedding day, a privilege reserved for those brides who went to their wedding beds as virgins. She was unsure as to what being a virgin implied, however, only that it had to do with not letting a man touch her. Where babies came from was beyond her sphere of knowledge.

11

The wedding took place the following spring, complete with an overflow of food and drink, music and dancing, lasting the usual three days. By the end of the first evening a goodly number of the men were so drunk that they slept wherever the *brännvin* finally felled them: on chairs, slumped in corners, curled up on the floor. For once, Roland Sjöström only drank moderately. Ester had been putting him off for over half a year and he had grown impatient. Now that she belonged to him at last, he could hardly wait to take possession of her. While the more sober guests were whirling around the dance floor to the fiddler's tunes, he took Ester by the hand and pulled her into the adjoining room, locking the door behind them.

"Take off thy shoes," he ordered once they were alone.

Obediently she bent over with her back to him to unfasten their buckles. Without warning, he swooped the skirt of her bridal dress up over her back, exposing her nakedness,[11] and took her from behind. His thrust was so unexpected and so painful that it caused a primeval scream to rise from a place deep within her that she hadn't known existed. Nor could she stop screaming. It was as if she had been split in two. She struggled to free herself, but Sjöström had gripped her around the hips, leaving her powerless against his jabbing. When she could take no more, her body mercifully let her pass out. She never heard the chorus of hurrahs and wild clapping from the men listening outside the door.

Once Roland Sjöström had taken possession of his new bride he straightened up and let go of her, whereupon she collapsed onto the floor like an empty feed sack.

"Get up, Ester," he said in a voice edging on a command.

When she failed to move, he became impatient.

"Good God, get up!" he demanded. "Ester should't 'av made me wait so long."

When Ester made no response, he yanked her skirt down over her bloody thighs and, leaving her on the floor, went to find her mother.

"Mor[12] Britta," he said nervously, "something's wrong with Ester."

"Has Sjöström been with her?" she asked.

"She's in the other room," he continued, ignoring her question.

Britta gathered her long black skirt around herself hastily and left the room. She found Ester huddled on the floor crying.

"Why did Mamma not tell me?" she sniffed.

---

11. Underwear was uncommon in those days.

12. Mother. Common way of addressing a mother-in-law.

As usual when faced with sexual matters, Britta stiffened her back with a little twitch, as if to cut off any empathy she might have felt.

"One speaks not of such things," she informed Ester in a hard voice. " 'Tis a wife's duty and she cannot refuse. Such is a woman's lot in life. Ester'll get used to it. Get up and put thy clothes right! Ester's a married woman now like the rest of us and she's got guests to attend to. She has already brought shame upon Sjöström by crying like a baby. From this day onward her behavior reflects upon his honor. Do not forget that!" She turned on her heel and marched out, slamming the door. The hardness of her voice echoed through the empty room.

Without being told, Ester understood that she no longer belonged to her mother and father; she belonged to Roland Sjöström and his family. Her parents had suddenly become like distant relatives.

Ester had known the Sjöströms her whole life, but she could not imagine them becoming her family. There had been six children. Roland was the oldest, followed by four sisters, the youngest of whom was just a year older than herself. The last child, a boy, had died shortly after birth. The sisters were all married and living in the surrounding parishes with their own families, only meeting on special occasions. Mor Dagmar, as Sjöström's mother was called, had been a widow for a number of years, her husband having been killed by a runaway bull. As a child, Ester had always been afraid of her because of her harsh temperament. One did not disobey Mor Dagmar. And now she was living in the upstairs of Ester's new home. Luckily her weakened legs did not permit her to come downstairs often, but just knowing she was up there made Ester uneasy.

Like the other married women of her day, Ester was forced to accept her new role. She had no choice but to resign herself. It wasn't only a matter of serving her husband and caring for her mother-in-law. As a newly married woman she had the eyes of all the other married women upon her; sharp eyes which were quick to see anything she failed to do or did wrongly. It was impossible to have any secrets within the village, for the women watched each other like hawks, their eyes and ears missing nothing. One's behavior was not confined to one's self or even one's immediate family; it affected the larger family, whose relatives extended in all directions. And it particularly affected the man of the house, for it was he who was responsible for his wife's actions. Although men had recently lost the legal right to beat their wives, the new law did not change old traditions over night. Men still believed that it was the

13

threat of being beaten that kept their womenfolk under control. It was not, however, the fear of being beaten that made Ester obedient. She had stood up to Sjöström by refusing to give herself to him before they were married, but she had paid the price for her lack of submissiveness. Her wedding night had broken her spirit. Overnight she became lethargic, unable to face the thought of spending the rest of her life serving a man she loathed.

During the first months of their married life Sjöström took her every night "to make up for lost time," as he said. He paid no heed to her tears and protestations.

"Does Ester think I married her just so I could sit an' look at her?" he remarked roughly. "Ester is my wife and 'tis I who decides what she will do and not do."

She was forced to surrender, for she was powerless against Sjöström's size and strength. But she never ceased to wonder why her own body did not belong to herself. Had Sjöström treated her more gently she might not have found the act so distasteful. But he was rough, even violent at times, thinking only of his own needs and pleasure. Contrary to her mother's proclamation, Ester did not get used to it. The only way she could endure his nightly attacks was to let her body lie under him like a rag doll, absorbing his thrusts, while her spirit took flight to the ring of lilac bushes where she had played as a child. Only when she felt Sjöström roll off of her, did she return to her body.

Ester worked hard to perform the never ending household tasks that were required of every farm wife. Björkdalen was by no means an estate with an extensive staff of servants, but rather, simply a prosperous farm run with the help of the old cook Svea, the young kitchen maid Pia, and the milkmaid Maria, as well as a number of farmhands. It was Ester's duty to see that the household ran smoothly and efficiently. Like the women before her, when she became the mistress of Björkdalen she was entrusted with the heavy iron keys to all the storage buildings, cellars, pantries, and cupboards. She was responsible for overseeing their contents and making sure that the doors were kept locked at all times. No one, not even her husband, was allowed access to them without her permission. Thievery was not uncommon, even by one's own employees. When times were hard a person's first loyalty was often to one's own stomach, rather than to one's master and mistress.

There was one key that Sjöström had not handed over to his young wife, however, the brass key to the cupboard hanging in the corner of the best room. She was told that her husband was very particular about that cupboard because it had been made by his great great grandfather and namesake. The spray of flowers painted on the door was barely visible, its once-bright colors having faded with the passage of time, while the wood around the keyhole was worn satiny smooth, as if it had never seen a touch of paint. But on the inside of the door the black numerals of the date were still clearly visible: 1761. The two shelves in its musty-smelling interior held numerous small glasses, below which stood a cut glass *brännvin* decanter, the water-clear contents reaching up to its shoulder. Beside it stood a matching glass slightly larger than the others.

Ester paid little heed to the fact that she was not given the key to the corner cupboard and thus would have no control over her husband's drinking habits. More importantly, she clung to the hope that, if she performed her household duties to perfection, perhaps she would be freed from her nightly duties. But Sjöström never seemed to notice how the household was run. He had his own work to attend to outdoors. What was most important to him in regards to Ester was that she was available in his bed at night.

Several months after the wedding Ester realized she was with child. At last Sjöström would be forced to leave her alone at night. But when she broached the subject he just laughed.

"It does no harm in the least. What'd men do if they had ta wait till the child is born. And then wait till the churching's taken place. And then wait while she has her unclean days. And then before a man knows it, there's another one on the way and he's once again banned from exercising his marital rights. 'Tis never ending. No, that's just a woman's way of trying to avoid her duty."

Once again, Ester resigned herself. There was no one in whom she could confide. She was no longer a young maiden with a long braid bouncing down her back. Yet, even though she now wore her hair pinned up under a married woman's kerchief, she did not belong to them either. A married woman's function was to produce children for her husband and until she did so she was not fully accepted into their company. Nor could she confide in any of the servants, for they belonged to a lower class. And even if she had had someone she could confide in she could never have brought herself to mention what was troubling her. Women talked about many things woman to woman, but not about their sexual relationships with their husbands. Sex was like defecation; everyone did it, but no one spoke of it.

The days crept past slowly, as they do when one is unhappy. Ester performed the duties that were expected of her, but otherwise she kept to herself. To her relief, Pia and Svea took care of Mor Dagmar's needs, as they had done since the death of Roland's first wife. Now and then she went upstairs to visit the old woman, but she didn't seem to want her company. The criticizing sharpness of her tongue left Ester feeling unworthy of being mistress of Björkdalen.

At last the hot, extremely dry summer cooled into autumn. The birch leaves faded from green to golden yellow, then floated to the ground, followed by the first snow flurries. By December the cold was extreme and the snow unusually deep. A devastating famine was an undeniable fact. Although it had disastrous consequences for the poor, who made up the majority of the population in the countryside, the landowners managed to maintain some semblance of their higher standard of living. As much as possible, the priests continued to collect their tenth, in money or in kind, that was due them from each of their parishioners. For them, life went on as usual, as did life at Björkdalen, thanks to wise rationing. They were not starving. Nor was Sjöström experiencing any form of abstinence. He continued to carry on his nightly ritual, often forcefully, despite his wife's growing discomfort.

One gray afternoon at the beginning of the new year, Ester was suddenly overpowered by a stomach cramp much like those that accompanied her monthly bleeding. But it couldn't be that. She hadn't bled during the months she had been with child. Nor was her confinement due for another month. Could it be something she had eaten? When the pain ceased she wondered if she had only imagined it. But when a new pain came sometime later, she knew it had not been her imagination. The third pain forced her breath to catch in her throat. Old Svea looked at her questioningly.

"Has thy time come, *Fru'n?*"[13] she asked hesitantly.

"I know not," Ester answered nervously. "I should suppose that Svea knows more about such things than I. Has she not had children of her

---

13. Old form of address. Equivalent to Ma'am.

own in her day?"

"Oh, yes. Ten of 'em."

"Then perhaps she can help me when my time comes."

"The truth be known, I have never helped anyone. 'Tis other women who have helped me. But these things take many hours and *Fru'n* has only begun. No need to inform Sjöström yet. He's already anxious, as it is. There's plenty of time. Someone can go for Sister Alma in the morning. *Fru'n* should try to sleep this night so she's got all her strength for the morrow."

By the time everyone had finished their evening porridge the weak winter sun had disappeared behind the trees, taking with it the gray daylight, and replacing it with a sudden heavy wind. To be on the safe side, as soon as Sjöström and his two farmhands went to the barn to see that everything was in order should there be a storm, Maria and Pia hurriedly brought in as much water as possible, filling every available container, as well as the cauldron that hung over the fire on its swinging arm. At the same time, Svea took from the chest the embroidered bands that had swaddled many generations of newborn Sjöströms and, together with several clean towels, set them on the sideboard within easy reach. Hidden underneath them she placed a pair of scissors, a linen string, and a candle stub for cutting, tying, and securing the cord. That done, she set a basin of water, in which to wash the child, at the end of the raised hearth. Lastly, she raked the coals together and lay two pieces of wood on them, hoping to keep a little more warmth than usual in the room. As on all farms, the entire household, including the hired help, slept in the kitchen during the winter and any extra heat would be more than welcomed.

When the men returned from the barn everyone pulled out their respective box beds from under the benches and prepared themselves for the night. There was the dull rustle of straw as each of them tried, unsuccessfully, to fluff up the matted-down contents of his or her mattress bag. They should have been refilled long ago, but what straw there was must be kept to feed the animals. No amount of fluffing-up was going to prevent shoulders and hips from resting on the hard bed boards for the remainder of the winter.

Finally, everyone crawled into bed fully clothed, not only out of modesty, but for the sake of warmth, and pulled up their various animal hides and quilts: Sjöström and Ester in the built-in cupboard bed along the kitchen's back wall, Maria and Pia in the *utdragssoffa*[14] behind the table, the farmhands, 16-year-old Sven and his younger brother Nils, in the *utdragssoffa* nearest the door, and Old Svea in a narrow bed which pulled out in sections from a bureau on the far side of the hearth. Upstairs Mor Dagmar was already asleep. She spent most of her time in bed and paid little attention to what went on downstairs. She was tired of the struggle called living and prayed each night that she would not wake up in the morning.

Ester slept between her pains. But in the middle of the night she was woken by her own cry. She sat up. The room was ice cold and a storm howled outside, rattling the windows and sending clumps of snow thumping against the glass. Now and then a faint hiss rose from the hearth when snow fell down the open chimney onto the banked fire. Sjöström awoke with a start.

"What is going on?" he whispered loudly.

"Me thinks 'tis the child," Ester told him.

"How can that be? Ester has only been my wife for eight months."

"I know not, but it seems so."

Sjöström sat up and grabbed her roughly by her upper arm.

"Has Ester lain with another before she became my wife?" he yelled.

"Of course not!" she replied, as if he were joking.

"How am I to know if she speaks the truth?" he continued, slapping her across the face.

His sudden violence frightened her.

" 'Tis the honest truth, Sir," she cried, cowering before him.

"That's enough, Roland!" came Svea's voice from across the room.

Sjöström fell back against his pillow obediently.

By now everyone was awake. Old Svea got up and made her way through the darkness to the hearth. Gently she blew on the pile of ash-covered coals until a wavering finger of flame shot up. Once it began to greedily devour the sticks she fed it, she went to Ester. Reaching under the covers, she placed her hands on her belly.

"It has moved quite far down now," she remarked. "Someone must fetch Sister Alma."

Sjöström turned to Sven.

"Pull on thy boots and coat and hitch up Stella," he ordered. "Take the small wagon and go ta the village for Sister Alma as fast as possible!"

---

14. A bench or sofa found in almost all kitchens on which one could sit during the day. At night the seat was folded up against the back and held in place with a peg, while the box section underneath was pulled out ot make a bed. *Utdrag* means to draw or pull out.

18

His master's tone of voice was all too familiar to Sven. As much as he dreaded going out in the storm, he did not wish to incur Sjöström's wrath. Even though whipping and flogging had been forbidden by law,[15] Sjöström never hesitated to use his whip on those who displeased him. He knew that no one would dare take him to court for having broken the law. He held a high position within the community and in court his word would always win over the accusation of a poor peasant. Even if he were guilty. Sven was familiar with the sting of Sjöström's whip and didn't care to feel it once more. Reluctantly, he got out of bed and pulled on his boots. Before going out, he took one of the torch sticks that he and Nils had made earlier that evening and lit it in the fire. The resin flared up, lighting the room as he made his way between the pulled-out beds to the entranceway. But when he opened the outside door, a wall of snow hit him in the face. Pulling his coat tightly around his body and hunching forward into the storm, he managed to wade through the hip-deep drifts. But upon reaching the stall he could go no further. The snow was so deep and hard-packed against the front of the building that it was impossible to pull the door open. The other doors into the stall were to no avail, for there was no way to get a horse—much less a wagon—through them. At the same time, he dared not go back into the house. When Sjöström gave an order, he expected it to be carried out, even if it were impossible. How it was to be accomplished was not his problem. That was why he had farmhands.

Rather than return to the house and face Sjöström's anger, Sven set out on foot. In normal weather it took a little over an hour to walk to the village. He was used to walking. Everyone walked everywhere, aside from the rich with their horse-drawn carriages. It wasn't unusual for young men to walk ten miles to go to a dance on a Saturday night and then walk ten miles home again afterwards. They usually walked in groups, which made the miles shorter, and on the way home they helped those who had had too much to drink, while discussing the girls they had met. But to trudge through hip-deep drifts in a howling snow storm alone, with temperatures far below freezing, was not at all the same thing.

Even in the best of weather the road past Björkdalen was nothing more than two wagon tracks with deep ditches along both sides. And now, every trace of it had disappeared under dune-like drifts. But Sven had grown up in a workman's cottage belonging to the estate and knew every twist and turn of the road from childhood. Or so he had always

---

15. The law of 1858 forbid corporal punishment, except for boys under eighteen and girls under sixteen.

thought. At first he managed to plow though the drifts, but all too soon his torch, which had been struggling valiantly against the storm, began to burn low. Finally, seeing its chance, the wind killed it in one blow. Still Sven felt sure of the way in the darkness and swirling snow. Then suddenly, without warning, his foot sank, as if in a hole, and he fell. By the time he struggled to his feet the wind had already covered his tracks with snow, causing him to lose his sense of direction. Stumbling aimlessly, he knew that in such weather he must never stop moving. By keeping the wind in his face, as when he had started out, he hoped he would come back to where he had gone wrong. But nowhere did his feet find the road. After a while the wind began to make him dizzy as it beat at his face. Then his legs began to tire from pushing through the drifts. Finally he understood that he was lost; not only in terms of direction, but worse, in terms of survival. Exhausted from his efforts, as a last resort, he fell on his knees and beseeched the god whom he had so often blasphemed to save him, yet knowing it was sacrilegious to do so. He had no right to expect help.

For Ester, the night was endless. Her pains were coming closer and closer together, each one worse than the one before. She waited anxiously for Sister Alma to arrive, while clutching to the belief that Old Svea must know more than she let on. She had to, after having given birth to ten children. Pia and Maria, on the other hand, were young and had never even been present at a birth.

When Sven had not returned with Sister Alma by daybreak it was clear that something had happened. It was also clear that the child was not going to wait much longer. The wind had abated as the sky lightened, and because witnessing a birth was not for men's eyes, Sjöström and Nils set out in search of Sven and Sister Alma.

In spite of her lack of experience, Ester was convinced that something was wrong. She couldn't remember when she had last felt the child's kicking. Her body was telling her to push, but when she did she felt as if she were pushing against a wall. To her relief, Old Svea proved to be more knowledgeable than expected, for she had grown up around sheep and cows, often having assisted when they had difficult births. However, it was believed that a woman should give birth herself, without assistance. A midwife or wise woman was only there in case a problem arose.

Without Sister Alma's presence, it fell to Old Svea to make the necessary decisions. Finally, disregarding the taboo against assisting, she examined Ester hesitantly, only to discover that it was not the head that was down, but rather, one of the feet. By now Ester was nearing exhaustion and could no longer push properly. Svea realized that the only chance was to do as one did with sheep and cows. As gently as possible she slid one finger in until she could hook it around the foot. Then she told Ester to push as hard as she could. Slowly, amid Ester's screams, she managed to pull the child out. The head came last, with the cord wrapped tightly around the neck. It was a tiny boy-child, that appeared to have been dead for some time.

Upon reaching the stall, Sjöström found the door blocked by a huge snowdrift. Quickly he and Nils set about clearing away enough snow to peer inside, in the hope that Sven had managed to drive the horse and wagon out before the snow had piled up. But before they could pull the door wide open Bruno's soft whinneying told them otherwise. Without digging further, they hurried out to the road, but found no trace of Sven. Any tracks he might have made were completely obliterated by the layer of new snow lying innocently over the landscape, hiding every trace of the night's drama. It was obvious that fetching Sister Alma was impossible. Even if they could reach the village they could not possibly bring her back to Björkdalen.

Sjöström and his farmhand looked at each other, sharing the same thought.

"Go and find Sven!" Sjöström ordered. Like Sven, Nils obeyed reluctantly, out of fear of his master.

On his way back to the stall another sort of fear crept over Sjöström, one that was unfamiliar to him. Was Old Svea capable of delivering the child? And why was it coming so early? Was Ester lying to him? Had she been with another man before him? He would soon find out. Women who refused to confess the name of the child's father invariably cried out his name when their labor became unbearable, in the belief that doing so would ease the pain and quicken the birth. What if he should lose Ester, as he had his first wife? Many women, as well as newborn babies, died in childbed. He had paid a dear price for Ester, nor did he want to have to find yet another wife. And if the child were a son he certainly did not want to lose it. To realize that he was not in control of the situation made him feel both weak and angry.

Having fed and cared for Bruno, he was on his way to the house when he heard Ester's screams. He took the porch steps two at a time and flung open the door.

"What's going on?" he cried.

Before anyone could answer him, he caught sight of the child lying on the table, the cord still around its neck.

"My son! What's Svea done to my son?" he yelled, taking a step towards Old Svea, his eyes wild.

"He was stillborn," Svea replied calmly. "And Sjöström is going to lose his wife also if he does not leave the house and let us take care of her in peace."

She had worked for two generations of Sjöströms and had been like a mother to Roland as he was growing up. She was not afraid to stand up to him; she was the one person who could make him back down. He cast a quick glance in the direction of the child.

"To lose two sons 'tis a blight upon my name," he remarked, then left the room meekly, with not so much as a glance in Ester's direction.

Having made his way through the hip-deep snow to the woodshed, he picked up an axe and began splitting wood with quick, violent strokes. In some obscure way, his manhood had been tarnished by the fact that his offspring were too weak to live, coupled with a sense of shame in the fact that his wives had failed to give him an heir.

Nils continued plowing through the heavy snow aimlessly, searching for some trace of his brother in the endless sea of whiteness surrounding him.

"Sven! Sven!" he called, over and over until his throat grew tight and his voice hoarse. But the only answer he got was Sven's name echoing back to him from the edge of the forest on the far side of the barren fields. Just as he was about to give up, he caught sight of his brother's cap lying on the snow some distance away. Relieved that he was on the right track at last, he waded toward it as fast as the deep snow would allow. To his horror, when he bent down to pick it up, he discovered that it was still on Sven's head! Even though he knew it was too late, he began digging frantically, slinging away the snow from around his brother's lifeless body with his bare hands. He found Sven on his knees, frozen, his hands pressed together as if in prayer.

Nils returned to Sjöströms several hours later, his eyes red and his brother's cap in his hand. That afternoon they brought Sven back to

Björkdalen, where Nils had fashioned a coffin for him. Because of the weather, and the fact that Nils was Sven's only remaining relative in the village, it was decided that there would be no viewing. Instead, once Sven was laid out, the lid was fastened on the coffin and it was taken to the shed to await the funeral on Sunday.

That evening when he left for the inn, Sjöström picked up the bundle containing the child, that Svea had placed in the cold of the entrance-way, and took it out to the shed. Prying open the coffin, he lay it beside Sven, then refastened the lid.

Immediately after the birth Ester fell into a deep depression. She had failed as a wife by not giving Sjöström an heir. At the same time, she was hurt by the fact that he had only cared about the boy-child and ignored her completely. That and Mor Dagmar's "When is Roland going to get himself a decent wife!" when she was told of the stillborn child. It was then that Ester understood that she was but a vessel for carrying Sjöström's heir. She wished she had died along with the child. Curiously, she never inquired as to what had happened to it.

Mor Britta

Björkdalen, Summer 1869

Although the day was sunny and warm, Ester froze. She had been frozen with fear since she had heard Pia call "she says she's the child's mother" to her husband from the kitchen door. Her worst fear had become reality: The girl had come to take her child, the child Ester had nursed as her own throughout the spring.

She had had such pain in her swollen breasts after the loss of her still-born child that she had wished she could die. Consequently, it had been a relief when Sjöström had come home from church with the news that there was a child in the parish who needed a wet nurse. The famine had taken so many that each new life was vital to the community, hence he had been rewarded with a wave of respect from the congregation for having offered his wife.

"Whose child might it be?" Ester had asked, disinterestedly.

"Her mother is a fifteen year old maid. Ester can guess the rest. The same old story; a roll in the hay and no father."

"Is it a boy-child?"

"No, and 'tis just as well. My son must be of my own flesh and blood."

"Does Sjöström mean that we are going to keep the child?"

"I don't know. Let us wait and see how things develop."

"Has she been baptized?" she questioned. The thought of nursing a heathen child was repugnant. One avoided contact with heathens at all costs.

"Oh, yes. She's not a heathen, although apparently her mother is. The child is baptized Stina-Kajsa, but is just called Kajsa."

Later that day he had returned with the child. When Ester unwrapped it she found an infant as apathetic as she herself. It was too weak to even cry. She held it to her breast mechanically, but no avail. It seemed to be beyond reach. However, its proximity caused Ester's milk to begin to flow. Not knowing what else to do, she let it drip onto the child's lips at short intervals. After what seemed like an eternity, Little Kajsa's mouth opened ever so slightly, letting the milk run into it, only to let it run out again. But the relief from the pressure in her breasts was so great that she was reluctant to let go of the child.

For the next few days Kajsa hung onto life by a thread, while Ester coaxed milk into her drop by drop, both day and night. Slowly life took a hold on her and she began to swallow awkwardly. At the same time, as Kajsa came back to life, she pulled Ester up out of her depression and gave her a reason to live. After several weeks she was nursing normally and gaining weight rapidly. By that time, Ester had become attached to her as if she were her own child. She was secretly glad that the boy had not survived, for Sjöström would have taken him from her at an early age to school him for his future responsibilities. For Ester, the boy's death avenged the manner in which he had been conceived. Soon the memory of the still-born child slipped from her mind entirely. For her, it was Kajsa who was born out of the pain of that night.

And now the sudden appearance of Kajsa's biological mother had jarred her back to reality.

The latch clicked as the door shut. Ester slumped onto a nearby chair, her shaking legs refusing to hold her upright any longer. Roland Sjöström remained standing in front of the kitchen window, his hands shoved deep in his pockets and a satisfied expression written on his face. His eyes followed the girl making her way down to the road where Johan, his new stall boy, waited with the farm wagon. He watched as the boy offered his hand and hoisted her up onto the board that served as the driver's seat. With a light slap of the whip on the horse's rear, they set off. Once they were out of sight, he turned to his wife. The baby she still clutched to her breast had started to cry. Ester herself was somewhere else, her eyes squinted shut, out of reach of reality's grasping fingers.

"Be careful with the baby!" he reprimanded. "Ester's squeezing it too hard."

She appeared to not hear him.

"Ester!" he repeated, his voice a little harder. "Listen to me! It's all right. She's gone now."

Ester's eyes opened slowly and she looked around, making sure the girl was no longer in the kitchen. She had had no choice but to let her hold Kajsa while they drank coffee, but the conversation had drifted past her like a fog rolling out to sea. She had kept her eyes riveted on Kajsa, fearing the girl would suddenly run out the door with her. And when the child was finally returned to her arms, she nearly fainted from relief.

"Ester can stop her worrying now."

"But what if she comes back?" she whimpered.

"She shan't be back. By the time she's frittered away all the money I gave her, she'll have forgotten about Kajsa."

"But did I not hear Sjöström tell her that once she gets her life in order an agreement can be reached?"

"Yes, but I didn't say what sort of agreement. Besides, she is only fifteen years old and has no idea how to handle money. Just as she gets used to having it, it'll be gone. By the time she's twenty she'll most likely be a prostitute."

"But what if she does try to take Kajsa back?"

"She's smart enough not to try. Even if she went to court, she's got no chance of winning."

Ester relaxed her grip on the child. She knew Sjöström was right. No one ever won against him. Several years before his first wife died, he had been taken to court by a young kitchen maid who had worked at Björkdalen. She claimed that he had forcefully taken her maidenhead while she was in the best room cleaning up after the New Year's Eve festivities and that he was the father of the boy-child she had given birth to the following September. The event had been witnessed by another maid, who had heard her cries and rushed into the room. But when she had seen their master moving on top of the girl she had backed out the door hurriedly, knowing her involvement would cost her her job. But Sjöström had seen her. The following day he called her into his office and threatened her into silence. When he was later taken to court, he stated that there had been no witnesses. Therefore the process became a matter of an illiterate maid's word against his. He had had no trouble convincing the judge of his innocence. Not only did the girl fail to be awarded the usual financial compensation for her misfortune, but Sjöström then turned around and sued her for defiling his good name and reputation—and won! As a result, the girl was fined 40 daler in silver coin. But because she owned nothing beyond the ragged clothes she was wearing, having been fired when her pregnancy became obvious, she was unable to pay the fine. Instead, she was sentenced to two weeks in prison on bread and water. After the first week of isolation in a dark, unheated stone cell, with only rats for company, she became crazy, screaming over and over that Sjöström was a lying swine. Once released, she was sent to live with her family. But her constant ravings made it impossible for them to keep her at home. Eventually she was locked away in the attic of the poor house, where she was all but forgotten.

And although the child was raised by her parents, he was always regarded as an outcast within the parish. But none of this had touched Roland Sjöström. To him, the poor lacked feelings and were no better than animals. The court had freed him and therefore his conscience was clear. Through the entire ordeal he had had the backing of the others of his class, for the majority of them never thought twice about taking advantage of their female employees when it suited them. If a girl got pregnant and named her master as the father, he automatically denied having had anything to do with her, maintaining that she was just trying to extract money from him in order to support some farmhand's bastard. Everyone, rich and poor alike, knew the truth, but the rich were not about to change the pattern and the poor where powerless to do so.

Secure in the fact that no one could take Kajsa from her, Ester continued to build her life around the child, eager for the day when she would become a helpmate. Kajsa was hers and hers alone. Sjöström paid her no heed, for she served no function for him. Having her to care for made Ester feel less alone. Even Sjöström's eternal striving after a son ceased to bother her. She let him open her legs without a struggle, as duty required. And when she became pregnant once again, she hoped, for Sjöström's sake, that it would be a boy. Nor could she imagine having to divide her attention between Kajsa and another girl-child.

Like her son-in-law, Mor Britta also hoped that Ester would again become pregnant with a boy-child. For the sake of her own honor. As far as she was concerned, a stillborn child did not fulfill the requirements for her daughter to be regarded as a mother. Nor would a girl-child satisfy Sjöström's needs. And taking in someone else's bastard girl-child as one's own did not serve anyone's needs.

When the news reached Britta that Ester had been sick several mornings she suspected that she was finally pregnant again. Gathering together some of her dried herbs that served to alleviate such "sickness," she set out for Björkdalen. Although the two farms bordered on each other, their respective houses lay nearly a mile apart. The road connecting them was nothing more than two wagon tracks that had turned to mud in the rainy November weather. By the time she reached Sjöström's her shawl clung to her back like a wet blanket, soaking her to the skin, and her feet were mud-caked and freezing. But one look at Ester confirmed her suspicion: she was obviously pregnant. Giving Old Svea the herbs, she instructed her as to how to make tea of them, as well as a poultice to lay on Ester's stomach. Then, because the wind had come up, accompanied by a driving icy rain, she took her leave without waiting for her clothes to dry. Ester watched her disappear down the road towards Lunna, shoulders hunched against the weather while holding onto her shawl with one hand and her scarf with the other. They had barely exchanged a dozen words.

Three days later Lilly appeared at the door unexpectedly, clearly upset.

"What's happened?" Ester asked immediately.

" 'Tis Mother. She's sick in bed."

"Sick in bed? She's never before been sick in bed."

"I know. Father is so worried that he went all the way to town for the doctor last night."

"What's wrong with her?"

"The doctor thinks it's pneumonia. He gave her some pills and powders, but could do nothing more. We just have to wait for her fever to break. But I thought I should come and tell my sister. Mother thinks she's dying."

Ester dressed in her warmest clothes and followed Lilly home, instructing Svea to send Sjöström to get her in the little cart as soon as he came in.

She arrived to find her mother burning with fever and struggling to breathe.

When Mor Britta heard Ester's voice she opened her eyes slowly and lifted her hand towards her. Ester took it dutifully.

"Forgive me," was all Britta managed to say.

Bitterness welled up inside Ester. Suddenly her mother wanted to make everything right between them so she could die in peace. She jerked her hand free.

"I shall come again tomorrow," she said simply.

As she turned to leave, she bumped into Reverend Holmgren, who had been standing in the doorway, having come to give Mor Britta the holy sacrament. Without so much as an "excuse me," she rushed past him and out the door. Had she stopped to look, she would have seen that Holmgren's horse stood with its head hanging down, a sure sign that death was standing at the foot of Mor Britta's bed. But instead, all she could think about were all the times her mother had let her down.

The next morning Ester filled a container with Svea's freshly made soup to take to Mor Britta. Half way to Lunna Gård she heard the village church bell begin to strike. Automatically she began to count each clang, as she had done as a child, thinking it must be ten o'clock already. But when she got to eleven she stopped short. The church bell wasn't ringing the hour, it was ringing to announce that someone had died. Mor Britta! Clutching her long skirt higher above the muddy track, she began to hurry, even though she understood that it was too late. As she came nearer, the sound of hammering could be heard from the little carpenter shop across the field. The *budkavla*[16] must have gone around at dawn, for someone was making a coffin.

One-eyed Klara, an old woman who lived in a hut in the forest, was there when Ester arrived, her father having sent a wagon for her; not so much for Klara's comfort, but because the dead must be washed and laid out as quickly as possible. It was a painstaking task, for the diseased must be as clean as a new-born baby when standing before God. To be asked to wash a corpse was an honor that was given to someone outside the family for, as everyone knew, the dead wanted company on their last journey, causing relatives to keep a distance.

When Ester came in she saw that the windows in the best room had been covered with sheets, except for one that was left open enabling the spirit to depart, and all the pictures with worldly motives, as well as the mirror, had been removed. Even the big Mora clock standing in the corner had been stopped. The door to the little room where her father took his midday nap had been lifted from its hinges and set across two sawhorses. On it lay Mor Britta, covered with a sheet except for the arm which Klara was washing. The lid from an *utdragssoffa* was leaning against the wall, waiting to replace the door under Britta once she was clean. In the meantime, the room in which she had died was being smoked to kill any remaining remnants of her illness. Out in the yard the straw that had been her last mattress was smoldering. Each member

---

16. A wooden stick with the names of all the farms in the parish carved on it. When something needed to be done (in this case, funeral perparations) the *budkavla* was passed from the last farm to have had it to the next farm on its list of names, whose duty it was to serve on the village burial group. This involved notifying the priest, helping with the laying out, ringing the church bell, making the coffin, digging the grave, etc.

of the household watched surreptitiously, to see if the smoke went straight up, indicating that she was on her way to heaven. But, although there was scarcely a breath of wind, the smoke only rose several feet before veering off towards the north. No one was surprised, for Mor Britta had not been particularly well liked, due to her hard and unsympathetic nature. In fact, when the word spread amongst the village women, there were even those who secretly rejoiced to know that Mor Britta was going to meet the devil rather than her maker.

As soon as she was finished, Klara called in the women from the farm that had received the *budkavla* that morning and whose turn it was to help with the preparations. Together they lifted the door with the body on it from the sawhorses and laid the *utdragssoffa* lid across them instead. Then they carefully moved Mor Britta from the door to the lid, where they would lay her out in her wedding dress.

Like most women, Britta had long ago made provisions for her own funeral, according to parish protocol. Because it was important to be properly dressed when one stood before God to be judged, most women chose to be buried in their wedding dresses (which, for practical reasons, were almost always black), a pair of stockings knitted especially for the occasion, and a simple cap. These Mor Britta had kept in her chest, wrapped in brown paper, along with the monogrammed handkerchief that was to cover her face just before the coffin lid was nailed on. Why its corners must be left sticking out under the edge of the lid no one remembered; that was simply how it was done. Further, the rest of the departed's clothes were to be given to the women who washed and had laid out the body. For One-eyed Klara, such a gift was a god-send.

When she came out of the room, Klara handed Lilly the basin of dirty wash water.

"Set this here out in the entranceway," Klara instructed. "When people hear that Britta's gone they'll be a wantin' some of the water she's been washed in."

"Why?" Lilly wondered, finding the thought distasteful.

"B'cause such water it has special powers."

"What kind of special powers?"

"It can cure the likes of *engelska sjukan*[17] and scabies, as well as killing the lice and fleas that everyone has in the bed. But sometimes people they get greedy and wash themselves with it. After that they see ghosts everywhere. So pay attention, so that no one takes more than her share."

---

17. English sickness or rickets.

Dressing Britta proved to be no easy task for the village women. Not only had her arms already become stiff, but over the years she had grown stouter. But because she had been used to having her own way, rather than go against her wishes by dressing her in her ordinary Sunday outfit, they opened the back seam of her wedding dress and arranged it on the front of her body, leaving the open back hidden beneath her. To make sure that she wouldn't "go again" and haunt the living, they stuck "corpse pins" in the bottoms of her feet, insuring that people would hear her cry out in pain should she try to walk. And just to be on the safe side, they sewed the toes of her stockings together.

The wake was held on Saturday. All the villagers, as well as folk from the surrounding area, came to say good-bye, including young children and those who had hardly known Mor Britta. Regardless of how they felt about her, she had been part of the community and her death had left an empty place. People touched the corpse, patting the cheek or hand, not only to overcome the fear of death, but to make sure that one would not be bothered by her ghost in the future. One could also have various pains healed by touching the affected place three times with the dead person's hand or finger while chanting, "When this finger has decayed, my pain shall be gone," for it was believed that the dead could take the illnesses of the living with them to the grave.

Before setting out for the churchyard on Sunday morning, the people who had taken part in the wake, and who were to follow the procession, were served breakfast. They sat around Mor Britta, eating and drinking and chatting quietly. Now and then one of the women leaned over and placed a morsel of bread or cooked potato beside Britta's folded hands to help her on her way. When everyone had finished eating, one of the men nailed the lid fast and six bearers lifted the coffin from the sawhorses, kicking them aside lest they should stand waiting for another coffin to be set on them. When they reached the front door they stopped and lowered the coffin twice in the form of a cross, before carrying Britta feet first out the door. To carry her out head first would allow her to see the door of her old home and thus find her way back again. Once out in the road, the bearers had several miles to walk carrying their burden, for it was unthinkable to travel to one's final resting place while bouncing on a horse-drawn wagon. Such transportation was only for paupers, whom no one wished to carry, and those no one cared about. On either side of the roadway to the village pine boughs had been laid out, their

31

needles not only pointing the way to the churchyard, but also threatening to stick the dead, should she try to return home.

Upon reaching the church they were met by a woman standing beside the open grave. Rather than funeral attire, she was dressed in rags like many a beggar. As soon as the casket was set down she approached one of the pallbearers, curtseying respectfully before him. Holmgren's face turned an angry red and he stepped forward to hinder her; then thought better of it.

"I had not the chance to go to Lunna to say good-bye to Britta," she explained. "I wonder if I might see her now."

"And who might thou be?" one of the pallbearers asked.

"Britta's younger sister Hildur," she replied in a voice loud enough for all to hear.

A gasp rippled through the by-standers. A number of the women mourners glanced sideways at each other, but no one dared say a word.

One of the bearers pried open the lid of the casket while the others stood at the graveside waiting. Leaning over the coffin, the woman gently caressed Britta's now cold face while mumbling unintelligibly. Finally, two of the men stepped forward and drew her back into the waiting group, where she continued her mumbling. Meanwhile, Ester wept, but not for her mother. She wept for her stillborn boy-child who, as an unbaptized heathen without a soul, had been "buried" without ceremony, probably behind the stone wall on the north side of the churchyard, near criminals, suicides, witches, and others who could not be buried in consecrated ground. As she watched Mor Britta's coffin being lowered into the grave, she wondered where the child lay, for such places were not marked. She was afraid to ask.

Once Mor Britta's coffin was *jordfäst*,[18] with a layer of earth covering it to prevent her from "going again," everyone went into the church for the Sunday service.

In his "corpse sermon," as it was called, Reverend Holmgren's praise of Mor Britta went far beyond his usual praise for departed parishioners; not because she was so much better than them, but because Lars Engelholm had paid him well. Such praise was a commodity which could be bought for the good of the deceased person's soul.

"In conclusion," Holmgren remarked, his eyes resting on Ester, "I would like to add that, on her death bed, Mor Britta was so humble as to ask to be forgiven by someone she had treated poorly, but that person committed the unforgivable sin of turning her back and refusing to

18. Literally "fastened to the earth."

forgive her. But she will pay dearly for her lack of respect. No mother deserves such arrogant treatment!"

Ester's face burned with shame. She felt as though she had been publicly disrobed and beaten in front of everyone. The thought of facing people's scorn after the service was unbearable. But she needn't have worried. The entire congregation rose as one and filed out past her without so much as a glance in her direction. She had ceased to exist for them. Even Lilly and her father ignored her and Roland Sjöström hurried out to his waiting carriage, telling his stallboy, to drive him home without waiting for his wife. Ester stood in the *vapenhus*[19] listening to the voices of the departing parishioners until they faded into the distance. When she finally dared to venture out the door, the woman who had claimed to be Mor Britta's sister was sitting on a bench by the gate. Since there was no other way out of the churchyard, Ester was forced to pass her. Keeping her eyes on the ground, she walked as fast as she could, set on ignoring her presence. But just as she reached the gate the woman got to her feet and blocked her way.

"Hold thy head up, my child. Thou need not go in shame," she said gently. "Pay Holmgren no heed. He himself is the greatest sinner of us all." She paused a moment, then continued, half questioningly, "I assume thou art Britta's Ester?"

Ester nodded.

"My name's Hildur Unosdotter," she continued. "Has Ester never heard my name mentioned?"

"No, Ma'am. Never."

"That doesn't surprise me," Hildur replied with a little snort of bitter laughter. "Come and let us sit down on the bench here and I'll tell Ester something that I think she should know."

"But what about the *gravöl?*[20] Ester protested, feeling that she was obligated to take part in it.

"Does Ester really want to face more of the same kind of treatment as she's just experienced?" Hildur asked her.

Ester shook her head.

"People will talk, whether one is present or not. 'Tis best not to have to listen to them."

Glad to be relieved of what she had seen as an unpleasant duty, Ester

---

19. Weapon house; the entranceway to the church where, in the old days, one's weapons were left during the service.

20. Literally "grave beer"; a gathering on the same scale as a wedding or baptism, beer being the main drink (for the men.)

sat down on the bench.

"I imagine Ester is wondering about Britta's sister," Hildur began mysteriously.

"I think everyone is wondering," she replied. "I never knew that Mamma had a sister."

"No, she did not want anyone to know about me."

"But why?"

"Certainly Ester is aware of the fact that Britta was extremely concerned about how things looked to others. Honor. Her own and her family's..."

"Yes, but..."

"It was the same old story that has happened countless times throughout history."

Ester looked at her, unsure as to what she meant.

"We were extremely poor when we were growing up," she began.

"Poor?" Ester interrupted. "I thought my mother came from a well-to-do family."

"Yes, that's what she wanted people to believe, which was made easy by the fact that we came from another parish and she was not known here. And I think she eventually believed it herself. But such was not the case. Originally we were nine siblings, but a cholera epidemic took the two oldest, whom I never knew. Then there were several younger children who died in infancy. I've a vague memory of babies who never stopped crying and I suspect that they died from starvation, for all of us were always hungry. As for those who survived, one sister went to Stockholm, got married, and died in childbirth. The other two, both boys, went to America. One of them was never heard from again and the other was supposedly killed in an Indian raid. Like many people in those days, both our parents drank *brännvin* daily. Our mother excused her use of it by maintaining that it kept her consumption at bay, while our father was a straight-forward alcoholic, who never bothered with excuses. All men drank in those days, especially the poor, who tried to forget the misery of their poverty. At the same time, our poverty was the direct result of our father's drinking. Not only did he spend most of his spare time and money in the nearby tavern, but he also distilled his own *brännvin* in our one room cottage, which is where most of our potatoes and grain went, instead of into our stomachs. It was disgusting. Every time he opened the mash container to put in more grain or potatoes or to dump out the draff for the animals, it filled the room with steam and an incredible stink. He and our mother fought constantly over that apparatus. We children were scared to death to go near the hearth, even when we were freezing, because it stood there like an enemy soldier guarding the fire. Anyone who got near it was severely beaten. Actually we, girls and boys alike, were constantly being beaten, because our father was very violent when he was drunk, which was most of the time. Several birch whips of various thicknesses always stood at attention on the mantelpiece to forever keep the fear of his wrath alive in us.

"Britta could hardly wait to get away from home. Once she was confirmed she turned her back on the rest of us and walked out the door. When half a year had passed without a word from her, Mother swallowed her pride and went to Holmgren, who happened to be the priest in our parish at that time, since Britta would have had to obtain a pass from him in order to leave the parish. According to him, she had gone to Stockholm, although she had never sent him her new address for the church records. Sadly, Mother never saw her again. The following year our father drowned when he stood up in a rowboat while drunk, lost his balance, and fell overboard. By that time our mother's consumption was in its last stages and Father's death, coupled with having lost all her children but me, was too much for her. Her death left me with no one, so I decided to go to Stockholm in hopes of finding Britta. When I went to Holmgren to obtain a pass to leave the parish, he asked me if I wished to pay for it in the same manner as my sister had done.

" 'I did not know one needed money to pay for a pass,' I told him innocently, for I was but twelve years old and knew little of worldly things.

" 'One need not pay with money. One can pay in kind,' he replied.

" 'In kind? What does that mean, Sir?'

" 'Come into the other room and I will show Hildur,' he said. He put his arm around my shoulders and steered me through the doorway into the vestry. As soon as the door closed behind us he began pulling off my clothes. Just the smell of his closeness made me nauseous and I understood that he was going to do something bad to me.

" 'I changed my mind,' I cried. 'I do not wish to go to Stockholm.' I ran to the door, only to find it locked. I began banging on it with my fists and screaming as loud as I could. My guardian angel must have been with me, because just at that moment the parish clerk came into the building and heard my screams. He understood the situation immediately. Although he said nothing, the look he gave Holmgren when he unlocked the door from the outside was one of complete disgust. Obviously I was not Holmgren's first innocent victim, nor the last, I am sure. That sort of thing still goes on to this day, and will continue to do so as long as the well-to-do continue to look down upon the less fortunate and fail to see us as human beings."

"I always felt that Mother had no use for Holmgren. Now I understand why," Ester commented. "Did Hildur find her in Stockholm?"

"No. Britta never got there. Because our parish lay further to the west, she had to pass Lunna Gård on her way to Stockholm. I later heard that she had been walking with several young people who apparently got tired of her ways, for even at that age she could be unpleasant. They had slept in a barn somewhere around here, but when she woke up in the morning the others had gone on without her. Afraid to continue alone, she made her way to the nearest house, where Grandma Engelholm opened the door. Showing her a letter of recommendation from Holmgren, she asked if they had need of a governess for the two young boys that she could see playing in the kitchen. She was able to read and write and had had to help take care of us younger children at home, but I cannot imagine whatever possessed her to try to pass herself off as a governess. The only conclusion I was ever able to come to was that she had "paid" Holmgren well and gotten him to recommend her for such a job. Much to her surprise, she was given the position, the children having been Granny's grandchildren, whose mother had died from TB. Granny's oldest son, Lars, and Britta soon took a liking to each other and before long Britta had a big stomach. Whether it was Holmgren's or Lars' has never been determined, but Lars was man enough to make an honest woman of her. Shortly thereafter she gave birth to Ester's older brother Albert. Some time after Albert's birth Lars' brother, the father of the two young boys, was killed by a run-away horse. And so it was that Lars became guardian of his two nephews, whom he and Britta then raised as their own. A few years later Britta gave birth to Lilly and finally little Ester."

Ester was silent for a while, struggling to take in all she had heard. But there was still her unanswered question.

"Why did Mother not want anyone to know about her sister?" she asked.

"I shall continue my tale," Hildur told her, getting to her feet. "But I'm getting cold. Come, let us walk a bit. We've plenty of time. Sjöström will think Ester has gone to the *gravöl* and the people at the *gravöl* will think she has gone home."

They walked along the road away from the village. After a while Hildur spoke.

"It was not until years later that I discovered that Britta never gotten

36

further than Lunna Gård. Although I had refused to pay Holmgren 'in kind' for a pass to leave the parish, I was determined to go to Stockholm in the hope of finding Britta. I packed the few clothes I owned, as well as some of my mother's things, in a large cloth sack that she had supposedly carried me in when I was a baby. While looking around for something of value that I could perhaps sell along the way, I came across a little box filled with coins. To me it seemed like a fortune! Then it came back to me, how once when I was a little girl my mother had shown the box to me, explaining that the money was for her funeral and that I should not tell anyone about it until that day came. But since her funeral had already taken place, paid for by the parish, I had no bad conscience about keeping the money. It would certainly lighten my journey. I tied the coins tightly in a bit of cloth to prevent them from jingling and stuck them in the pocket of Mother's skirt at the very bottom of the sack, with the other clothes neatly folded on top of it. Lastly I took a few pieces of dry bread to eat along the way.

"Since it was summer, I was able to walk at night in the twilight. It must have taken me two weeks. Whenever I was stopped and questioned I explained that my pass had been stolen, but that I was on my way to Stockholm to live with my sister, who was the only remaining member of my unfortunate family. I even gave her name and a made-up Stockholm address. By the time I got that far in my story I was weeping and my interrogators never failed to take pity on me."

She paused, as if lost in the past.

"My life would have been so different, had I never gone to Stockholm," she murmured, more to herself than to Ester.

HILDUR

Stockholm, summer 1844

The sun looked down from a cloudless sky, warming the day. Just outside the entrance to the city Hildur fell in with a family who had left the countryside to seek a better life in Stockholm. Upon reaching the customs gate through which everyone must pass, the man of the family was questioned as to his business in the city. He replied that they were going to his son, who had a job waiting for him in the Old Town, and gave an address. The customs official assumed that Hildur was with them, for she was dressed as poorly as they were; indeed, as poorly as most of the country folk who passed by him in the course of the day. Therefore he let her pass without question.

Once inside the city, Hildur was met with a shock. Never before had she seen so many people in one place! She quickly understood that she was not going to simply bump into Britta on the street, as she had assumed; not amongst the hundreds of people milling about. Nor had she any idea of how or where to go about looking for her. Turning around to seek advice from her new-found friends, she discovered that she had become separated from them. She tried to stand still, hoping they would come back for her, but was soon swept along by a stream of people all moving in a single direction. The crowd swelled as it progressed, with people shouting wildly, although she couldn't make out whether they were glad or angry. Soon she was pressed into a group of men, women, and children who were gathered impatiently in a simi-circle at the bottom of a low, treeless hill. Looking up, she caught sight of a wooden platform with a bench in the middle. Below one end of the bench lay a pile of thin branches, their wilting leaves still clinging to them.

Presently a wagon drew up and a man in chains was led up the steps of the platform to where a priest and a man holding a huge long-handled axe awaited him. The spectators became wild with excitement, as if they were about to take part in a great festive event. Suddenly Hildur understood what she was about to witness. Horrified, she turned to flee, but found herself fenced in by the crowd.

"Don't go now," a boy about her own age shouted at her. "The fun's just startin'. Sometimes he don't get the head all the way off on the first try."

Hildur looked at him in disbelief. Was she having a bad dream? Were people actually enjoying such a spectacle?

Meanwhile, the man was tied down on the bench, the priest recited

The Lord's Prayer loud enough for all to hear, and the executioner raised the axe above his head. Hildur looked up just in time to see it come down across the man's neck and his head fall into the branches with a thud. The crowd cheered. A stampede of women rushed forward to catch the blood in bowls or to dip the corners of their aprons in it, for the blood from a person who had been executed could cure many diseases. Hildur, for her part, vomited the little breakfast she had eaten and collapsed, her body jerking violently. A few people moved aside, more out of fear than to give her space, while others ignored her. When the crowd had finally dispersed, Hildur was left lying on the ground, frothing at the mouth.

Presently two constables approached and ordered her to move along. Getting no response, they grabbed her by the upper arms and jerked her to her feet, demanding to know her name and where she lived.

"Hildur Onosdotter," she told them absently, and gave the name of her village.

"And what is Hildur doing here?"

"I'm going to my sister Britta."

"Where's she live?"

Hildur shrugged. Her head was spinning and when they let go of her arms she collapsed.

Failing to get any further information out of her, they concluded that she must be a vagrant, without any means of support apart from selling her body, and was probably drunk. Under the *Tjänstehjonsstadgan* [21] of 1664, vagrancy was against the law. Everyone who was capable of working was obligated to work to support themselves. To fail to do so called for immediate arrest and eventual imprisonment in the notorious *spinnhuset.* [22] Likewise for public drunkenness. No considerations existed as to sex, age, or physical condition.

Hildur woke up in a foul-smelling room surrounded by darkness. Struggling to sit up, she discovered her arms and legs were tied down—like those of the man on the bench before his head was chopped off!

"No!" she screamed. "No! No! No! I did nothing wrong!"

---

21. The Hired Household Servants' Act.

22. Spinning mill which served as a women's prison.

She tried to jerk her arms free, but they were too tightly bound. The more she tried to free herself, the more hysterical she became. Presently she heard footsteps approaching, then a door opened, letting in a faint ray of light. Two men entered and stood on either side of her, staring down into her face. Hildur squinted her eyes shut to avoid seeing the axe, which one of them must have. She was so frightened she could hardly breathe.

"*Fallandesjuka,*"[23] one of them concluded, as if she weren't there.

"Hardly," replied the other. "She's just one of them bitchy dames who likes ta play theater. Best we keep her tied down till she's broken into submission."

The door closed behind them and once again she was left in darkness.

Because Hildur had no address or proof of employment, much less a pass from her home parish giving her permission to travel to Stockholm, she was convicted of vagrancy, as well as probable prostitution and drunken behavior, and sent to the *spinnhuset.* There she spent the next few months confined to a cold damp seven square foot stone cell containing only a wooden box bed with a bit of musty straw on which to lie, a rough horse-hair blanket, and in one corner a bucket that was only emptied once it was full. A tiny barred window up near the ceiling let in a slight draft, but no light. During the day she was sometimes untied and allowed to move freely about the room in the darkness, with nothing but her thoughts and her growing insanity for company. And a herd of hungry rats. To keep them at bay, she spent hours walking round and round the edge of the room, first clockwise, then counter clockwise, while they scampered around her feet. But worst of all, she was followed by a crowd of jeering spectators who were waiting for night to come, when she would be tied down and beheaded. Nor did sleep offer any refuge, for it was then that the nightmares took possession of her. Over and over again the executioner stood with his axe poised above her head while she begged for mercy. Or Reverend Holmgren chased her, tearing at her clothes. Or the devil himself prodded her from behind with his pitch fork, while a myriad of evil creatures, the likes of which were depicted on the walls of her parish church, crawled into all her bodily openings and gnawed at her innards. And always the executioner waiting in the background with his axe. Nor could she wake up from such nightmares, for they followed into her waking hours. There was no escaping them. They consumed her, erasing

---

23. "Falling sickness," epilepsy.

her past and offering no future, leaving nothing but the horror of the endless present.

Each night when the warder came in to strap her arms and legs down she kicked and fought with all her strength, but to no avail. He showed no mercy towards her, treating her as though she were a wild, insensitive animal rather than a human being.

"The more she screams and fights, the longer she'll have to stay in the cell," he told her.

But she had no control over her body. Inevitably, spasms took over, causing her to chew her tongue until blood-red froth bubbled from her mouth. Then, just when the axe was poised over her and about to fall, she mercifully slipped into unconsciousness and the straps were pulled tight over her arms and legs.

One night a new warder came into her cell, a giant of a man with a long red scar down one cheek. As usual, Hildur fought frantically against being tied down, yelling and spitting at him, but he was much stronger than she was.

"Hold still, *din hor djävel!*"[24] he commanded.

But she continued fighting to get lose.

"Maybe this'll calm Hildur down," he remarked calmly.

Grasping her by the ankles, he dragged her to the end of the bed and spread her legs as far apart as he could before tying them down. Before she realized it, he had dropped his britches to his knees and rammed himself into her. Her back arched in pain, her body contracted, and once again she lost consciousness.

The next morning when she was untied she could hardly stand up for the pain in her lower abdomen.

Not long afterwards, without any explanation, Hildur was moved from the isolation cell into a large room where the woman prisoners both worked and slept.

"If Hildur doesn't want to be sent to the dark cell then she'd better pay attention to the rules," she was told. "The first rule is that one must always be polite and respectful to the warders and obey them without

---

24. Equivalent of "you bitch."

question. Second, there shall be silence at all times. All talking, laughing, and singing is forbidden, as well as any contact with one's fellow prisoners by the use of words, signs, letters, or presents. Third, prisoners are required to help with the housework: carrying in water, bringing in fire wood, cooking, and cleaning, as well as keeping one's own body and sleeping quarters clean. The work day begins at 5:00 a.m. and ends at 8:00 p.m. during which time each woman shall perform the tasks assigned her: carding wool, preparing flax, spinning, knitting, or sewing. Any lack of respect or infringement of these rules will result in being confined to either the light or the dark cell, as well as a reduction in food rations."

Once Hildur was out of the dark cell and no longer strapped down at night her nightmares abated somewhat. Even the picture of the man being decapitated receded far enough into the background that it no longer caused her to have convulsions. Thus life in the *spinnhuset* was almost bearable—at first. However, she had failed to understand the seriousness of the rules until she unknowingly broke one of them. When given a set of cards and a basket of wool she remarked that she would rather spin than card wool. Not only was she locked into a cell to ponder her disrespectfulness toward the warder who had given her the wool to card, but she was forced to card for the entire two years that she was in the *spinnhuset*.

"Hildur must learn to submit her will to those above her," she was told over and over again. " 'Tis her place in society to respect and obey her betters."

Combing wool between cards fifteen hours a day, day after day, week after week, month after month, was exhausting, as well as the eternal rasping sound that raked her ears. It quickly became a form of torture. Regardless of the weather outside, the room was always stuffy and filled with dust, making breathing difficult. The few existing windows were covered with years of dust and never opened. The inmates never saw a tree or the sky, yet they were aware of the changing of the seasons: in the winter they froze and in the summer the heat was unbearable. That, coupled with the poor quality and quantity of the food, undermined the health of most of the long-term prisoners. Any epidemic that found its way into the *spinnhuset* was guaranteed to reap a goodly number of victims before moving on.

In spite of the rule of silence, a great deal of communication was carried out under cover of darkness. After working hours the fire on the open hearth, which was the only source of light, was banked to save wood. Consequently, no warder could watch the women's every move and they were able to whisper quietly amongst themselves without being observed. Hildur soon discovered that she was living amongst women and girls of all ages and backgrounds. Some were simply vagrants, who had had the bad luck to be arrested because they had no place to live or no means of support. Others had supported themselves as prostitutes, or as petty thieves, stealing to feed and clothe themselves or their children. Some begged instead of stealing. Others sold *brännvin* illegally or had been picked up for being drunk in public. But the consequences were the same: incarceration in the dreaded *spinnhuset*. There were even murderers amongst them, unmarried girls who had suffocated or drowned their illegitimate babies immediately after birth and hidden the bodies in the hope of saving their reputations. To be an unwed mother was to be an outcast in society, with very little hope of finding a job.

One day a new girl was assigned to the bed next to Hildur's. Under the cover of darkness she confessed to Hildur that she had been so hungry that she had picked up an apple that had fallen into the gutter from a heavy-laden tree on the far side of a wooden fence. Before she had even had a chance to bite into it she was grabbed by a manservant from the house behind the fence. He propelled her to his master, a well-to-do man of great importance, who had no sympathy for the poor.

"Stealing is a punishable crime," she was told harshly.

"But Sir, it was lying on the side of the street in the gutter," she replied.

"It did not belong to her. To take something that does not belong to one is stealing," was his answer.

She was given a month in the *spinnhuset* for stealing and lack of respect for the upper class who were her superiors.

For Hildur, time stood still in the silence of the *spinnhuset*. The only sound was the rhythmless rasping of the cards scraping together, hour after hour. It was a torment that forced many to the edge of their sanity. One day, when she had been carding continuously for a year and a half, Hildur crossed over that edge.

"I cannot stand this deadly silence one more minute!" she yelled at

43

the top of her lungs. "Let us all sing!"

She began singing "la-la-la" off key, as loud as she could.

Immediately one of the warders grabbed her by the hair.

"Shut up, Bitch!" she commanded, dragging her out of the room and down the hallway to the dark cell. Hildur stumbled along behind her, still singing.

By the end of the day she was still singing in the darkness as though she were drunk. Finally a priest was sent to talk sense to her, whereupon she showed her lack of respect by turning her back on him. But when the night warder came on duty he declared braggingly that he would take care of her.

"Time ta quiet down," he ordered upon entering the cell.

Hildur was huddling in the corner, by now just singing gibberish. She gave no indication that she noticed his presence. Without warning, he grabbed her and threw her on the bed. Only when he had strapped down one of her arms did she come to her senses.

"Let go of me!" she screamed, swinging wildly with her free arm. By the time he had managed to catch it and tie it securely he was already aroused.

"I see she wants the same treatment as last time," he remarked with a laugh.

She kicked and spit like a wild cat, but was powerless against him.

This time she wasn't spared the pain and degradation by losing consciousness. She was fully aware of the disgusting manner in which he invaded her. After he left the room she turned her head as far to one side as her restraints allowed and vomited onto the floor.

With the coming of summer, Hildur was informed that she had served her two years and was now free to leave. She was given the clothes she had been wearing the day she was arrested, along with the bundle of possessions she had been carrying, in exchange for her prison clothes. The fact that her dress fit more snugly than it had previously didn't strike her as strange. She was fourteen now and had surely grown in the past two years. She had no idea of how emaciated she had become, thanks to the prison food.

Before being set free, she was sent to the director of the *spinnhuset*. When he questioned her about her plans, she said she was going to look for her sister Britta.

"That lie will get Hildur nowhere. When Hildur was first arrested we

44

checked all the parish registers in the Stockholm area for someone by the name of Britta Unosdotter. There is no such person. Therefore, I suggest that Hildur quit lying and return to her home parish before she lands in the *spinnhuset* again." His voice was hard and unfriendly.

Hildur started to protest, but thought better of it. Instead, she watched as he wrote something on a paper, tossed a bit of blotting sand over it, then handed it to her.

"What is this?" she asked, for she had never learned to read.

"It's a pass permitting her to travel back to her home parish."

Without further explanation, he stood up and ushered her from the room. A waiting warder guided her to a door, opened it, and told her good-bye. She heard it shut behind her, followed by the click of a key turning in the lock. Suddenly she found herself standing alone in the world she had been taken from two years earlier. It was as if no time had passed. The weather was warm and the sun looked down from a cloudless sky, as it had the day she had walked through the customs gate into the city. Without so much as glancing at it, she folded the scrap of paper she had been given and put it in her pocket along with the few coins she had been paid for her endless carding.

Hildur had no idea what to do or where to go. Ignorant of the rules of the city, she was terrified of unknowingly doing something wrong and being sent back to the *spinnhuset.* She wondered if it were true, that Britta was not in Stockholm, but quickly concluded that even if she were, it would be impossible to find her.

Walking against the stream of wagons and people coming into the town, she found her way to the toll gate and began the long journey home. But as she walked, it occurred to her that there was no reason to return to her old village, for she no longer had a home or family there. Better that she try to find work as a maid somewhere along the way. But how did one go about such a thing? She was afraid to simply knock on a stranger's door. What should she say when asked about her past employment? Or asked for recommendations. Or why she was not in her own parish. Usually a girl's parents arranged her first position and spoke for her, but without parents, she was going to have to do such things herself. Yet everytime she paused before a farm, instead of going to the door, she promised herself she would try the next one instead.

Finally, after having walked for several days, she gathered her courage and knocked on the kitchen door of a large farm house. The door was opened by the cook who summoned her mistress.

"I heard that Madame is looking for a servant girl," she lied.

The woman looked her up and down.

"And where'd she hear that? We've no need of more help," she replied haughtily. "And even if we did, we'd never hire a whore with a whore child."

"But I have no child," Hildur told her.

"Does she think that I can't see that pregnant belly bulging out from underneath her dress!" she declared.

Hildur looked down at herself and gingerly touched her belly. Was that why her old clothes no longer fit? She had never looked at herself without her clothes on. To look at one's own body was sinful. She turned around and ran down the steps as the door slammed shut behind her. Once out of sight of the house, she sank to the ground, shaking, with her back against a tree. It couldn't be true! It must just be a bad dream. Gingerly she slid her hands over her belly. It was no dream. But how could it have happened? She had never been together with a boy. Then suddenly she remembered. Of course! The guard. When he had her tied down. That it had been done to her without her consent made it less shameful somehow, yet she couldn't tell people that, that it wasn't her fault. To have been in the *spinnhuset* was nearly as shameful as being an unmarried mother. Shame turned life black. She had heard about girls who found themselves with child, how some of them "went into the lake" to escape their shame. No one hired a pregnant girl, and if she had been lucky enough to have a job, she was fired when her condition was discovered. And how could she take care of a baby when she had no family to help her and no place to live? She would end her days in the god-forsaken poor house, amongst old people who were sick and dying or crazy. Suddenly she understood why girls went into the lake.

After a while she got to her feet and continued walking while mulling over her situation. She had heard about girls who gave birth secretly, then murdered the baby and hid the body. But it seemed as though they always were caught. When she was a child, a housemaid in the village had managed to keep her growing stomach hidden and, after giving birth in a little-used shed, had suffocated the child and buried it under the floor. For months afterwards every time someone went into the shed they heard a baby crying. Finally one day the village elders decided to tear up the floor and, sure enough, there lay a rat-chewed child's body. By that time the girl had moved on to a job in another parish and started a new life. Eventually she was found, but denied having given birth to an illegitimate child. But when she was taken back to the shed and shown the body, she broke down and confessed. That she had been raped by her master had no bearing on the situation. In court he called her a liar and denied having ever touched her. She was a murderer. Her trial was straight forward and her execution took place shortly afterwards. The event had been followed closely by everyone in the village. Although she had been well-liked and known to be a hard worker, her sin was unforgivable in people's eyes. For years afterwards her fate was thrown up before the young village girls to frighten them. Hildur was not willing to take the risk of following in her footsteps. Although the thought frightened her, the lake seemed a better solution. In the meantime, she kept walking.

Now and then she stopped at a farm to beg or buy a bit of bread and cheese or occasionally a slice of smoked sausage. Most people scorned her and, if the woman of the house was pregnant or had small children, she was told to go away from behind a locked door. It was a well-known fact that the presence of an unwed mother could cause *engelska sjukan* in a child.

One afternoon she was stopped by two policemen on horseback. They pinned her between them as if she were a runaway convict, while their horses stamped and snorted, their sweaty hair sticking to her bare arms.

"Name!" one of the barked.

"Hildur Unosdotter," she answered politely.

"Parish?"

"Svartsjö."

"What's Hildur doing outside her parish without a pass?"

"I have a pass," she replied, digging in her pocket and handing him the paper the director had given her.

"Hmmm," he murmured when he had read it. "So she's been in Stockholm. And what, pray tell, was she doing there?"

"I was looking for my sister Britta."

"Does she not know that Britta Unosdotter is married to Lars Engelholm and is mistress of Lunna Gård?"

"She is? I had no idea," she replied, shocked.

Suddenly Hildur felt a great weight lifted from her shoulders. She was headed the right way. Her big sister Britta, who had taken care of her as a child, would know what to do.

The following day she caught a glimpse of Lunna Gård from the top of a hill and within several hours she was standing in front of the house.

Even though she had never been there, it felt like home.

She straightened her dress as much as possible, then knocked on the front door timidly, rather than go to the kitchen door. She was family, not hired help.

At the second knock the door was opened by a housemaid.

"Who is it?" she heard her sister call from the depths of the house.

"Best that Madame comes to see for herself," the girl answered.

But Britta had been warned, for the news traveled faster than Hildur walked.

"No!" Britta screamed when she saw her younger sister. "Get away from here! Thou art no longer my sister! Hildur's big belly and her pass written out by the *spinnhuset* director have brought shame upon me. And upon my husband and his family as well. Go! Let the rest of us live in peace and Godliness."

"But 'tis not as it appears," Hildur began. "I can explain."

"No words can explain away Hildur's belly and the *spinnhuset*. Get out of here before my good man or his mother sees thee. Do not ever darken this door again or claim to be related to me! Is that understood?"

"Yes, Britta," she replied humbly, looking down at her feet. Britta's wrath always unnerved her.

"Be gone!" Britta ordered. Her right arm flew straight out, index finger pointing toward the road.

Hildur walked away stunned. She felt as if she had been physically kicked and spat upon. Never had she imagined that her own sister would turn her back on her. From what she could see of the farm, Britta had certainly *"kommit upp i smöret,"*[25] which had always been her dream. She wondered if Lars Engelholm was aware of her poverty-stricken background and alcoholic parents. Perhaps not, for Lunna Gård was far away from where they had grown up. Knowing Britta, she had probably presented herself as the woman she had always wanted to be, and in so doing, had become that woman.

If she were to be honest, Britta's reaction did not entirely surprise her. In any situation, Britta always thought of herself first. Compassion for other people and their misfortunes had never been a part of her make-up. And now it was clear that she had finally left her past behind her, hopefully well buried.

---

25. Literally, "come up in the butter," to have become well-to-do. Peasants often ate their porridge from a large communal bowl. In an indentation in the center of the porridge was a pat of butter, which was a luxury. Everyone must begin by eating around the edge of the bowl. Whoever reached the melted butter first was said to have "come up in the butter," which was everyone's aim.

Hildur continued down the road in a daze, without knowing where to go or what to do. Not far beyond Lunna Gård she took a road she had never traveled, for, more than ever, she did not wish to return to her home parish. People there had not been particularly kind to Uno and his family when she was growing up. They were not like everyone else. Her father had refused to marry her mother, even though he had fathered all the children. After each birth the parish priest had tried to force him to marry her, but each time he had refused. Also, the village elders were constantly after him because of his drinking. People's comment through the years had always been, "No good will come of Uno's brats." For Hildur to return with her belly in the wind would provide them with proof of their prophesy.

She never knew how many days she walked or where she was or where she was going. She simply walked, convinced that, if she walked long enough and far enough, one day she would wake up from the nightmare and there would be no baby inside her. The summer days were long and warm. There were people on the road and in the fields. Many who saw her spat on the ground three times. Others looked the other way, pretending not to see her. It was as if she were carrying a sign that said "HOR."[26] Every morning she awoke into the nightmare. Rather than escaping from it, it grew larger and larger, consuming her.

By now her flight had taken her past a number of lakes, but she could never quite make up her mind to take the final step. There was plenty of time, or so she thought. One day the road suddenly narrowed into a seemingly endless forest. There were no more lakes. As night approached she came upon a woodsman's hut beside a stream. Inside it was equipped for winter, with a sleeping ledge, firewood, a kettle, tin basin, wooden plate, mug, a hunting knife, and in a sealed tin, a few phosphorescent matches that could be struck on a stone. She could hardly believe her good luck. For the first time since leaving the *spinnhuset* she slept with a roof over her head instead of under a tree.

Towards morning she was woken by a sharp pain in her back and abdomen. She understood immediately that she had missed her chance to go into the lake, that she would have to find another solution. As it was, she barely had enough time to make a fire and set the kettle to boil. Several of the women in the *spinnhuset* had talked about having given birth alone, leaving her with some idea of what to expect and what to do. With shaking hands she laid two of her mother's dresses on the floor and covered them with an apron, then tore off one of the strings with

---

26. Not a prostitute, but one who is promiscuous or has committed adultery.

which to tie the cord. Beside them she lay the hunting knife and a clean apron. Yet all the while she kept asking herself why she was going to so much bother. The only alternative she had now was to smother the child once it was born. It wouldn't matter if it landed on the hard floor. In fact, it would be better. "Born dead." At the last minute, she decided it would be better to give birth outside, so as to be able to easily cover her tracks. Then she would take them both into the first lake she came to. Taking a basin of warm water and an apron, she hurried outside. She could feel the baby pressing to come out. Hunkering down above the apron, she let her body tell her what to do. When it told her to push, she pushed with all her might. She felt the child slide from her body and drop onto the apron. Looking down between her legs she met two big, somewhat surprised eyes looking up at her from a perfectly formed girl-child. It began to cry, the arms and legs flailing wildly. Without thinking, she picked it up and cradled it in her arms comfortingly.

When dawn came, she washed both herself and the child and buried the afterbirth, then lay down in the shade beside the stream, with the child at her breast. Several hours later she awoke to discover that she was no longer imprisoned in the nightmare, that the baby was not inside her anymore. Her fear and anxiety were gone. Looking at the child, she realized that it was the only blood relative she had left in the world. Kneeling by the edge of the stream, she dipped her hand into the water, then placed it on the child's head.

"I baptize thee Signe, in the name of the Father, the Son, and Holy Ghost. Amen." she repeated solemnly. She never questioned her right to do so or whether it was valid. If God gave a disgusting man like Reverend Holmgren the power to baptize people in His name, then surely He would accept her simple act when no priest was available. Now the child was safe from the many dangers surrounding it. And neither of them was going to go into the lake. That night, in spite of a gnawing hunger, she fell into a deep and peaceful sleep.

The following morning she gathered her few possessions and swaddled Signe in some of her mother's clothes that she had taken when she had left home so long ago. Laying the child on top of her bundle, she hoisted it over her shoulder and set out, hoping to beg a bit of bread somewhere. The day was warm and before long she felt weak from hunger, her legs barely holding her upright, her bundle heavier than before. And now she had another life to care for besides her own. Realizing what lay ahead, her thoughts once again turned to the lake. But just when she felt too weak go on, the road emerged from the forest onto an open plain. In the distance she could make out a group of people cutting hay and hanging it to dry. As she approached, they stopped working and moved into a grove of trees to drink coffee. One of the women motioned her to join them. Hildur hung the sack from the limb of the tree furthest from the group and went to her.

"And who might this be?" the woman asked, motioning her to sit down.

"Hildur. Hildur Unosdotter," she answered, immediately regretting that she had given her family name. She was ashamed to be related to Drunken-Uno, as her father was referred to behind his back.

The woman handed her a piece of dry bread and a tin cup of poor man's coffee made from roasted rye rather than real coffee beans. Although the farmhands and maids were helping take hay on a large, prosperous farm, real coffee was considered to be too good to be wasted on peasants who wouldn't appreciate it. But Hildur couldn't imagine that real coffee could have tasted better.

"And where might Hildur be going?" the woman asked.

None of the others appeared to be interested in the new-comer, for which Hildur was thankful.

"I know not," she replied quietly. "I need to find work somewhere."

"What sort of work?"

"Anything."

"Excuse me for asking, but what does Hildur have in the sack that she hung on the tree over there?"

Hildur hesitated, reluctant to answer. She looked down at her hands holding the tin cup.

"Hildur need not answer. I can see the truth by the milk stains on her blouse," the woman told her kindly.

By now the others had gotten to their feet and the women were packing together the coffee things.

"I must go back to work now," the woman said. "If Hildur continues on down the road a piece she'll come to a dilapidated cottage with a thatched roof on the far side of the road. The key hangs beside the door. Go in and make thyself at home. Eat the rest of the porridge in the pan standing on the hearth. I shall come as soon as I'm finished here."

By now Ester and Hildur had come to a crossroads. Hildur stopped.

"If it had not been for her, I know not how Signe and I would have survived. She took us into her home, the most humble abode imaginable, and cared for us until I was well enough to go on. I shall never forget her kindness. And I took Britta at her word and stayed away, for she would have been more ashamed of me than I was of our father. But I have always wondered if Lars Engelholm ever learned the truth about her background. At any rate, her lies enabled her to live the luxurious life she'd always dreamed of.

"But here's where we must go our separate ways," she continued. "I've a long way to go before dark and Ester should return home. But now that Britta is no longer making the rules, I hope that we may meet again. I live just beyond the next parish. There I am known as Arvidsson's *käring*[27] because I'm ten years older than my husband Sten Arvidsson. I doubt that people there even know my real name, which is just as well."

"I have no chance to go so far from home," Ester told her, "but *Moster*[28] Hildur would be most welcome to visit me at Björkdalen—or Sjöströms, as it is called."

"I'd like very much to, if I survive the winter."

"I shall look forward to that day!"

And with that, they parted with a handshake, each glad for their all too brief meeting.

When she got home Sjöström didn't bother to ask where she had been for so long. She had behaved badly and Holmgren had been right to shame her, although much of the shame went out over he himself for not having had better control over his wife. However, several days later, when he happened to hear that she had not been present at the *gravöl,* he demanded to know where she had been and what she had been doing.

"I was with *Moster* Hildur," she told him.

"*Moster* Hildur!" he snorted. "That old beggar woman? Does Ester really believe that story about her being Mor Britta's younger sister?"

"Yes, because it is true. Besides, why would she come all this way to say good-by if she was not Mor Britta's sister? There is nothing for her to gain by doing so. Did you see Reverend Holmgren's face when he saw her? He knows who she is. Ask him."

"Has Ester no respect? One does not ask the parish priest such things."

"Both Mor Britta and *Moster* Hildur came from Svartsjö Parish. Uno's daughters. Write to the present priest in Svartsjö Parish and ask

---

27. Old lady.

28. Mother's sister, aunt.

52

about them."

"Be not childish, Ester. A man of my standing cannot do that."

"Then I shall do it," she told him.

A week later Ester received a letter, confirming Hildur's background.

RAOUL

Björkdalen 1871

Winter had seemed never-ending. For months the fields were a sea of white, edged with drifts like frozen waves. But as the sun rose higher in the sky with each day, nature began to creep out of hibernation. Thin green shoots pushed their way up through the snow, dragging buds behind them, which were soon to open into dangling bell-like snow drops. In more protected nooks and crannies, where the snow had already melted, reddish-brown heads peeked out from under soggy autumn leaves, then burst into bright yellow coltsfoot blossoms. Winter was over at last.

Ester's second confinement occurred in much more favorable circumstances. The weather was warm, the child's head was down, and Sister Alma arrived in good time. And Ester was surprised by the sense of fulfillment she experienced when Sister Alma announced to Sjöström that she had given him a boy-child. Without consulting her, he named his son Raoul.

Ester's maternal instinct blossomed. Having two children to care for gave her a life somewhat independent of Sjöström. Like most husbands and wives, they shared very little; and even less than ordinarily because of the twelve years difference in age. Marriage was a practical and economical arrangement, with each partner having his or her separate functions and jobs. More than anything else, their joint effort was that of producing offspring. While Ester loved Raoul with an instinctual mother love, she loved Kajsa in a deeper way. She had saved Kajsa's life as an infant and in so doing, Kajsa had given her back the lust for life she lost when she married Sjöström. And as the girl grew, she spread joy all around her with her sunny disposition.

Raoul, on the other hand, proved to be a difficult baby. He nursed poorly and cried much of the time, both day and night. Nothing seemed to help. Ester held him as long as possible after he had finished nursing, but was careful to put him down before she could be accused of spoiling him. But as soon as she laid him in the cradle he began to howl. As time went on she became more and more worried, thinking there must be something wrong with him. It was not at all uncommon for a child to die before reaching its first birthday. Her fear was not so much for Raoul, for he would surely go to heaven and escape all the sorrow and suffering of earthly life, but rather, she feared Sjöström's reaction if the boy should die. He would consider it to be her fault, no matter what the circumstances. He was obsessed with having an heir who would take over his name and the farm. From the day he was born, Sjöström guarded the boy jealously, forbidding anyone but Ester and Svea to go near him.

Kajsa did not share her father's enthusiasm for Raoul, however. She couldn't see anything special about him. He couldn't walk or talk or feed himself; he just cried, causing her mother and Old Svea a lot of worry. Nor was she allowed to go anywhere near him. If she should happen to go close to the cradle when her father was in the room, he yelled at her threateningly. Once, when he smelled of *brännvin,* he slapped her so hard that she fell and hit her head on the edge of the hearth. Crying, she turned to her mother for comfort.

"Leave her alone!" she heard her father yell. "She must learn to obey."

She saw her mother shrug, then pick up Raoul and begin to nurse him.

Although she had no actual memory of her first year, seeing her mother hold and rock Raoul while nursing him awakened a longing she had hitherto not experienced. If she could only crawl up into her mother's lap and be rocked! Kajsa wished they had never gotten Raoul.

Upstairs, Mor Dagmar had soon had enough of the child's crying. One afternoon she thumped her cane angrily on the floor above the kitchen. Old Svea hurried up to her.

"I cannot take any more of that child's wailing!" she informed Svea so loudly that Ester could hear her down in the kitchen. "Shut him up with a few drops."

"As Ma'am wishes," Svea answered. Although Mor Dagmar was more or less confined to her room, she still ruled the household when it suited her. To encounter her displeasure was unpleasant.

"Can Ester find a clean rag," Svea said when she came back downstairs. She disappeared into the best room, returning with the *brännvin* decanter. Ester looked at her questioningly, for she had assumed that her husband possessed the only key to the cupboard.

"There is an extra key, kept for emergencies," Svea explained.

Kajsa watched curiously as her mother dug through her sewing basket until she found a scrap of newly woven linen left over from the towels she had recently woven.

"Is this alright?" she asked, handing it to Svea.

"Perfect."

In the meantime, Svea had poured a bit of *brännvin* from the decanter into a glass. Tying a knot in one corner of the cloth, she let it soak up the *brännvin,* then placed it in Raoul's open mouth. When his tongue touched the wet cloth a surprised expression crossed his face. Then his mouth closed around it and he began to suck. A minute later he was asleep and the room was silent at last. Kajsa watched enviously. She would have liked to have a taste also, but her mother and Svea seemed to have forgotten her.

"That age-old method always works when all else fails," Svea remarked. "I hope Mor Dagmar is satisfied now." The tone of her voice was disquieting.

From that day on, whenever Raoul cried Mor Dagmar's cane thumped the floor angrily, often accompanied by an even angrier, "Shut him up!" and he was given "a few drops" to keep peace in the household.

However, to Svea's way of thinking, Raoul was getting too much *brännvin* for his age. Instead, she suggested they try something else, at least during the daytime.

"Bring me a rag that is a little larger than the one we use for the *brännvin,*" she instructed Ester one afternoon when Raoul began crying as usual.

While Ester fetched a rag, Svea went into the pantry and returned with a *sockertopp.*[29] Laying it in the wooden sugar box, she cut off a piece about the size of the end of her thumb, and handed it to Ester. Kajsa waited anxiously, for she was always given a little piece of sugar whenever the *sockertopp* was cut. But to her disappointment, no one took notice of her.

"Put this in thy mouth and loosen it up with thy saliva," Svea instructed her mother. "Then spit it out into the rag."

That done, she tied the melting sugar securely in the cloth and put it in Raoul's mouth. He immediately began to suck frantically.

"Perhaps we should try a *dihorn.*[30] It is more practical," Svea decided. "If I remember right, there is one in the top drawer of the cupboard there."

Ester hunted through the miscellaneous objects in the drawer until she found a hollow, slightly curved cow horn, its yellowish surface

---

29. A cone-shaped sugar cube about 8 inches high. Pieces were cut from it into a special wooden box with a built-in hinged knife. The small grains fell through holes into a drawer below and the larger pieces stayed in the upper box.

30. An early form of baby bottle made from a hollow sheep's or cow's horn with a leather-covered hole in the pointed end. It was filled with milk mixed with sugar or thin porridge, and placed in a holder in the child's bed. (Di is pronounced 'dee' and means suckle or nurse.)

polished so smooth that it was almost translucent. Over a hole at the pointed end was tied a bit of what had once been soft chamois-like leather, but which was now dry and brittle.

"Is this it?" she asked, holding it up.

"Oh, yes. Good," Svea assured her. "Now see if Ester can find the holder for it. It should be a rather long flat piece of wood, bent at one end, with a hole large enough to set the horn in."

Ester found it lying inconspicuously on its edge along the side of the drawer, looking like any ordinary long forgotten scrap of wood. But when she pulled it out she discovered that the front side was decorated with delicately carved flowers twisting from one end to the other.

"Who has made this?" she wondered. "It is beautiful!"

"Probably Sjöström's grandfather. From what I heard when I first came to work here, they had had many children, all of whom were fed with the *dihorn*. Women of a little higher standing didn't nurse their babies in those days, especially not those who had access to cows' milk. Many of Grandma Sjöström's children became sick and died soon after birth. Personally, I think it is because they should have been nursed, which is nature's intention. Some of the things that were put into a *dihorn* cannot have been good for a newborn child."

"What sort of things?"

"Rye porridge thinned out with milk and often laced with a bit of *brännvin*, for one. That must've been hard on a newborn baby's stomach. However, Raoul is past that dangerous age now." She handed Ester a knife. "Here. Cut off the old piece of leather."

Once Ester had removed the leather she held the horn up to the light to look through it, but the small end was blocked.

"What's stuck in here?" she asked Svea.

Taking it, Svea peered into the horn, then poked at it with a darning needle. When that didn't work she tried pouring hot water into it. Eventually a slimy black clot fell out onto the table.

"It's no wonder babies died, if this is what was being given to them. If Ester's going to feed Raoul with this, she must make sure to wash it thoroughly after each time it is used. Don't let anything spoil in there."

Once the horn had been washed and a new chamois cloth tied over the end, Svea filled it with a mixture of watered down milk and a little sugar and set it in the holder, which they then wedged between the side of the cradle and the mattress, within reach of Raoul's mouth. In no time he had found it and began sucking contentedly.

By the time spring came, Raoul was old enough to be given more solid food, as well as cows' milk. Traditionally, the oldest member of the household was assigned the task of masticating the child's food between toothless gums until it was mashed to an easily swallowed paste. But when approached on the matter, Mor Dagmar put her foot down.

"Never!" she declared. "That child has cost me hours of sleep and I do not take kindly to him. Mark my words, he is never going to be capable of taking over Björkdalen."

Thus Mor Dagmar had had her final say on the matter. Instead, the job went to One-eyed Klara. She was over 80 and had at one time been a kitchen maid at Björkdalen. As with all servants, when she became too old to work, she had been forced to move to a *backstuga,*[31] a tiny cave-like hut built into the side of a hill on the edge of Björkdalen's forest. No longer having an income, she lived the life of a pauper, barely subsisting by doing odd jobs that now and then came her way: helping with the big twice-yearly laundering and the slaughtering of the Christmas pig, or the enormous pre-Christmas baking, as well as occasionally washing and preparing the dead for burial. For such jobs she was given a little rye flour for porridge or bread and sometimes a couple of salted herrings or potatoes. But never any copper coins. In spite of her bad back, which prevented her from standing straight, she was clever and able to make do with what little she had. But she couldn't help experiencing a sting of resentment every time she was forced to accept what she looked upon as alms. Such scraps were hardly payment for the time and effort she put into helping others. She felt degraded. However, she didn't consider masticating little Raoul's food as work, for certainly some of it might slip down her own throat at the same time. Besides, she had no choice. She was told simply to present herself in the kitchen on the second day of Easter.

"Who's that?" Kajsa asked from where she knelt on the kitchen *utdragssoffa,* peering out the window. She was two and a half and curious about everything and everyone around her.

Ester went to the window. "Oh, 'Tis One-eyed Klara," she answered.

"Why's she coming?"

"She's going to chew Raoul's food for him."

Kajsa looked at her mother as though she had said Klara was going

---

31. Literally "back cottage," usually in very poor condition, where the poorest, mostly old people, lived when they could no longer work.

to fly to the moon.

"Raoul has no teeth yet, so he can't chew his food himself," her mother continued.

Such an explanation was hardly enlightening, but there was no chance to ask more, for Klara was already standing in the entranceway. Kajsa had never seen such a person. She was so bent over that she looked like she was searching for something on the ground by her feet. It was only by leaning heavily on her two sticks that she could keep from tipping over frontwards.

"Good day," she declared cheerfully. Her gaze fell on Kajsa. "Is this Little Kajsa? My, how she has grown! She was just a baby when I saw her last."

"Yes, Ma'am, Kajsa's big now," Kajsa told her proudly. She liked the old woman immediately. Most adults ignored children. But Klara had not only noticed her, she had spoken directly to her, even before speaking to her mother.

"And this is the baby," Ester interrupted, nodding toward the cradle.

Klara gave Kajsa a friendly pat on the head before going over to look at Raoul.

"Is Ester going to wean him now?" she asked. "He looks big enough."

"Yes. I have had a lot of trouble with him crying, so he's been getting extra milk with sugar in a *dihorn,* as well as my milk."

"There's one thing Ester must understand if she is going to wean him: Once she stops nursing him she must never again give him the breast. If she does, he will have misfortune the rest of his life."

"Misfortune? What sort of misfortune?"

"He will become a *tvedägging* [32] and will fail at everything he tries to do. Any creature he touches'll wither away and die. And if he comes into a house where someone is churning, the cream'll never turn to butter. Also, his very words can harm others. Mark my words, 'tis bad luck for anyone who meets him."

Ester nodded absently, not wanting to believe the old woman's words. Kajsa, on the other hand, failed to understand the words, but felt a darkness come over the room. She watched as Klara was given a piece of dried bread to masticate between her toothless gums. Once it was the consistency of mush, Ester gave her a spoonful of sugar to add to it. Finally, when no lumps remained, Klara spit the entire contents of her mouth into the palm of her hand, formed part of it into a ball, and placed it in Raoul's mouth. A happy gurgle and smacking of the tongue

---

32. Literally, "double suckler."

indicated his approval. Like a small bird, his mouth remained open in eager anticipation. And like a mother bird, Klara continued to chew and fill it until his eyelids grew heavy.

And so it was that One-eyed Klara came to Björkdalen's kitchen every afternoon. Because she had such difficulty walking, she spent more time going to and from the house than she spent feeding Raoul. Although her hut was isolated, there was a wagon path which passed close to it. Yet it never occurred to Sjöström to send one of his men to fetch her in the two-man cart. Once a person was relegated to a *backstuga* he or she ceased to exist for him. That she was keeping his son and heir alive was immaterial; there were many toothless people around who could do that. Kajsa, however, was fascinated by *Tant*[33] Klara. She always noticed Kajsa and stopped to talk with her, whereas her own mother never had time for such things anymore.

Several nights after Klara's first visit, Raoul once again began to howl. Ester was tired and rather than get out of bed and take out the *brännvin,* she lifted him out of the cradle and held him to her breast, glad that her milk had not yet dried up. Klara's warning passed through her head, but she ignored it. Surely once wouldn't hurt.

The following summer was late in coming and people began to look upon it with foreboding, afraid that another famine was on the way. Usually the hay would have been cut and dried by this time and many of the wild flowers would have finished blooming, but it was as if spring stood still and refused to give way to summer. Then suddenly, over night, the weather changed. The sun came out and burned away the clouds, the sky turned blue, and flowers burst into bloom. Kajsa was enchanted. Looking out the window, she saw that the yard was a sea of yellow.

"Mamma, can I go out an' pick those flowers?" she asked. "I's big enough to go by myself. I's more than three now. I won't go far away from the house. Please."

"Yes, Kajsa may go out, but she must keep a lookout in case *Gråben*[34] should be feeling hungry for little girls."

---

33. Used in the same way a child would use "aunt" for an older woman who was no relation.

34. "Gray legs," the nickname for wolves.

It was highly unusual for a wolf to come near a house in broad daylight, especially that time of year, but it was necessary to frighten children with the possibility of being eaten alive, in order to make sure they obeyed their parents.

Kajsa lifted the latch to the outside door gingerly, suddenly feeling not at all as big as she had thought she was. Cautiously, she put one foot out onto the stone step, then the other. The warmth of the stone under her bare feet was enticing after the winter's cold floors and she ventured further out. A light breeze made its way across the fields, gently swaying the tall grass which would soon be cut for hay, and causing the flowers in the yard to nod to her as if she were expected. *Gråben* was forgotten. She quickly became engrossed in picking a bouquet of dandelions for her mother. Her tiny fingers grasped each stem by its middle, stretching it toward her until the stem popped loose from the leaves below, then adding it to those in her other hand. As the bouquet grew, she squeezed the stems more and more tightly in her fist until the white "milk" ran down over her wrist. All the while she sang softly to herself, an off-tune melody whose words she made up as she went along. It wasn't until the crunching of gravel behind her broke into her reverie that she remembered her mother's warning. She jumped to her feet, too terrified to run.

"Mamma!" she screamed.

" 'Tis just me," a voice called out behind her.

Turning around, she saw Post-Anders on his way up to the house, bearing his huge leather mail pouch over one shoulder by its wide strap. He walked his five mile mail route three times a week, often bringing her mother a post card from one of her childhood friends. It was the only way they had of keeping in touch with each other, aside from meeting in church, if they happened to live in the same parish. Her mother would let her eyes go back and forth across the back side of the card before glancing at the picture on the front. All the while Kajsa waited anxiously, hoping that it would then be given to her. She loved the pictures: sometimes they were of flowers, other times buildings or drawings of children or animals. She saved them in the box in which she kept her special things, taking them out on rainy days and arranging them on the floor in front of her.

"Does Post-Anders have a pretty card for Mamma today?" she asked curiously.

"No cards today," he replied. "But I have a real letter for Kajsa's father. The kind that comes in an envelope without a picture." He held it up so she could see it.

"Oh," she mused. She had never seen such a letter before. She stood up and brushed off her dress with her free hand before following him into the kitchen.

"A letter for Sjöström," he declared, handing it to Old Svea.

"I'll see that he gets it," she answered, laying it face up on the table.

When Ester came into the kitchen to arrange for supper she saw it immediately.

"Who has written to Sjöström?" she asked Svea.

"I've no idea. Maybe there is a return address on the back." She hadn't bothered to look, for she had never learned to read.

Ester picked the letter up and turned it over. Written on the back flap in child-like penmanship was the name Fru E-C. Engström and an address in Stockholm.

"Hmmm," she muttered, perplexed. "Has Svea ever heard of a Fru E-C. Engström?"

Svea turned around and their eyes met briefly, the same thought going through both their minds.

"Surely it can't be someone's wife accusing him of..." Ester began. Quickly she dropped the letter back on the table as if it were hot and busied herself with preparing Kajsa's porridge.

Sjöström was as puzzled as they had been when he saw the letter. Kajsa watched curiously as he ran his thumb under the flap and pulled out the single piece of folded paper. He opened it and read aloud:

> *Dear Herr Sjöström,*
> *Herr Sjöström said that when I got my life in order, and perhaps even found a husband, that we could come to an agreement about Kajsa. In the past three years I have had a job, saved money and found myself a wonderful husband. Next month we are emigrating to America, together with the rest of his family. I would like to know when I can come and get Kajsa.*
> *Sincerely,*
>
> *Elsa-Carolina Engström*

"No!" Ester gasped and began to cry. Kajsa understood nothing except that someone was going to come and get her.

"Mamma, I don't want to go away!" she wailed.

"Get a hold on thy selves!" Sjöström told them roughly. "There's nothing to worry about. No one's going to take Kajsa away."

He turned to Ester.

"Even if she tried to go to court, it couldn't be settled within a month. Such things take time, as well as money. But she's made it easier for us by emigrating. Once she's gone I can become Kajsa's legal guardian,[35] claiming that the child was abandoned. That way she'll belong to us permanently."

"Is Sjöström sure?" she asked.

"Absolutely."

But he could see that neither Ester nor Kajsa was not completely convinced.

The next day he answered Elsa-Carolina Engström's letter, congratulating her on her marriage and wishing her well. In regards to Little Kajsa, he made it clear that her home was with them and requested that Fru Engström refrain from attempting to have any further contact with her or them.

Several days later he received a letter from Stockholm. Once again Ester became nervous, worried that Fru Engström was taking legal action. Without opening it, he scribbled "return to sender" across the envelope in bold letters and handed it to her.

"Give this to Post-Anders next time he comes," he told her.

But still Ester could not relax. She became over-protective, careful to never let the child out of her sight.

To appease her, once he was able to ascertain that the Engström family had left Sweden, he went to the officials and became Kajsa's legal guardian. Thereafter he visited the parish priest, requesting that he change the child's last name in the official records "for my wife's sake," as he expressed it. He watched as Reverend Holmgren drew a thick black line through Elsdotter, the shortened form of Elsa-Carolina's-daughter, and replaced it with Sjöström. Both Holmgren and Sjöström agreed that it was a relief to be rid of Elsa-Carolina once and for all.

"Now I've done all that I can possibly do," he told Ester when he came home. "Kajsa belongs to Ester now and no one can take her from thee.

---

35. Legal adoption did not exist at that time.

63

So I don't want to hear any more worrying and fussing over the matter." His voice had a slight edge to it, indicating that the matter was closed.

Ester was relieved, knowing Sjöström was in control of the situation. But it was a long time before Kajsa ceased to fear that someone was going to come and take her away. For weeks she stayed close to her mother, afraid to even go outdoors to pick flowers.

One morning several days later Kajsa was woken by the sound of talking and laughing out in the yard. She sat up and tried unsuccessfully to rub the sleep from her eyes, unable to wake up.

"Who's here?" she asked her mother, who was already up and dressed. "Kajsa wants to sleep more."

" 'Tis only the neighbors who have come to help take hay," Ester told her. " 'Tis way too early for Kajsa to get up. Lie down and go back to sleep. I'm going out to help, but Svea will be here to take care of Kajsa and Raoul when it's time to get up."

With that, Ester disappeared out the door and the voices faded into the distance.

It was the ringing of the *vällingklocka*[36] that woke Kajsa several hours later. The kitchen door was open and Pia and the milkmaid Maria were helping Old Svea carry out bread and cheese, a crock of salted herring, boiled potatoes, and a pot of porridge, as well as a bowl of raw-stirred lingonberries and sugar, to the long table under the giant maple tree. The aroma of freshly boiled coffee filled the kitchen and the cut-glass *brännvin* decanter stood waiting on a tray, like a soldier at attention, surrounded by a ring of tiny glasses. Hurriedly she got up, pulled her dress over her head, and went outside. Women and maids from the neighboring farms were gathered in the yard, wiping the sweat from their faces with the hems of their long skirts, while the men took turns splashing water from the horses' watering trough over their heads to cool themselves. They had been cutting and raking hay since the sun went up at 3:00 a.m.

"Come and sit down to breakfast," Sjöström called to them. "It'll soon be time to go back to work again."

People took their places on the long benches on either side of the

---

36. A large bell on the roof of an outbuilding on an estate or large farm, used to wake people and call them to work and to meals.

table, men on one side and women on the other, with Sjöström at the head. *Brännvin* glasses were filled for the men and farmhands, coffee cups for the women and maids. Sjöström stood up and raised his glass.

"Here's to what looks like the best hay harvest in recent years!" he declared. *"Skål!"*

The men and boys raised their glasses.

"Skål!" they repeated, emptying them in a single swallow. A couple of new farmhands, who were not more than ten or twelve years old, choked as the alcohol burned their throats. But they were doing men's work and thus must behave like men, as best they could.

All the while two year old Raoul stood beside his father proudly, his golden curls shining in the sunlight. Setting down his glass, Sjöström turned toward him as if he had suddenly become aware of his presence.

"And here we have the next Sjöström in the long line of Sjöströms!" he declared, picking him up. He reached for the *brännvin* and filled his glass once more, then passed the decanter along the men's side of the table. Following his lead, each of them refilled his glass.

"Three cheers for Raoul!" he cried, handing his glass to his son. "Drink up and show them what a man Raoul is already!"

Raoul shook his head.

"Come now," he insisted, holding the glass to the boy's mouth. " 'Tis high time Raoul learned to drink like a man."

"No, Papa!" he protested, turning his face away. "Raoul no sleep!"

"Is Raoul refusing to obey his father!" Sjöström declared. He grabbed the child's jaw with his huge hand, forcing his mouth open, and poured the contents of the glass down his throat. At the far end of the women's bench, Ester watched, horrified. When Raoul coughed and gagged Sjöström pushed him down hastily, fearing he was going to vomit.

"Run to thy mother," he ordered, giving him a shove in Ester's direction.

Raoul only managed two steps before his legs buckled and he collapsed, crying, in the grass. Ester rushed to pick him up.

"Let the child be!" Sjöström commanded. "He must learn to be a man."

"But..." Ester began, only to be silenced by her husband's look.

Not daring to defend the child against Sjöström in front of everyone, she backed away and sank down on the end of the women's bench.

"Not to worry about Raoul," someone comforted. "He is nothing but a child."

But Ester couldn't take her eyes off her son where he lay gagging and crying in the grass.

Presently Old Svea came out bringing fresh coffee. When she saw the child she instantly sized up the situation. Casting a disgusted look in Sjöström's direction, she lifted Raoul up and carried him inside. Roland Sjöström dared not try to stop her, for he knew she would ignore his command. It would only make him look weak in front of his neighbors. Just the simple act of her picking up the boy had already belittled him sufficiently. But as soon as breakfast was finished he sought her out.

"Svea can be thankful that there is now a law against beating one's servants, because I would like nothing more than to pull up her skirt and make her pay for degrading me in front of everyone!" he declared, puffing himself up.

"Yes, I am sure Roland would like that," she said quietly, looking him straight in the eye.

Deflated, he left the room, staring at his feet as he went.

That was just the first of Sjöström's efforts to harden his son into a man, a task that was to become unpleasant not only for the boy, but for the entire family. Unfortunately, Svea was not always able to protect Raoul from his father's training methods.

Such was the case when Sjöström went outside one winter night to relieve himself off the edge of the porch, as usual before bed. When he opened the door to go back inside, the moonlight followed him into the room, falling upon Raoul who was curled up on his side sound asleep. Only his head was uncovered. Roland Sjöström exploded, tearing the blanket from the sleeping child and jerking him upright by the arm.

"How many times has Raoul been told that he is to sleep on his back with his hands on top of the covers!" he shouted, slapping him on the back of the head with the flat of his hand and waking everyone in the room.

Raoul blinked sleepily, both perplexed and frightened. He understood that he had done something wrong, but he didn't know what. Nor did he dare ask.

"Raoul is to keep his hands off his organ. Otherwise the *nattman*[37] will cut it off. It's not a plaything."

Raoul understood the message, but not what he had done wrong. He hadn't touched his organ.

The next night he was placed on his back, his arms tied to the sides

---

37. Another name for a class of men at the bottom of society, who carried out executions, slaughtered horses, skinned animals, buried carcasses, emptied latrines, and carried out jobs that others found disgusting.

66

of the bed, and given a severe warning by his father concerning the dangers of touching himself. After several nights of such warnings, Raoul became so nervous about touching himself that he was unable to pee during the day. Consequently, he began to wet the bed in his sleep. Ester and Svea were able to hide the fact for some days, until one morning when the whole room smelled of urine. Without having to be told, Sjöström grabbed the birch rod from where it stood on the mantel, eternally at the ready to sting the backside of any child who had done wrong. Before Raoul realized what had happened, Sjöström had him over his knee, his *kolt* [38] hanging open on either side of his hips, and was whipping him mercilessly with the birch. The louder Raoul cried while struggling to get free, the harder his father beat him.

Svea tried to intervene, but was told to mind her own business if she wanted to keep her job. Even Ester, who generally avoided confrontations with her husband, begged him to leave the child alone, only to be told that Raoul was his son and that he intended to make a man out of him.

"I'm not going to have a son who is a weakling and wets himself like a girl," he informed her. "Ester can spoil her daughter, if it so pleases her. But she has nothing to say about my son. Besides, Ester knows full well that children are uncivilized creatures and need to be beaten into submission."

Ester said nothing. She, too, must submit to her husband.

When the news of Raoul's bedwetting reached One-Eyed Klara, she picked up her broom, along with a tiny piece of dry bread crust, and went out to her cowshed. Although she no longer had a cow, she still had a number of rats who fled for cover when she opened the door. Placing the bread crust on the floor in front of her, she sat down on the three-legged milking stool to wait, with the broom raised above her head. Presently a small rat ventured out from its hiding place and made its way across the earthen floor towards her. Just as it reached the crust she brought the broom down on it with all her strength, killing it instantly. She picked it up by the tail, wrapped it in an old rag, and set out for Sjöströms.

"This is the best cure for bedwetting. It's been used everywhere since the time of Christ," she explained to Ester and Svea. "If Svea will lend me a knife, I'll prepare it."

---

38. A smock-like garment that was open down the back, worn by small children, with nothing underneath it. It was very practical for toilet training, as well as spanking.

That said, she butchered the rat in the same manner as one butchers a cow or pig. The choicest part she gave to Svea, instructing her to fry it well. Ester and Kajsa watched with revulsion.

"The only other cure that I know of," she said consolingly, "is to fry part of an undigested fish that was extracted from the stomach of a pike. But I'm better at catching rats than pike who have just eaten."

Once it was fried, Svea was sent to get Raoul.

"Just between Ester and me," Klara whispered while Svea had gone, "Ester looked down into Mor Britta's grave as they lowered her casket, did she not?"

"Yes, of course."

"So there is the cause of Raoul's bedwetting. Did Ester not know that looking into an open grave when she is pregnant would cause the child to become a bedwetter?"

"Is that really so?" Ester gasped.

"Yes, of course. 'Tis common knowledge. Did Mor Britta never tell her daughter that?"

"No, she never talked about such things. I never even knew where babies came from till it happened to me." She paused a moment, considering. "Does Klara mean that I have caused Raoul to be a bedwetter? That it's my fault that he is being beaten?"

"I shan't say it for sure," Klara said half reassuringly.

"Oh my lord! What shall I do?" Ester cried.

"All we can do is hope that this age-old cure works."

Just then Svea came in carrying Raoul.

"Come, Raoul. *Tant* Klara has made something good for Raoul to eat," the old woman said.

She offered him half a spoonful of the fried rat meat, which she had chopped so finely that it could be swallowed without having to be chewed. Raoul looked at it warily, then at the three women hovering around him. After much coaxing, he opened his mouth, while Kajsa looked on suspiciously. She didn't like it when adults tried to fool her brother.

"Just swallow it right down like porridge," he was told.

Raoul swallowed, gagged, and vomited it up again.

"Not good!" he declared.

Klara took a smaller amount of the meat and mixed it with a bit of left-over porridge.

"Just eat a tiny bit," she told him while holding his lower jaw. "It will stop Raoul from peeing in the bed."

Perhaps it was this last bit of information that changed his mind, for he gave up and opened his mouth. This time he gagged, but did not vomit. Kajsa, however, ran outside just in time to be sick to her stomach.

"Now it's just to wait and see if he swallowed enough for it to work," Klara concluded, wiping his mouth with her thumb.

"Oh, I do hope it works!" Ester replied, her voice shaking. She could never forgive herself for having caused her child such pain!

"I'd best be going," Klara said. " 'Tis getting late."

Ester went into the pantry and came out with a *hålbröd*[39] and a small piece of the previous summer's cheese in payment for her efforts.

"Thank you, Ma'am," Klara said, curtsying as best her back would allow.

The following day, when it was too cold for Raoul to go outdoors, Seva kept her eye on him to see how often he peed. Much to her surprise, by evening he had not peed once the entire day. As soon as Sjöström left for a night of drinking at the inn and Ester had gone out to the barn to give the cows a little extra hay, she set the chamber pot on the floor in front of him.

"This is how men and boys pee," she told him.

She took his hand and wrapped his fingers around his little penis.

"When Raoul feels that he needs to pee, he takes a hold of his organ like this and steers the pee into the pot or onto the ground. When he is done, he shakes off the last drop. That's the only time he touches his organ. It's alright for him to hold on to it when he pees, but not any other time. Does he understand?"

By now he had let go of his penis, still nervous about touching himself.

"Now, let's see if Raoul can fill the pot with all the pee he has been holding in all day."

When he hesitated, she assured him once again that it was alright to hold onto himself when he peed; that he must do so in order not to wet his feet. Finally, he took a hold of his penis, aimed at the pot and, taking Svea at her word, nearly filled it.

The next morning when Sjöström yanked the covers off of his son as usual, to his surprise, the bed was dry. He seemed almost disappointed. It never occurred to him to praise the child, however, for praise made

---

39. A small round bread about an inch thick with a hole in the middle. These were hung up to dry on poles hanging from the ceiling and thus could last for many months without getting moldy. Such hard bread was dunked in coffee or gravy. Soft bread was only for special occasions.

children vain. Raoul tried to tell him that he had learned to pee properly, but he so feared his father's reaction to his having touched himself that he could only stammer. Svea said nothing, letting the credit go to Klara's cure. Sjöström made no comment whatsoever, and after a few days he gave up checking the bed. But Raoul never got over the fear he experienced every morning upon waking. Nor could he ever speak in his father's presence without stammering.

At first Sjöström didn't notice Raoul's stammering, for he was more interested in the boy's obedience than in what he had to say. It was Mor Dagmar who drew his attention to it.

"What is wrong with that child!" she declared when he took Raoul upstairs to visit her one Sunday. "Can he not talk like a normal person? Or did something frighten him and cause him to stammer?"

"What does Mor mean?"

"He stammers."

"He does?"

"Yes. Listen to him."

He looked over at Raoul. Raoul looked at the floor.

"Say something, Raoul," he ordered.

"I-I can't," Raoul answered in a whisper.

"Speak up!"

"I-I c-can't," he stammered a bit louder.

"Speak properly!" Sjöström demanded.

Raoul cowered in front of his father, unable to utter a word.

"Send for Klara," Dagmar intervened. "She's good at curing things. As Roland saw, she cured his bedwetting."

Two days later, when everyone was gathered for the noon meal, Klara appeared carrying a package wrapped in brown paper. Kajsa was immediately curious, but Raoul, who had heard his grandmother's suggestion, was apprehensive. Everyone watched as she laid the package on the table and untied the string. Slowly Raoul's curiosity began to get the better of him. He inched closer as Klara folded back the paper.

"What is it, Raoul?" Sjöström asked from the far end of the table.

Raoul wrinkled his nose.

"Ugh! I-It's a...it's a s-slimy f-fish," he answered.

In the same instant, Klara lifted the fish by its tail and slapped him across the mouth with it. He was so shocked that he stood as if paralyzed, his mouth hanging open and his eyes bulging.

"Why did *Tant* Klara hit Raoul?" Kajsa asked, horrified.

"Because that is how one cures a person who stammers," Klara told her.

"But why does he stammer? He didn't used to."

"Because something has fightened him."

"But *Tant* Klara frightened him with the fish."

"Yes, that's how it works."

Such logic Kajsa found hard to understand. She felt sorry for Raoul, for he looked more frightened than ever.

Everyone but Svea had great hopes that Raoul had been cured. But such was not to be the case.

Björkdalen 1874

As every winter, the sun began to climb higher in the sky after the solstice, faster and faster for every day, until it reached the equinox in the middle of March, whereupon day and night were of equal lengths. From there daylight took over, all but shutting out the night, culminating with the summer solstice in June. By then people were breathing more easily, thankful for having made it through the winter and spring without starving.

Ester was once again with child. This pregnancy weighted her down more than the previous ones. Often she was forced to take to her bed and leave the running of the household to Old Svea and Pia. And now that Kajsa was 5½, it fell to her to take care of Raoul, a task for which she had mixed feelings. For the most part she disliked him because he had taken her place in her parents' eyes. Thus she was not always as kind to him as she could have been. At the same time, taking care of him, as well as carrying out the small jobs entrusted to them, made her feel grown up.

One such job was carrying the slops to the pigs. She and Raoul had to carry the pail between them, but because Raoul was small, he could never hold his side up high enough, so that the contents often spilled out into the ground. At first she had tried to compensate for his shortcomings by bearing most of the weight, but finally gave up and, with a certain amount of delight, let the unpleasant contents slop out over his bare feet.

Raoul's favorite job was collecting the newly-laid eggs from the hen house. He had become quite good at picking them up gently and placing them in his basket. But one day there was a strange object lying in one of the nests amongst the eggs.

"What's this?" he asked.

Kajsa turned around to see a long black viper hanging from his hand, wiggling wildly.

"No, Raoul!" she yelled. "Drop it! 'Tis a snake!"

But too late. It had already sunk its poisonous fangs into the boy's hand. He dropped it, screaming. No sooner had it landed on the dirt floor than it slithered out of the hen house through a hole in the wall.

In the meantime, Raoul had also dropped his basket, breaking all the eggs. Kajsa picked him up and ran toward the house as he clung to her crying. But whether he was crying from the pain or the fear of what his father was going to say about the broken eggs, was impossible to know.

Svea had heard his screaming and had come out onto the steps.

"What ever's happened?" she called out.

"Raoul was bit by one of those black snakes with the zig-zags on it."

"Oh, no!"

Svea grabbed the child and, pulling up his *kolt,* ordered him to pee on the bite, but he just whimpered.

"Do as I say!" Svea ordered, but he refused.

"Usch! Why does he have to pee on it?" Kajsa wondered aloud.

"To make it clean and hopefully wash away the poison," she was told.

Just then Sjöström came out of the barn, having heard the commotion.

"What's going on out here?" he demanded to know.

"Raoul was bitten by a viper," Svea told him.

"Oh my God!"

He dropped the shovel he had been carrying and ran to them. Already Raoul's hand had turned purple and was swelling rapidly. Kajsa watched as her father pulled his organ out of his pants and peed on her brother's hand, not caring who saw that private part of himself that he always kept hidden. Raoul screamed even louder when the urine stung the bite.

"Give him a shot of *brännvin* to calm him," he told Svea, "and then put him to bed."

Suddenly he turned to Kajsa, who was still standing on the steps.

"And what was Kajsa doing when she was supposed to be taking care of Raoul?" he shouted, grabbing her roughly by the upper arm. "Does she think he should suffer while she, who let it happen, goes free? When Kajsa is told to watch Raoul, that is what she is to do and I'll see to it that she doesn't forget it! Svea!" he yelled, "bring out the birch rod from the mantle. Now!"

Without giving her a chance to explain what had happened, he threw her across his knee, pulled up her skirt and whipped her violently.

"Whore child!" he hissed through clinched teeth. "If my son dies because she did not take care of him as she was told to do, she'll pay for it! And it'll be far worse than this!"

By the time he had drawn blood, Kajsa had already fainted. When he had finally exhausted himself, he left her on the steps for Svea to collect and went in to his son. Ester sat beside the boy, wiping his

73

forehead with a wet cloth in an attempt to bring down his rising fever. For the first time in his adult life, Roland Sjöström was afraid, for the situation was out of his control. He turned to Kajsa who lay whimpering on the kitchen soffa where Svea had lain her.

"Get up!" he ordered. "Run and fetch *Tant* Klara!"

When Kajsa failed to respond, he jerked her to her feet by the arm.

"Do as thee are told!" he roared.

Kajsa could hardly stand, let alone run, for the pain was almost unbearable.

"Get going!" he snapped.

She stumbled out the door and across the yard to the path leading into the forest. She had never gone through the forest to *Tant* Klara's hut alone. In fact, she had never been in the forest by herself. She knew that was where *Gråben* lived, as well as bears who liked eating little girls even better than eating honey. And she had often heard big people talking about trolls and the forest nymph who lured folk, especially children, into hidden caves so that they could never go home again. Yet she was more afraid of her father than she was of creatures in the forest that she couldn't see. Maybe living in a cave with trolls and the forest nymph wouldn't be so bad. She had heard that the nymph was a beautiful lady with a long tail hanging under her skirt, but that her back side was like a hollow log, although she had no idea how a hollow log looked.

By now she had slowed her pace because it was so painful to walk.

"*Tant* Klara!" she called out. "Is *Tant* Klara at home?"

Presently she heard Klara's old voice making its way through the trees.

"Who is calling me?" she called back.

" 'Tis me. Kajsa."

"What's the matter?" she asked, her voice coming nearer.

"Raoul...a snake...." she panted. "Papa says *Tant* Klara must come."

"Kajsa has to help me. I only have one walking stick with me," she replied.

But when she looked up and saw the child limping towards her she was horrified.

"What has happened to Little Kajsa?"

"Papa says 'tis my fault," was all she could manage.

With her free hand Klara lifted Kajsa's bloody skirt.

"Oh, my lord!" she mumbled to herself upon seeing the bleeding welts on the child's buttocks. "Come. We must take care of Kajsa's backside first."

"No," Kajsa protested. "Papa says to hurry. Raoul is very hot from the snake biting him. He'll be angry if we don't hurry."

"No need to worry. I shall take care of Kajsa's papa. I care not about what Kajsa has done or not done, he must not beat her like this."

She led the way into her hut, indicating that Kajsa should lie down on the pile of rags which served as her bed. Carefully she removed the girl's skirt, which was beginning to stick in the drying blood. Then she applied a salve that she had made from various flowers, in order to staunch the blood and quell the stinging pain.

Once Kajsa had become quiet, Klara went to an old cupboard in the corner of the room. Aside from a little table and a chair, it was the only furniture in the hut. An air of holiness surrounded it, almost as if it were an altar. Pulling out a key that hung on a string between her sagging breasts, she unlocked the cupboard door. The shelves inside were filled with every imaginable kind of dried leaves and plants, some lying uncovered and others wrapped in newspaper, brown paper, or rags. The top shelves held small jars of various salves and ointments that she made from nature's gifts. Quickly she hunted through the cupboard, plucking out a number of herbs and salves which she placed in a cloth bag. When she was finished she closed and locked the cupboard door, replacing the key in its hiding place.

"Kajsa must stay here and rest. I shan't be gone long," she told the child.

Taking her two walking sticks, she went on her way, the bag dangling from one shoulder.

By the time Klara arrived Roland Sjöström had gained a degree of control over himself. But she had never seen him so scared and helpless. Like Svea, she had known him since he was a child. What little liking she might have had for him had completely evaporated at the sight of Kajsa's buttocks. She showed him the outward respect required by social protocol, but in reality, she had no respect for him whatsoever. She found his way of treating those below him to be disgusting, as was his way of manipulating people's feelings towards him, by kicking them and then handing them a few potatoes to show his generosity. When he first took Kajsa, Klara had actually considered that perhaps he had done it out of the kindness of his heart. But as Kajsa grew older, it became obvious that he had taken her for the same reason many people took foster children: they were cheap and expendable labor. If he had cared about the child, he would have sent Pia or Maria to fetch her instead of Kajsa. The only thing slowing Kajsa's fate was the the fact that Ester, in her innocence, stood in the way.

" 'Tis about time that Klara got here!" Sjöström declared when she hobbled through the kitchen door. "What took her so long?"

Ignoring him, she made her way to where Raoul lay in an *utdragssoffa,* a wet cloth still covering his forehead in an attempt to bring down his burning fever. Ester stood up on shaking legs, her face ashen gray, and motioned to Klara to take her place. She, too, was frightened, but for more than just her child's well-being. Klara could see that she was afraid of her husband. She wondered if this was the first time she had witnessed his explosive violence. Or had she witnessed it all too often?

"Kajsa?" Ester whispered to Klara, her back towards Sjöström.

"She's all right. She's in my hut," the old woman whispered back.

"He's so cruel," Ester dared to reply under her breath.

Klara laid a comforting hand on her arm, then opened her bag.

"Klara had better save my son!" Sjöström warned her from across the room.

"I shall do what I can, but I'm not God," she told him. "Has Sjöström sent for Dr. Ljungkvist?"

"Of course I've sent for him," Sjöström told her rudely. "We need a real doctor!"

Ljungkvist was the only doctor in the area, living two hours away by horse and wagon.

Shooing everyone away from the bed, Klara set to work, mumbling to herself while applying herbs to draw out the venom. The women huddled around the table waiting anxiously, while Roland Sjöström stood staring out the window with his back to the room, fists jammed deep into his pockets, watching for the doctor.

When Dr. Ljungkvist finally arrived he looked at Raoul's hand in amazement.

"I could not have done better myself," he declared. "What has she used?" he asked, turning to Klara.

"Just some herbs and salves; things I've gathered from nature. And a few prayers."

"There is nothing left for me to do," he concluded.

Without having opened his black bag, he went to the door. Sjöström held out the usual sum for a house call.

"I have done nothing," Ljungkvist, remarked waving away the gesture. "Give it to the old woman. She's the one who saved Sjöström's son."

Roland closed the door after the doctor and returned the money to his pocket.

Klara packed her things into her bag, leaving some herbs and ointments with Svea, with instructions as to when and how they should be applied. She bid everyone good-bye and, taking her walking sticks, stepped out onto the porch and down the few steps to the yard. She heard the door close behind her, then suddenly open again.

"Where's Kajsa?" Sjöström yelled after her.

"In my hut," she yelled back. "And if Sjöström ever beats his daughter again I shall report him to both the village *sexman*[40] and Reverend Holmgren."

"Klara shall mind her own business if she knows what is good for her! As the man of the house, I have the legal right to beat those who are disobedient. Besides, she's only a foster child."

"Yes, and we all know why one takes foster children and how they're treated," she shouted back, no longer caring about the consequences of her disrespectful action.

Sjöström was left standing on his porch with his fists clinched. No *backstusittare*[41] had ever dared to speak to him with such lack of respect, yet he was at a loss as to what to do about it. He suspected that Klara possessed certain magical powers and, although he would never admit it, he was afraid to cross her.

That night Ester was woken by a sharp pain in her stomach. On her way around the corner of the cottage to relieve herself in the undergrowth as usual, something wet ran down the inside of her thigh.

Instinctively, she put her hand between her legs. When she held it up in the late summer twilight she saw it was covered with sticky blood. She hunkered down against the pain, waiting for it to subside. When she finally stood up she could see a tiny object lying in a pool of blood. Sjöström's son, most likely. She crept back into bed, dreading the thought of having to tell him. She knew that he would blame Kajsa for letting Raoul get bitten, which in turn had upset her and caused her to miscarry.

Rather than tell her husband, Ester confided in Old Svea. She in turn took Roland aside and informed him of what had happened, impressing him with the fact that it was over and done with and that no one was to

---

40. One of the six (sex) village elders whose responsibility it was to keep a watchful eye on people's morals and report their misdeeds.

41. The term for people who lived in utter poverty in tiny cottages or huts *(backstugor)*.

blame, especially not Kajsa. She had already paid dearly for that snake bite.

"There will not be another word uttered about it!" she told him decidedly. "Does Roland understand that?"

"Yes," he replied meekly.

She had no idea what she would do should he ignore her and punish Kajsa anyway, yet she didn't need to threaten him. He obeyed her just as he had done as a small child.

Kajsa remained in the hut for several days while Klara tended her wounds, relieved to be away from her father's unpredictable violence. Each afternoon the old woman took her bag of herbs and made her way through the forest with the help of her walking sticks to check on Raoul's progress. No mother could have been more attentive, for it was simply an act of caring on her part. Sjöström offered her no compensation for her efforts. In fact, Roland Sjöström avoided crossing Klara's path when she came to see to Raoul. He only took on confrontations that he was sure of winning. He had no desire to submit himself to possible humiliation by the tongues of such old women as Klara and Svea.

When Kajsa returned home Svea scrubbed her thoroughly from head to toe in the zink tub in front of the fire.

"Why do I have to be washed now?" she complained. "I just had a bath in the wash house tub before midsummer."

"*Tant* Klara's hut only has a dirt floor," Svea replied, "so Kajsa has come home with dirty feet."

"But why must Svea wash all of me—even my hair—if 'tis only my feet that are dirty?" she persisted.

"And why must children ask so many questions?" Svea retorted evasively.

God knows what sort of lice and flees the child had brought home with her! Although such vermin were part of everyday life, even for the well-to-do, Klara's hut must surely be crawling with them.

By the time both children were healed, life had returned to normal at Björkdalen. For as long as she could remember, Kajsa had looked forward to starting school. Ester had taught her the alphabet when she was five and she quickly began sounding out words on her own. But there was nothing for her to actually read. Only upper class homes had books, although most peasant homes at least contained a copy of *Luthers lilla katekes,*[42] a little book of questions with complicated answers about the Lutheran faith, to be memorized for conformation. Kajsa could read many of the words, but their meaning was beyond her understanding. Nor were the psalm book or Bible any easier.

One winter day Svea handed her a letter that had come for her father, instructing her to put it on the desk in his office. Beside the shaker containing his blotting sand lay a thin book with the words *Bonde-practica eller wäder book*[43] printed on the tattered cover. She knew she must not touch it, yet she could not resist the temptation. Gingerly she lifted the cover. Inside was written Roland, 1720, in neat brown script. She slipped her finger between the pages, opening it at random. "About the Twelve Months of the Year" was printed at the top of the page. Below there were verses for each month. She read the first one: *Januarius Torsmånad /Bliver himmelen röd på morgonen nyårsdag /Då bliver det år stor sorg och klag.*[44] She could both read the words and understand the message. It gave her an uncomfortable feeling. She regretted having opened the book. Quickly she closed it, laying her father's letter on top of it, and hurried back to the kitchen.

"Post-Anders left a letter for *Herr'n,* "[45] Old Svea remarked when Sjöström came in at supper time.

No sooner had he gone into his room to get it than he was back again, mad as a hornet.

"Who has moved my *Bonde-practica?"* he demanded. "That book is very old and fragile. It was passed down from my great great grandfather Roland. No one is to touch it!"

Kajsa grasped the edge of the table, where she had been scrubbing potatoes, and braced herself.

"I looked at it when I came in with *Herr'n's* post," Svea told him. "I

---

42. *Luther's Little Catechism.*

43. Equivalent to *The Farmer's Almanac.*

44. January, Thor's month/If the sky is red in the morning on New Year's Day/Then there will be great sorrow and complaining that year.

45. Mister or Sir.

thought it might be something Kajsa could read. *Luthers lilla katekes* is too difficult for her. Or does Roland perhaps have another book more suited to her age? Something more interesting than *Bonde-practica?*"

She looked him straight in the eye as she talked, for she knew full well that he had a copy of *Grimms sagor* [46] in the shelf along side his farming manuals. Although her reading ability was limited, she had recognized the word *sagor* [47] on its spine when she was dusting.

"Something with fairy tales, for example," she concluded, then went back to washing the dishes.

Without further ado, he disappeared into his room and returned with the Grimm book, tossing it onto the table in front of Kajsa.

"Be careful with it," was all he said, casting an angry look at Svea's back.

"Oh, many thanks, Papa!" Kajsa exclaimed curtseying respectfully.

"Thank Old Svea," Roland Sjöström muttered as he left the room.

"I shall," Kajsa called after him.

When he was out of sight she went to Svea and simply hugged her, for she had no words with which to adequately express her gratefulness.

After wiping her hands thoroughly on her apron, she sank down onto a near-by chair and opened the book. The first story was "Hansel and Gretel." Slowly her finger made its way across the page under each line, her lips moving imperceptively as she read. A whole new world had opened itself to her.

Kajsa could hardly wait for the first day of the new year, when she would turn seven. Then it would only be a few months before she could start school. Every day she asked Svea how many days were left until her birthday.

"None," Svea told her one morning. "When Kajsa wakes up tomorrow morning she will be seven years old."

That night she lay awake for a long time, listening to the snow storm wailing outside as it piled drifts up against the side of the house. Beside her in the *utdragssoffa,* Raoul whimpered in his sleep. She hugged him against her, wondering who was going to take care of him once she went to school. He seemed so small and fragile. But before she could contemplate it further, his even breathing lulled her to sleep.

---

46. *Grimm's Fairytales.*

47. Fairytales.

She was wakened by the sound of spilled water hissing on the fire as Svea filled the cauldron that hung over the open fireplace. She could feel the warmth coming from the hearth even before she opened her eyes.

"Look," Svea said when she saw that Kajsa was awake. "God has made the world beautiful for Kajsa on her birthday."

Slowly she opened her eyes. The entire room was bathed in a reddish glow. She sat up and looked out the window. The sun was on its way up, sliding under long rolls of clouds, turning them fire-red.

"It looks like a good omen for the coming year," Svea concluded.

But, remembering the *Bonde-practica's* verse, Kajsa wasn't so sure.

It was still summer when school started in August. Kajsa was so excited when she set out on the first day that her bare feet hardly touched the hard-packed ruts in the road as she hurried along. At last! Over her dress she wore a brand new white pinafore that Svea had sewn for the occasion and down her back bounced her long blond braid with a bit of yarn tied on the end. A basket containing her dinner,[48] a piece of dry bread, a bit of cheese, a hard boiled egg, and a small bottle of *blå mjölk,*[49] swung from one hand.

When the school house came into sight she slowed down hesitantly. Although she had seen the small wooden building a number of times, it had always been in passing. She had never been inside. Outside the entrance groups of children were running around, yelling and laughing. All of them seemed to know each other, except for several her age who were also new-comers. Suddenly she felt shy.

Presently a large man with dark hair and a long black coat opened the door and rang a hand bell.

Magistern.[50] After the priest, he was the next most respected-through-fear man in the parish.

"Line up according to class," he ordered.

Suddenly the atmosphere changed. The laughing and yelling ceased, a line formed, and he led them into the building, indicating their respective seats.

Kajsa looked around. The school house consisted of one room,

---

48. The noon meal was referred to as dinner and the evening meal as supper.

49. Skimmed milk. The cream was almost always skimmed off milk and churned into butter, a source of income.

50. The name by which a male teacher was addressed.

furnished with several rows of long tables and benches that could accommodate 10 to 20 pupils, depending on how tightly they squeezed together. *Magistern's* desk stood on a platform in front of the blackboard, giving him a clear view of all that went on in the room. In the corner, beyond his desk, a huge green tiled *kakelugn*[51] reached almost to the ceiling. In the wintertime the crackling of burning wood behind its brass doors would slowly take the chill from the air, warming those who sat closest to it. In the corner near the door stood a pail of water on a stool, a common drinking scoop hanging from its edge.

Kajsa was given a seat in the front row with the other six pupils in the first class, three boys and three girls, none of whom she knew. The remaining nine children sitting behind them made up classes two and three. While the others tittered amongst themselves, Kajsa sat at her desk patiently, waiting for school to begin.

"Silence!" *Magistern* roared. The room fell silent. "Everyone stand and bow their heads while we recite The Lord's Prayer together."

Some recited loudly and clearly, others mumbled unintelligibly to hide the fact that they didn't know it, and still others just moved their lips silently. But everyone joined in at the amen, after which they sat down.

"Now, let us hear how many new pupils can recite the alphabet. Axel shall begin," *Magistern* said, waving his ruler at the small boy at the end of the first row whose clothes hung in tatters, more patched than whole.

"Ah...ah..." was all Axel managed to say.

"Stand up!" *Magistern* snapped, slapping his desk with the ruler, so hard that the pupils in the front row jumped. "One must stand up when called upon!"

Axel got to his feet meekly. But no matter whether he was sitting or standing, he could not recite the alphabet.

"Does Axel not know the alphabet?"

"N-n-no."

"No, Sir!" he was told.

"N-n-no, Sir," Axel repeated.

"Sit down. Axel shall have learned the alphabet by tomorrow. Next!"

The girl next to Axel stood up nervously.

"Name?"

"Anna," the girl answered barely above a whisper.

"Speak up!"

"Anna," she repeated a little louder.

"Anna, Sir," she was told.

---

51. Tiled stove.

"Anna, Sir."

"Begin."

"A, B, C…" but she got no further.

"Next."

While the rest of the pupils in the first class stumbled though the first few letters in the alphabet, Kajsa stared into space, bored. When her turn came, she stood up and repeated the entire alphabet quickly and perfectly. The other children looked at her with disdain, thinking her to be bragging. They all knew she came from Björkdalen which, in their eyes, made her rich. The rest of them were from poor *torpare* [52] homes, where they lived in in varying degrees of poverty. Kajsa had been vaguely aware of the fact that the others were "less fortunate" than herself, but had no idea what that meant. Nor did she know that the *torpare* homes from which they came belonged to Björkdalen, and were ruled over by Roland Sjöström; that her own father was, to a large extent, responsible for their conditions. The *torpare* children, however, were well aware of that fact.

At noon everyone was sent outside to sit in the grass and eat the midday meal. Kajsa sat down beside Anna, with her dinner basket in front of her, while the other two girls, Kristina and Alva, settled on the other side of Anna. No one said a word. Feeling uncomfortable and not knowing what to do, Kajsa reached into her basket and took out the piece of cheese. She bit into it self-consciously, swallowing it without chewing, then took another bite. She could feel the eyes of the other three on her.

"Shall thee not eat?" she asked finally to break the silence.

Anna pulled a piece of dried bread from her apron pocket, but the other two shook their heads.

"We eat at home," one of them said.

Failing to understand, Kajsa went on eating. But by the time she got to the hard boiled egg she had lost her appetite.

On her way home that afternoon she puzzled over the situation, wondering why the two girls only ate at home. It never occurred to her that perhaps there was no food for them to take to school for dinner. Such a thing was simply not possible in her world.

The next day when Kajsa sat down in the grass with the three girls, they turned their backs on her. The day after that they got up and walked

---

52. A person living on a *torp* consisting of a small cottage, a cowshed, and a bit of land, all of which belonged to a larger farm. To pay the rent the *torpare* had to work on the large farm a certain number of days per year.

away, leaving her to eat the contents of her basket alone.

From then on, the three girls spent the dinner hour huddled together on the far side of the school yard. They needn't have bothered to move so far away however, for Kajsa understood that she was not welcome. She did her best to ignore them, too proud to show how hurt she was. At home, when asked about school, she pretended that all was well, while at the same time trying to figure out what she had done wrong. Was it because she knew the alphabet? Or because she was the only one in the first class who could read? Or perhaps it was because her clothes were nicer than the other girls' clothes? Before the week was out, school had lost its glow. She no longer cared about learning. She only wanted to be like and liked by the other girls.

On her way to school one rainy day, without thinking, Kajsa suddenly pulled off her white pinafore, threw it down in the road, and ground it into the mud with her bare feet. When it was sufficiently dirty, she pulled it back on and continued on to school. By the time she arrived, her dress had soaked up much of the muddy rainwater. Her legs and arms, as well as her hair, were streaked with mud. No one said a word when she took her seat. She had already ceased to exist for the three girls.

By the end of the school day the mud had dried, leaving her clothes looking like they had been worn for months without being washed. On her way home, before she had time to consider how she would explain their condition, her father drove up behind her with a wagon load of hay.

"Climb up!" he called to her. "I'm on my way to the barn."

He reached down and, taking her hand, pulled her up onto the driver's seat. Immediately she regretted having joined him. He reeked of *brännvin*.

He glanced over at her as she sat down.

"What in the hell has Kajsa done to her clothes?" he cried.

She shrugged her shoulders without answering.

"Answer me!" he yelled.

Still she said nothing. She hadn't the words to explain what lay behind her dirty clothes.

"Did Kajsa go to school looking like that?"

She nodded.

Without warning, he slapped her so hard that she nearly fell off her seat.

"I have given Kajsa nice clothes and I expect her to take proper care of them. I will not have her looking like a dirty *torpare* brat!"

"I do not like nice clothes," she heard herself say. "I want to look like a *torpare* brat."

Both she and Sjöström were shocked by her unexpected words. Never before had she talked back to him.

Roland Sjöström jerked the horse to a halt, furious at her lack of respect. Grabbing her by the upper arm, he dragged her over his knee, pulled up her dress, and whipped her with the ends of the reins while she cried out, begging him to stop.

"I do not ever want to see Kajsa in dirty clothes again. What will people think! She is a disgrace to me!" he told her, then pushed her off the wagon onto the ground.

She wandered the rest of the way home dejectedly. No one at school liked her, she was a disgrace to her father whom she feared, and her mother never defended her against her father's anger. The only person she could depend upon, and who she knew liked her, was Old Svea. And *Tant* Klara, of course, but she didn't live with them. She wished she had a different family.

Although the three girls continued to ignore Kajsa, they never teased her openly, having been warned that they lived at the mercy of Roland Sjöström. Should he discover that they were treating his daughter badly, he would not hesitate to take reprisals. All the *torpare* were familiar with an incident that had occurred several years earlier.

Life on a *torp* was anything but secure, yet the poor had no choice. Because it was against the law to be without work and a place to live, a *torpare* was forced to accept whatever conditions his landlord chose to put upon him, if he wished to keep his job and his home. To be fired was to be blacklisted, making it impossible to find a new job. He paid the rent by working for the landlord a stipulated number of days per year, as well as putting in extra time whenever he, or his wife, was needed. It was common knowledge that the landlord could appear at a *torp* any time the man of the house was away working and demand "favors" of his wife. For her to refuse could have serious consequences for the entire family. Almost every landowner had bastard children here and there in the cottages on his land, none of whom he ever recognized as being his. Although husbands were well aware of his activities, they were powerless to prevent them. To go to court was unthinkable, for the rich always won. They had no choice but to accept the resulting child and raise it as their own. It had always been so between the rich and the poor in the countryside.

And thus it was that one day Roland Sjöström had appeared at a *torp* he owned in the surrounding forest. He knocked with an impatiently firm hand.

"Who might be at the door?" Ellen called out.

" 'Tis thy landlord," Sjöström answered. "Let me in. I have some potatoes for Ellen."

"I can't come to the door, for I'm not well," she answered. "Can he not give them to my husband instead?"

"No. I wish to give them to Ellen personally."

Taking a large key from his pocket, he put it in the empty key hole and opened the door. The stench of *brännvin* followed him into the room.

Ellen huddled in the bed, surrounded by her three small children. She knew why he had come. It was not the first time.

"Please, Sir, let me be. I'm not well. And Sjöström has already given us one extra mouth to feed. Besides, my husband will be coming soon."

"Ragnar has been given an extra job to take care of today. He'll be later than usual."

Realizing the danger of being in the bed, Ellen got to her feet.

"Please," she begged, "let me be."

At once he saw by the bulge under her apron that she was with child.

"Well, well. This time it shan't be I who has given her another mouth to feed," he remarked with a smirk.

"Leave me alone," was all she managed to say.

"As Ellen wishes," he told her, going towards the door. "Such a pity. She'll regret it."

He paused, hand on the latch, waiting for her to change her mind. But she remained silent.

When Ragnar came home that evening several of Sjöström's drinking companions had been there and had moved all of the family's possessions, as well as Ellen and the children, out into the yard and then torn down the cottage before their very eyes.

Nor was it the first such episode in the countryside. Such was the manner in which the rich dealt with the poor when they were uncooperative.

However, there were a few *statare*[53] school boys whose lives were in no

---

53. In opposition to a *torpare,* a worker on a farm who was paid mainly in kind (stat) and quartered on the premises in one room and kitchen, regardless of the size of his family.

way subject to Roland Sjöström's whims. Always on the lookout for someone to tease or degrade, especially if the victim were a girl, they gladly took over where the three girls left off. Because Sjöström had made a point of keeping Kajsa's background secret, a number of rumors had grown up. Some believed her to be one of his bastards, born of a *torpare's* wife or a young maiden he had seduced or raped. Others maintained that it was Ester who had stepped out of line and that Sjöström had saved Lars Engelholm's honor by taking his pregnant daughter in exchange for a piece of land. Still others were convinced that Kajsa belonged to neither Sjöström nor Ester—that an unknown unwed mother had left her new-born baby outside the church, rather than murdering it, as was so often the case. One way or another, Kajsa Sjöström was seen as a bastard child. The boys delighted in poking her and hissing *oäkting*[54] or *hor unge*[55] in her ear, words that had no meaning for them beyond the fact that they knew they referred to something taboo. While Kajsa did not understand such words either, she understood that they meant something bad, yet there was no one she dared ask. She simply knew that she was being ostracized.

Kajsa quickly became disillusioned with school. When Magistern wasn't sitting behind his desk filling the room with clouds of smoke from his pipe, he walked amongst the pupils, slapping his ruler in the palm of his free hand, warming it up to use on some unsuspecting victim. Although there was no shortage of victims, he seemed to take special delight in chastising Axel.

Every morning he told the boy to stand up and repeat the alphabet, that he was supposed to have learned at home. But Axel never got further than B, or at best, C. At first his knuckles were rapped sharply with the edge of Magistern's ruler. When that failed to produce the required result, Magistern worked over the palms of his hands with a small whip until the boy cried out in pain. After that Axel became so fearful that he could barely utter a sound. Such refusal to speak further angered Magistern, causing him to seek other teaching methods: pulling the short hairs on the back of the child's neck, slapping him, banging his head down on the desk while calling him a stupid donkey, and showering him with similar insults. One day when Axel was too

---

54. Bastard.

55. Whore child.

frightened to even stand up, Magistern hauled him to the front of the room by his ear, commanded him to remove his tattered britches, and bent him over a chair, whereupon he whipped him with a cane until he drew blood. The other pupils paid little heed to the beating. It was the accepted manner in which to punish children who failed to learn or do as they were told. Everyone had suffered beatings. They were part of life.

To finalize the act, Magistern threw Axel's britches at him and told him to get out and never come back to school.

"Tell thy parents 'tis not possible to teach anything to their stupid donkey of a child!" he yelled after him.

Axel never spoke again and the word "idiot" was written after his name in the church records.

Hilda Maria

Björkdalen 1876

With the coming of autumn the days shortened quickly, as if in a hurry to reach the winter solstice and be reborn once again. Golden birch leaves covered the ground and otherwise invisible spider webs hung heavy with pearls of dew in the morning light. The harvest was in, the brown earth turned upwards in empty rows to await the spring. Roland Sjöström looked with satisfaction upon his well-filled storage buildings. Even after having delivered the required one tenth to the church they would have plenty to eat during the coming winter.

With that worry off his mind, he turned his attention to the child which was soon to be born. During the past year he had become more and more disenchanted with his only son, whom he saw to be weak, both in body and character. His attempts to make a man out of the boy were not succeeding. He feared that Raoul was going to be incapable of taking over Björkdalen after him. At times he even entertained the possibility that Raoul might actually be an idiot. He made it clear that the next child must be a boy of a different caliber.

Ester was well aware of her husband's disappointment in Raoul, for he made no secret of the child's failure to live up to his expectations, neither to her nor to Raoul directly. Thus she feared giving birth to a girl-child, for she knew she would be held to blame for not producing a son. That she herself might want a girl was not a consideration. Once married to Sjöström, she had ceased to have wants or desires of her own. Her duty was to back her husband; it was what he wanted that was important.

Kajsa, however, hoped for a sister, although she dared not say so for fear of angering her father. He didn't take well to those who disagreed with him. But if boys were like Raoul, then it was enough with just one in the family. She resented the burden of always having to be responsible for him.

The day that little Hilda Maria was born proved to be a disappointment to the entire family. Roland Sjöström celebrated his disappointment by getting drunk and cursing his wife loudly for not having given him a son. It was only Svea's intervention that prevented him from becoming physically violent towards her and the newborn girl-child. Ester wept out of fear in the face of her husband's anger, as well as in shame for having failed to produce a male child for him. Raoul didn't need to understand Sjöström's angry words to know that his father didn't like him. Kajsa, who had long ago learned to avoid her father when he smelled of *brännvin,* huddled in a corner as he raged. While she understood that his violence towards herself and her brother was because they were children, she had never imagined that he could possibly treat their mother in the same manner. And all because of the tiny bundle lying in her mother's arms. The fact that it was only a baby, and not the sister she had hoped for, was overshadowed by her father's unexpected violence. Even Mor Dagmar's thumping cane expressed dissatisfaction at the announcement of a girl-child.

Several nights after Hilda Maria's arrival a cold wind unexpectedly rushed down from the north, forcing its way into the cottage through the gaps around the windows and door, bringing with it the first snow of the season. The fire on the open hearth hadn't a chance of competing with the sudden chill filling the room.

Hilda Maria had been fussy ever since the wind came up and eventually began to cry. Ester waited nervously, not wanting to spoil the child by picking her up.

"Make that baby stop wailing!" Sjöström snapped finally, his voice thick with sleepy irritation.

When Ester dutifully reached into the cradle beside the bed, she was shocked to find that Hilda Maria's face was unusually cold.

"No wonder she's crying. She's cold," she told her husband.

"Then put her here between us," he remarked. "Anything, just so she shuts up and I can get some sleep."

Without getting out of bed, Ester scooped the child up out of the cradle and tucked her under the covers between them.

When the first morning light made its way into the room, Ester awoke to find the child wedged between them, stiff and cold.

"Sjöström!" she cried, shaking him awake, "The child is dead! One of us must have rolled over and smothered her."

"It was not me, thy stupid cow!" was all he said.

At the same time, she was sure that she had not suffocated the child. She was such a light sleeper that she would immediately have woken up had she lain on any part of the tiny body, even if it were only a finger. And it was unlikely that Hilda Maria had frozen to death there between them. It must have been Sjöström. It was not uncommon that infants were smothered when sleeping with adults, more often than not intentionally, should they be unwanted. Many an unmarried maid claimed to have accidently lain on her child, smothering it. An unprovable form

90

of murder. But would her husband take such a drastic measure simply because she had given him a girl-child instead of the boy-child he wanted? Ester was afraid to contemplate the possibility. Instead, she accepted the guilt and let Sjöström deride her for being so clumsy.

The day after Hilda Maria's death Ester was woken by sharp pains in her abdomen, accompanied by a throbbing headache and burning fever.

"I fear 'tis the childbed fever," she heard Svea tell Sjöström.

Such a fever often followed on the heals of childbirth, leaving the newborn child motherless. Even seemingly healthy women succumbed to it for no apparent reason.

In her half-delirious state, Ester experienced a sense of release. God was punishing her for not having forgiven her dying mother and for not having given Sjöström a son. And perhaps most of all for not loving her husband. It would be a relief to die and leave the burden of her irrevocable sins behind her.

This time Klara's herbal remedies, accompanied by her unintelligible mumblings, failed to have the slightest effect. Within three days Ester was dead. Because people lived so close together in cottage kitchens, birth and death were accepted as natural parts of everyday life and thus seldom hidden from children. Death, however, had not visited Björkdalen during Kajsa's short lifetime. Therefore, she was puzzled when she saw her mother sleeping in a wooden box, holding the baby in her arms.

But when her mother was still sleeping the next morning, Kajsa became concerned.

"Are Mamma and Hilda Maria going to wake up soon?" she asked Svea.

When Svea put her arm around her before answering, she knew something was wrong. Looking up, she saw that Svea was crying.

"Kajsa's mother is not going to wake up," the old woman said in an unsteady voice. "She and Hilda Maria have gone to heaven to be with Jesus."

"But they are right here. They have not gone to heaven."

She had never been able to understand the place people called heaven, nor this Jesus that they talked about all the time. And how could her mother have gone to heaven when she was lying in that box? None of it made any sense to her. But there was no one to ask. Certainly not her father, who was in an angry mood and smelled terrible. And Svea and Pia were too busy. Eventually some women from the village appeared, but Kajsa dared not approach them for fear her father would yell at her. Nor did they pay her any mind where she huddled in a corner out of the way. She watched silently as they lifted her mother from the box, laid her on the lid of one of the benches that had been placed between two chairs, and set about washing her. Kajsa watched for the slightest sign of life; a little helping movement as they removed her nightgown, the batting of an eye, or even a groan when they were too rough. But there was nothing. Her mother was like a wooden broom handle, stiff and unbending. The women had to struggle to get her into her church dress before returning her to the box. Just as Kajsa finally understood that her mother was not going to wake up, something dreadful happened. A man she had never seen before came into the cottage carrying a large board that looked like the top of a table. Without warning, he laid it on top of the box in which her mother and Hilda Maria lay, checking it for size. Kajsa scrambled from her hiding place and rushed toward him.

"No! No! Do not close Mamma in the box!" she screamed, clutching at his sleeve.

In the same instant a hand gripped her upper arm firmly and steered her towards the door in a seemingly gentle sweep.

"Come. This is no place for Little Kajsa," she heard her father say in the kindly tone he used in the presence of others, while the grip on her arm tightened warningly. Experience had taught her to respond to his grip rather than to his voice. As always, he was careful to present a loving face in front of the villagers, even when beating his children behind their backs.

Once out in the entranceway he let go of her arm with an angry jerk.

"Such behavior reflects badly on me!" he hissed between clinched teeth. "Kajsa will keep to her place and show respect for her elders!"

"Yes, Father," she replied, her head bowed in repentance, as she had been taught. "But Mamma?" she couldn't resist asking.

"She is dead. Kajsa no longer has a mother. Now go in and take care of Raoul," he ordered, giving her a shove towards the door. His tone made it clear that the subject was closed. She dared not ask more.

For the next two days people came from all corners of the parish to say good-bye to Ester Larsdotter. Unlike her mother Britta, she had been well-liked by all who knew her. Many of the women wept and patted Kajsa and Raoul on the head while mumbling *"stackars barn"*[56] as they

---

56. Poor children.

left. More confused than ever, Kajsa tried her best to stay out of the way and not ask the many questions for which she had no answers.

On the morning of the third day Svea woke Kajsa and Raoul earlier than usual.

"Hurry and put on thy best frock before thy father returns from the stall," she instructed Kajsa. "Then dress Raoul in his new jacket and britches."

"Why?" she asked, rubbing the sleep from her eyes.

" 'Tis thy mother's funeral today," Svea replied.

"What's a funeral?"

"I've no time to explain just now," Svea replied evasively. "I must get the fire going underneath the porridge so we can fill our stomachs with something warm before setting out. Kajsa will see soon enough."

Reluctantly, Kajsa crept out from under the covers. The fire on the hearth had not yet had a chance to warm the room and her teeth chattered uncontrollably as she pulled on her clothes. Raoul refused to get up into the cold room, protesting loudly upon being pulled from the warmth of his bed and fighting her attempts to dress him. Then suddenly, at the sound of his father kicking the snow off his boots in the entranceway, Raoul once again became a docile, sullenly silent little boy with large frightened eyes. Kajsa dressed him quickly and sat him at the table.

When they had finished eating, Svea set out with the children along the rutted snow-covered road towards the village church. Although the storm had abated somewhat, an icy wind still managed to press its way through Kajsa's thick hand-knit woolen stockings. At first the snow collecting around the tops of her leather boots melted from the warmth of her body, but soon it began to freeze again as she became colder. Ahead of them her father, *Morfar*[57] Lars, and two other men walked slowly, carrying the box containing her mother and Hilda Maria on their shoulders. Upon reaching the church, they continued inside, setting their burden down in front of the altar railing.

The members of Roland Sjöström's and Lars Engelholm's households were ushered to the front pews by one of the village elders. Kajsa pulled her shawl tighter around herself, for it was nearly as cold inside the church as it was outside. Once the service began she had a hard time sitting still, for her body kept wanting to move in order to stay warm. But every time she swung her legs Reverend Holmgren glared down at

---

57. Grandpa (literally mother's father).

her from his perch high above the congregation. She feared him almost as much as she feared her father when he smelled of *brännvin.* She was sure that neither of them had ever been children.

As usual, the service was long and filled with big words that had no meaning for her. Soon the monotony of Holmgren's voice, coupled with the chill creeping over her, began to lull Kajsa to sleep. At first her head drooped onto her chest, only to jerk upright a few seconds later. Finally her eyelids became so heavy that it was as if their weight held her head down. Even her father's grip on her upper arm failed to hold them open.

Suddenly Holmgren stopped talking and cleared his throat.

"There is someone in the front pew who has so little respect for her recently diseased mother that she cannot even stay awake at her funeral," he declared, his voice cold and devoid of compassion.

The words stung like a slap in the face. Even worse was the tightening of her father's grip on her arm.

Once the service was over, her father steered her outside to where everyone was gathered around a big hole in the ground. Presently the box was brought out, whereupon Reverend Holmgren threw dirt on it with a little shovel. Kajsa was shocked. How could he do such a thing to her mother who was so careful about dirt! But when the men began to lower the box into the depths of the hole it was more than she could bear.

"No! Don't put my mother in that hole!" Kajsa cried, pulling out of her father's grip and throwing herself over the coffin. Sjöström lunged forward to grab her, but was intercepted by a woman who had sat unnoticed at the back of the church. He failed to recognize her at first, for she was dressed as the other women, rather than in the rags she had worn at Mor Britta's funeral.

"I can take care of her," she told him, while pulling Kajsa off the slowly sinking coffin.

"Good. Take her away from here!" he declared under his breath, glad to get rid of the child before she caused him to lose his patience in front of those present.

"Come. Let us go into the parish hall where 'tis warm," she told Kajsa, taking her by the hand and leading her out of the churchyard. Kajsa followed in a daze, the vision of her mother disappearing into the ground still following her.

After stamping the snow off their feet, they drew two chairs close to the fire burning on the hearth. At last Kajsa dared to look up at the stranger questioningly.

"My name is Hildur," the woman said. "I'm your mother's *moster.*"

"I didn't know Mamma had a *moster*. Why have I never met *Moster* Hildur?" Kajsa asked, puzzled.

"We didn't know of each other until we met at *Mormor*[58] Britta's funeral. Kajsa was just a baby then."

"But that was long ago. Why has *Moster* Hildur never visited us?"

"Because I live far away in another parish. It takes me half a day to walk here and half a day to walk home again. I can't leave my daughter alone for that long."

"But could *Moster* Hildur not take her daughter along?"

"She can't walk very well."

"Oh," Kajsa replied, afraid to inquire further. She had been taught not to ask personal questions of grown-ups, although sometimes her curiosity got the better of her.

Sensing that her answer had not satisfied the child, Hildur continued.

"Her name is Signe and she's no longer a child. In fact, she's older than Kajsa's mother was. I shall tell Kajsa about her one day, but not now. People are beginning to come in for the *gravöl.*"

When they got home Sjöström let his pent-up anger roll over Kajsa.

"That is the last time Kajsa is going to embarrass me in front of other people," he told her harshly. "Me thinks 'tis high time that she goes out to earn her keep. There's no reason for her to stay here. She was her mother's child, not mine. I've enough on my hands with Raoul."

Kajsa looked up at Svea pleadingly.

"But where shall the child go?" the old woman asked Sjöström. "Who'll take her? She is too young to work as a housemaid."

"Nonsense! She's going on eight years old. There're those who would be glad for her. She's small and doesn't eat much. And she's used to working."

Svea thought for a moment.

"If Sjöström is serious about this...." Svea began.

"Of course I am serious! I always mean what I say."

"Well, then, what about Hildur, Ester's *moster*? She seemed to be quite fond of the child."

"I care not if someone is fond of her. I just want her off my hands. Svea knows as well as I that my taking her was for Ester's benefit, because she was so poorly after the birth of the first child. But now that she's gone...."

He was getting worked up, his voice becoming louder and louder.

"Calm down, Roland." Svea told him. "Nothing can be done about

---

58. Mother's mother or grandmother.

95

it at the moment, anyway. And Bruno's waiting out in the stall for his evening hay."

As always, when she addressed him as Roland he turned into the small boy she had mothered through childhood. Dutifully, he replaced the cap he had just taken off and went out the door.

That night Kajsa lay awake for a long time, listening to the unintelligible mumble of a discussion between her father and Old Svea. Gradually it became more distant, then disappeared altogether, along with the flickering of the firelight playing on the timber walls. At first she thought the fire had been banked for the night, causing the darkness. Then suddenly she realized that she was closed inside a narrow box, its wooden sides pressing against her so that she could hardly move. She was dead and had been buried like her mother and Hilda Maria! Frantically, she tried to scream for help, but her throat tightened around her words, blocking their way to her open mouth. The harder she tried, the more frantic she became. Finally her legs began to twitch in small jerks, followed by an inhuman wail that floated up from inside her.

"Be still and go to sleep!" her father shouted from his bed.

For once in her life, Kajsa was glad for his angry voice, for it woke her out of a nightmare which was to continue to plague her sleep for many nights to come.

The winter was long and cold, with snow reaching well above Kajsa's knees. She could never get warm, no matter how many sweaters and shawls she wrapped around herself. Cold, too, was the house without her mother. Even though much of her time had been taken up with caring for Raoul, there had been comfort in the fact that she was always there. However, Kajsa had sensed that her mother was just as afraid of her father as she herself was, for she never took her side against him. Rather, she backed away and pretended not to be aware of what was going on. It was Old Svea who put up an invisible protective wall between Kajsa and her father. As long as she was in the room Kajsa felt safe, for she knew Svea could reign in her father's ill temper before it could strike at her.

Although she was told nothing, Kajsa understood that her father and Svea were discussing what was to be done with her. She often heard *Moster* Hildur's name mentioned. Kajsa had liked her. She had been friendly and kind when no one else had had time for her. It might be nice to live in her house, without her father and Raoul. And perhaps she could sleep there without the constant nightmare greeting her each night. One thing she knew for sure: If she lived there she would go to a new school, where no one knew her. She also knew that she had nothing to say in the matter. It was her father who decided such things.

Sadly, Ester's death was not the only tragedy of that winter. One morning shortly after the beginning of the new year, Old Svea set out to do the milking as usual, a job she had taken over after the milkmaid Maria had been forced to leave Björkdalen when she could no longer hide the fact that she was pregnant. It was still dark outside, the only light being the myriad of stars pinned against the blackness, for the sliver of moon was already half hidden behind the ridge of trees to the west. Soon the sky would start to lighten in the southeast, but not quite yet. Holding her long skirt high above the surface of the snow with one hand and the milk pail in the other, Svea made her way along the partially drifted path to the cowshed. Already she could hear the cows calling out to her, anxious for her gentle hands to relieve the pressure in their udders. Letting go of her skirt, she yanked the heavy door partway open, setting an avalanche of snow cascading off the roof. The impact knocked her to the ground, where she lay dazed and half buried, too far from the house for her call for help to be heard. It wasn't until much later, when Svea should long ago have come in with the milk, that Pia realized that something must have happened. Quickly she pulled on her boots and grabbed her shawl.

"See to Raoul," she told Kajsa. "I have to see what has happened to Svea."

By now the sun had come up over the treetops, casting its light on the pile of snow in front of the cowshed door.

"Svea!" she shouted when she saw it. "Svea!"

There was no answer. She could see Svea's kerchief lying in the snow beside the overturned milk pail. Coming closer, to her relief, she saw that the old woman's face had not been buried. Immediately she began brushing the snow off her, all the while beseeching her to speak, or at least open her eyes. Getting no response, she ran to the stall after Nils. Together they managed to free Svea and carry her between them to the house. Having moved her bed as close to the hearth as was safe, Nils returned to the stall. As a man, there was no place for him within the intimacy of caring for Svea. Although Pia was well aware of the taboo against observing a naked body, one's own or someone else's, she never-theless removed all of Svea's clothes. The old woman's wrinkled body had taken on a slightly blueish tone, cold to the touch. Gently she wrapped her in the quilts that Kajsa had warmed in front of the open fire. Eventually Svea's eyelids flickered slightly, her first sign of life.

"Cows," she mumbled, "cows."

Suddenly Pia realized that they had not been milked.

"Kajsa's seen Svea milking many a time, has she not?" she asked, turn-ing to the child.

Kajsa nodded.

"Then she must know how it's done."

"Yes, I think so," Kajsa replied.

"The milk pail is lying in the snow in front of the cowshed. Stand all the way under the eaves before opening the door. That way any snow sliding off the roof won't fall on Kajsa," she instructed. "But first go to the stall and tell Nils to fetch One-eyed Klara."

Kajsa half-ran out to the stall, feeling very grown up at the thought of doing the milking all by herself, without anyone watching to correct her smallest mistake. For a moment she forgot that her joy was due to Svea's misfortune.

One-eyed Klara was ministering to Svea when Roland Sjöström came home in the late afternoon. By then Svea had become delirious, babbling incoherently.

"I've done everything within my power, but she's still cold," Klara told him. "Me thinks it is best to fetch the doctor."

Sjöström glanced at the woman he had known all his life.

"She'll be alright," he remarked, unconcerned, "Svea's a tough old bird."

And with that he went to the corner cupboard and poured himself a warming shot of *brännvin*.

That night Roland Sjöström slept soundly behind the curtain drawn across his cupboard bed. Meanwhile, Pia and Klara spent the night keeping Svea wrapped in hot towels and covered with all the constantly re-heated quilts and animal hides available. Kajsa lay awake watching the two of them moving quietly between the hearth and the bed. Only the crackling of the fire and Klara's soft chanting broke the silence. Finally, Kajsa could no longer conceal her anxiety.

"Pia," she whispered hesitantly, "is Svea going to die?"

"I know not," Pia answered. "We're doing all that we can do. The rest is up to God."

"I don't want her to die."

"Nor do I," Pia added. "But it's not up to us. We can only do our best to help. 'Tis God who makes the big decisions."

The next morning Roland Stöström awoke to regret his nonchalance the previous day. Towards dawn Old Svea's heart had given up, leaving her stiff and even colder than when she had lain in the snow. Too late he realized what she had meant to him. She had been the one person in his life whom he could depend upon, who always treated him fairly, never turning against him as both his mother and father had been prone to do. If he had only gone for the doctor....

Kajsa's grief was boundless. She had no one to turn to for comfort or protection from her father. There was only Pia, who was no more than a child herself. And Kajsa could see that she too was afraid of her father, at least when he smelled of *brännvin*. She didn't want to think about any of it, yet she couldn't not think about it.

One-eyed Klara stayed to help Pia and the village women with the funeral preparations. Björkdalen had been Svea's home for over fifty years. Before coming there, she had been married and had given birth to a number of children, several of whom had died in infancy. Later, after her husband and remaining children had become the victims of a cholera epidemic, she had come to Sjöströms as a kitchen maid and had quickly become part of the family. She was as deserving of a grand funeral as Ester had been. Perhaps even more so.

Kajsa sat in the corner with Raoul, watching the women wash and dress Svea. She wished she could help, even though it was not a child's place to do so. She was not afraid of death. To her, Svea looked happy while the women tended to her. Kajsa supposed it was because, while Svea had fussed over everyone in the family, no one had fussed over her until now. Like Roland Sjöström, Kajsa was just beginning to realize how much Svea had meant to her. The emptiness after her was even greater than that after her mother.

On the morning of the funeral her father informed her that she was to stay home with Raoul.

"I shan't risk witnessing any more of that embarrassing behavior that Kajsa displayed at her mother's funeral," he told her.

Kajsa said nothing. She was just as glad to avoid possibly once again being reprimanded in front of everyone by Reverend Holmgren. Nor did she wish to watch another box being lowered into a hole in the ground. At the same time, she didn't want to miss seeing *Moster* Hildur, should she appear. Finally, just as the others were setting out, she asked Pia to please invite her home, should she meet her.

Moster Hildur did not appear, but another woman appeared who was to seal Kajsa's fate.

As he was leaving the *gravöl,* a woman from another parish approached Roland Sjöström.

"Excuse me, Sir," she began. "I've been led to understand that Herr Sjöström is looking for a new housekeeper."

Sjöström was taken aback. The thought of replacing Svea had not yet crossed his mind. But of course! He couldn't take care of the women's work himself and Pia was too young.

"As a matter of fact, I am," he replied.

"My name is Agnes Svensdotter. I have worked for Bengt Adamsson in Laxberg Parish. Perhaps Sjöström knew him. He passed away recently and I'm looking for a new position. I'm afraid I have no letters of recommendation, however. My employer left very quickly and unexpectedly."

"If Agnes follows me home now we can discuss the matter," he told her simply.

With that, she picked up a bundle she had left in the corner of the entranceway and they started off.

When her father came home after the funeral he had a strange woman with him. Kajsa regarded her suspiciously. She was about the same age as her father, but unlike Svea, who had been big and soft, she was small and thin, with hard, unfriendly eyes.

"This is my son," he said, motioning Raoul to present himself as he had been taught. Stepping forward Raoul held out his hand to the woman.

"R-R-Raoul," he said, bowing.

"*Tant* Agnes," she replied.

"Kajsa," Sjöström continued, pointing towards her. "My wife's daughter."

Kajsa shook hands and curtsied. *Tant* Agnes's hand was ice cold.

The rest of the household was introduced in the same manner as they came in: Pia the kitchen maid, Nils the farm hand, and Johan the stall boy.

By evening *Tant* Agnes had prepared supper and installed herself in Svea's bed. But not, however, without having first issued a few orders. Pia was used to doing as she was bidden, but Svea's way of giving orders always began with, "Can Pia be so good as to...." Kajsa, too, was accustomed to Svea's gentle manner, and she resented being told she was lazy and ordered to bring in a load of wood quickly or to get outside and fetch a pail of water. And for her part, *Tant* Agnes was quick to detect a note of what she saw as surliness in the child. And thus their relationship was established, a relationship which did not improve with time. Kajsa was unable to hide her resentment towards the woman who had so insensitively barged into her life and not only pushed Svea aside, but also her mother.

One afternoon, not long after Agnes's arrival, Kajsa sat down as usual on the kitchen bench, pulled the little three legged table close to her and carefully removed the lace tablecloth before opening one of her school books on its bare surface.

"Get thy things off that table and put the cloth back!" *Tant* Agnes told her harshly.

"My mother always lets me do my school work here," Kajsa retorted without thinking.

"Kajsa's mother is dead and now 'tis I who decides what she can and cannot do."

"*Tant* Agnes is not my mother!" Kajsa screamed. "She's just a mean old woman! I wish it was she who was dead instead of my mother and Svea."

The flat of Agnes's hand hit the side of Kajsa's head so hard that it knocked her off the bench.

"I cannot have that child here!" Agnes announced when Sjöström came in that evening. "She's spoiled and lazy and disrespectful. Either Sjöström finds a position for her or I find a new position."

"I approached my wife's *moster* on the matter a while back and I'm still waiting to hear from her," he replied, closing the matter.

One part of Kajsa was afraid to hope, while another part of her could not imagine that *Moster* Hildur would refuse.

The day that Post-Anders delivered a real letter to her father, sealed inside an envelope, was a long one for Kajsa. Upon coming home in the evening, Sjöström picked it up off his desk and turned it over casually several times before sliding the tip of his ivory letter opener under the corner of the flap, slitting it open. Kajsa pretended to be absorbed in her school work, while watching out of the corner of her eye. He pulled a paper from the envelope, unfolded it, and let his eyes glide over it quickly, then returned it to its envelope. Not a flicker of expression crossed his face.

"Gather thy things," he instructed finally, without looking at her. " 'Tis too late to set out now. Kajsa can leave with the dawn."

Kajsa let out the breath she hadn't known she was holding.

Quickly she rolled her few belongings in the skirt of her extra dress, tied it with a string, and placed the bundle in a coarsely woven satchel.

That night the nightmare left her in peace.

At breakfast the next morning Kajsa looked excitedly from one person to the next, wondering who was going to take her through the forest to Stenstorp, where *Moster* Hildur lived. But without muttering a word, they all left the table one by one and went to their daily tasks.

"Who's going to take me to *Moster* Hildur's?" she asked, when only she and *Tant* Agnes were left in the room.

"No one," Agnes told her.

"How will I get there?"

"Kajsa will get there on her own two feet," she was told. "It will only take half a day if she walks quickly."

"But I don't know where *Moster* Hildur lives. How can I find my way?"

"Just stay on the wagon road through the forest," Agnes said, pointing in the unfamiliar direction away from the village. "There are a couple of villages along the way where she can stop and ask directions. But beware of strangers. There can be bandits hiding in the forest, ready to rob travelers, although they probably are smart enough to understand that a child isn't likely to have anything of value with her."

Suddenly the excitement of going to *Moster* Hildur's lost its glow.

"But what about the wolves and bears?" she asked. "And trolls and the *skogsrå?*[59] They'll see that I am alone."

"Everyone must learn how to deal with such things on their own."

Pride forced Kajsa to put on a brave face in front of *Tant* Agnes. Grabbing the satchel with her bundle of possessions, she marched out the door, slamming it behind her, and walked away without saying good-bye to anyone. Not even Raoul. Once out on the road she turned left, away from the village and all that was familiar, and began the long, cold walk. But as soon as Björkdalen was out of sight behind her, her brave face dissolved into tears of both anger and sorrow.

That day proved to be the longest she had yet experienced in her short life. She walked quickly to keep warm, but not so quickly as to tire herself. She knew she must save her energy in case she had to run from danger. Although the snow was not properly cleared from the roadway, passing wagons had left deep wheel tracks, with holes after numerous horse hooves between them. But no matter which tracks she walked in, it took all her concentration to keep her balance.

Very soon the road entered the forest. Although the trees growing on either side had intercepted much of the snow before it had reached the ground, making it easier to walk, they also served to hide dangerous creatures from sight. Kajsa had visions of hungry wolves hiding behind the trees, waiting for a chance to pounce on her and tear her limb for limb. She hurried as fast as she could, not daring to look up from the ground. Her heart beat so loudly that she was sure every creature in the forest could hear it.

At the first village she stopped to ask directions to Stenstorp of an old man.

"They say 'tis just into the next parish," she told him.

"Yes, 'tis so. Jest keep on this here road. It goes straight as an arrow, so she don't have ta worry 'bout making any turns." *Lilla Fröken*[60] has a long way to go today. But she must remember one very important thing."

"What is that, Sir?"

"She must never sit down to rest. The cold will make her sleepy and if she closes her eyes she'll fall asleep and freeze to death. No matter how tired and cold she gets, she must keep on walking."

"Many thanks for the warning, Sir," she said, then bid him good-bye. She was glad he had warned her, for surely she would have sat down to rest along the way; she had already been tempted to do so several times.

---

59. A beautiful woman who appears to folk in the forest and lures them into her cave. Her backside is like a hollow log and she has a tail.

60. Little Missy.

It was only her fear of wolves that had stopped her.

Beyond the village the forest thickened, its silence broken only by the occasional snapping of a dry twig under some unseen creature's foot. Now and then deer tracks crossed her path, and once she even saw the huge footprints of a moose, who had left behind a still-steaming pile of scat. Letting her gaze follow his trail, she saw him standing not far away, motionless beside an evergreen, staring at her. She, too, stood stock-still, staring back, too frightened to move. After what seemed like an eternity, he stamped his foot with a snort, then turned and trotted off through the forest in the same direction as she was going. His proximity unnerved her, for she had never before seen such a huge animal.

Deeper into the forest she came to a fork in the road. Neither alternative went straight ahead, as she had been told the road would do. After much humming and hawing, she took the left fork. She walked for what seemed like hours, expecting to see a cottage, or at least a cowshed, after every turn in the road. But there was nothing but trees. By late afternoon she was becoming both cold and tired from plowing through the snow. And hungry. If only she had taken a bit of dried bread with her, or a cooked potato, but her only thought had been to get away from *Tant* Agnes as fast as possible. All around her the forest was blanketed in snow. There were none of the blue or red berries that hid amongst the low bushes covering the forest floor in the summer. In fact, there were not even any new shoots at the tips of the fir trees' fingers. Not that they filled one's stomach, but at least chewing on them gave the feeling of eating. She continued walking, reluctant to turn back. Finally, when she could not take another step, she sat down on a large stone by the side of the road.

"Just for a moment," she told herself aloud. "I shan't close my eyes even a wink."

The next thing she knew, she was being taken back the way she had come by someone she could feel, but not see. She felt as if she were walking in a dream.

"Come along, now," she heard a voice say. "Kajsa went the wrong way. 'Tis lucky that she stopped close to my cottage. If I hadn't 'a found her, she'd 've frozen ta death for sure. She was warned about sitting down."

"Yes, I know," she heard herself say, "but I couldn't take another step."

At the fork in the road, she was pointed in the right direction.

"There's a cottage just beyond the bend in the road. Knock on the door and they'll give Kajsa something to eat. I don't think she'd like my food."

"Many thanks for helping me," she replied spontaneously.

"As she can see, we're not ta be feared, as people make us out ta be."

She turned around to see who was speaking to her, but all she saw was a small shadowy figure the size of a young child hurrying in the direction from which she had just come. She was alone once more, but no longer tired. It wasn't until long afterwards that she began to wonder about who it was who had saved her from freezing to death.

Upon reaching the cottage, she hesitated, unsure if it were the right one, for it looked as if it were falling down. Surely no one lived there. But when she finally knocked on the door, an old man opened it a crack and peered out.

"Who's it?" called a woman's voice from within.

" 'Tis the lassie we've been a-waitin'," the man answered.

He reached out and grasped Kajsa's hand, pulling her inside. The door closed behind her.

A small, wrinkle-faced woman dressed in tattered clothes stood by the hearth stirring a blackened pot hanging over the fire.

"Sit down, Lassie," she said, indicating the bench behind the little table. "The porridge is soon ready. 'Tis mostly water, but 'tis the best we've ta offer."

Kajsa obeyed. It was then that she saw that the table was set with nothing more than two wooden spoons. Quickly she untied her bundle and pulled out her own wooden spoon, setting it on the table in front of her.

"Good that she has her spoon with 'er," the woman remarked. "We've only our own two and the stirrin' spoon's too big for a child's mouth."

Kajsa looked around the cottage's single room while the porridge cooked. It was the tiniest room she had ever seen, containing, aside from the open hearth, only the little table, two wooden chairs with broken backs, the *utdragssoffa* where she was sitting and which served as the old people's bed at night, a large flat-topped chest, and a cupboard reaching up to the low ceiling. On the hard-packed earthen floor, a couple of hens searched in vain for crumbs. Such strange people. She couldn't help wondering how they knew she was coming.

" 'Tis not to worry 'bout how we knowed to expect Kajsa. News it travels in unseen ways here," the old man assured her, answering her unspoken question.

Suddenly, she feared she had fallen in with the small folk that people had warned her about.

"Be not afraid," he continued, as if reading her thoughts. "We's not evil like ig'rant people says we are."

"M-m-might thee be 'small folk?' " she ventured curiously.

"We's just folk," came the answer.

The woman poured the porridge into a large wooden bowl and set it in the middle of the table. As was customary in poor peasant homes, everyone ate from the communal bowl, each with his or her own spoon.

"Warm thy soul and fill thy stomach," she said with a wave of her hand. "We's wishin' we had some butter or lingonberries ta put in the middle for our guest, but 'tis not the case. We's jest glad for the porridge a' don't weep for what we don't got."

All three spoons dipped into the thin gruel. Kajsa had never eaten such watery porridge, nor porridge without butter melting in a hole in the middle or lingonberries whose juice ran in red rivers toward one's spoon. Nor had any porridge ever tasted so good and filled her stomach so completely.

When the communal bowl was empty, Kajsa licked off her spoon, wiped it on the apron she always wore, and returned it to her bundle while searching for something with which she could give the couple to show her gratitude. Once again the man read her thoughts.

"We want for nothin'," he said. "Kajsa's visit has given us more 'n anything we can hol' in our hands. But now she must be on her way. 'Tis gitten dark. Stenstorp's the first place other side of the forest."

She retied her things and placed them in her satchel without the pretense of further searching within it, for she knew she had nothing to give them, and took her leave. Nor did she dwell on whether or not they had been "small folk," for whoever they were, they had shown her great kindness.

The forest was never ending, without a clearing or a cottage in sight, nor a single soul traveling the wagon road. Before long Kajsa was so cold that she could hardly walk, her half-frozen feet aching unbearably with each step. The wind harried around her, relentless as a wild animal, tearing at her clothes, attempting to devour her. On either side of her the fir trees had turned into monsters, waving their arms threateningly. And out of sight behind them lurked hungry bears, just out of hibernation, stalking, looking for their dinner.

Slowly the light began to fade as the sun and moon changed places. Long shadows fluttered across the roadway menacingly in the moonlight, daring her to cross them. Did they belong to the small folk? Or possibly the *skogsrå* or a troll? She looked from side to side nervously, but saw nothing. Then suddenly a cloud passed over the moon, leaving her in semi-darkness, save for the whiteness of the snow. Almost as quickly as it had disappeared, the moon returned again, full and golden through the trees. Somewhere nearby a wolf howled, sending chills along her spine. Her heart beat so hard she could hardly breathe.

Just when she was about to give in to the creatures of the night, something unexpected caught her attention: the smell of smoke! Suddenly her strength returned and she quickened her pace. Before long the forest gave way to an open field. On its far side stood a ramshakle cottage alone in the moonlight. She began running, stumbling over the uneven ground, crying in relief.

The cottage was dark when she reached it, for it was late. Not stopping to knock, she opened the door and went in, as was customary for travelers arriving after the household had gone to sleep. Without a sound, she made her way blindly toward the heat coming from the banked fire and collapsed on the floor.

By morning the wind had abated, having shredded the previous day's clouds and allowed hesitant rays of winter sunlight to make their way to the ground. A few rays even managed to press through the tiny soot-covered window of the cottage to where Kajsa lay in front of the hearth, curled against the cold. Their sharp light reddened her eyelids, causing her to sit up and rub her eyes. All at once an icy draft engulfed her from the gaps between the rough uneven floorboards on which she had slept. Shivering, she pulled her shawl tighter and looked around the room slowly. On the hearth above her a low flame played under a three-legged iron pot, its gentle bubbling sending the aroma of porridge out into the room, while a thin stream of smoke wound its way up through the open chimney and disappeared amongst the naked branches of the overhanging trees. The room was tiny compared to Björkdalen, the smoke-blackened ceiling so low that she suspected even she could touch it, and the timber walls without wallpaper or even pasted-on newspapers. Here and there the remains of burnt-out light sticks stuck out from between the timbers along with the insulating moss. The furnishings were few and primitive: two cupboards, a chest, an open *utdragssoffa,* a couple of broken chairs, and a small table. Nowhere was there a kerosene lamp hanging from the ceiling. The whole room felt gloomy and unwelcoming, in spite of the shaft of sunlight coming in the single window.

"*Moster* Hildur?" she called softly. Getting no response, she called once more, this time a little louder.

Suddenly a dishevelled figure, with wild eyes and hair standing on end, sat bolt upright in the *utdragssoffa* behind the table.

"What inna hell's goin' on! Can't a body sleep 'round here?" an angry voice yelled.

"Is *Moster* Hildur here?" she asked with false bravery.

"How'n the hell should I know? An' whose the child come inta' my cottage without bein' invited?"

"I'm Kajsa from Björkdalen. I've come to serve as a maid with *Moster* Hildur."

"She's not needin' no maid. Be gone with ya!"

Just then Hildur appeared from the cowshed carrying a pail with a bit of milk in the bottom. Before she could greet Kajsa, the man began to shout.

"Who's she? What's she doin' here?"

"Stop thy yelling, Husband!" she retorted. " 'Tis my sister's *dotter-dotter*[61] come to stay."

"What'a we need her for?"

"She's gonna help me round here since my husband does nothin' but drink."

"How dare my wife speak to me in such a way!" he declared, while attempting to hoist himself up out of the *utdragssoffa's* bed.

Kajsa pressed herself against the hearth wall, petrified not only by the wild-eyed man, but also by the fact that *Moster* Hildur dared to speak so to her husband. Her mother would never have been so disrespectful of her father, no matter what his faults.

" 'Tis not to worry, Little Kajsa," Hildur told her. "When Arvidsson's seeing the world through the bottom of the bottle he has no strength to even stand up. And when he awakes on the morrow, he'll remember none of this."

Although her experience told her differently, for such was not the case when her father reeked of *brännvin*, Kajsa tried to convince herself to trust *Moster* Hildur. In the meantime, Arvidsson had fallen back down into the bed and was already snoring.

"Welcome. I hope Kajsa's journey was not too difficult," Hildur said while she laddled watery porridge from the *tre-footing*[62] into a wooden bowl and dropped a few lingonberries into it. "Come and warm thyself by the fire," she invited, setting the bowl on the chopping block in front of the raised hearth. " 'Tis more pleasant to eat here than to sit at the table and listen to that snoring."

They ate in silence for a while, each scooping porridge from around the edge of the bowl with their wooden spoons, leaving the lingonberries in the center until last.

Finally Kajsa could no longer still her curiosity. "Where is Signe?" she wondered aloud.

"She keeps to her room upstairs."

"Why?"

" 'Tis a long story, which Kajsa will learn in time."

Kajsa nodded to indicate that she accepted her explanation, but her curiosity was far from satisfied.

"However, Kajsa shall sleep upstairs also, so she'll have plenty of

---

61. Daughter's daughter.

62. An iron pan with three legs attached to it, which is set directly above the fire on an open hearth.

chance to get to know my Signe."

Kajsa's mood brightened immediately.

When they had finished eating, Hildur scraped the last of the porridge from the *tre-footing* into the bowl and added a few lingonberries.

"Bring thy belongings, my child, and follow me."

Reaching down into her bosom, she fished up a string with a key hanging from it, with which she opened a door at the far end of the room. Removing the key, which also served as the door handle, she pulled the door shut behind them until the lock clicked, then led the way up a steep stairway to a single attic room.

"Signe, my dear, here she is at last," she called out cheerfully.

She set the bowl down on a small table beside a *utdragssoffa* filled to overflowing with straw and covered with a white sheet. In it lay a frail woman who reminded Kajsa of her mother.

"And this is Kajsa's cousin Signe," Hildur continued.

Kajsa took the hand that Signe held out to her, surprised to find that her fingers were as small and child-like as her own.

"Later on we must fix a bed for Kajsa," Hildur said. "I just haven't had time to do it yet. Perhaps an animal hide on the floor and a quilt will do for the time being," she said half questioningly.

"She can gladly share my bed," Signe said, "if she does not mind, that is. 'Tis warmer that way, also."

"Oh, I do not mind," Kajsa answered. "I have never slept all alone."

And so it was decided to everyone's satisfaction, for Signe welcomed company during the long cold dark nights.

Throughout her adult life Signe had passed the long dark winter days in front of her small hearth, trying to keep warm while carding and spinning by the light of the fire. Although her legs were all but useless due to an undiagnosed illness in infancy, only allowing her to move haltingly between her bed and the hearth, there was nothing wrong with her hands. With seeming ease they transformed the pile of fleece in her basket into yarn, which she then knit into woollen stockings and mittens. During the warmer summer months she sat by the open window, hemming Hildur's newly woven sheets and towels by hand and decorating them with embroidered monograms. Almost all of her handwork was pre-ordered by women who could afford to pay a few coppers so as to avoid having to do such tedious work themselves. The pay was hardly worth Signe's time and effort, but her customers maintained that, handicapped as she was, she should be thankful for any work that came her way. And indeed, she always managed to present a cheerful countenance to those who came up to her room to leave or fetch an order. People assumed she was happy, having accepted her fate in an almost saintly manner. In truth, she suffered not from her physical condition but, rather, from extreme loneliness, for she had no friends. As a bastard child, other children had been kept away from her. And in adulthood the women who came to her spoke only of the work they wished to have done. No one stayed to drink coffee. Consequently, her days were consumed by the monotonous tasks of carding and spinning, knitting and stitching, beginning and ending with a verse from the Bible. At best there was nothing to read in peasant homes aside from religious tracts. Anything else was considered dangerous or sinful. Only the rich could afford books.

And now, Kajsa's arrival had awakened Signe from her dreary, never-ending attic existence. For the first time in her life, she had something that craved her caring, aside from that which her hands could produce. She quickly became attached to the child, unable to imagine living without her.

Kajsa soon became integrated into the daily routines of life at Stenstorp. After each meal Hildur unlocked the door to the stairs and Kajsa took what food was left up to Signe; usually thin porridge or half a salted herring and one or two boiled potatoes, along with what remained of the roasted rye ersatz coffee. After several days of Signe's eyes following her as she left her to eat alone, Kajsa began taking her own meals upstairs also. It wasn't only that she felt sorry for Signe; she had also grown fond of this woman who reminded her of her mother, not only in looks, but also in gentleness.

At first they slept *skavföttes*,[63] as housemaids did when sharing a bed. Then one night Signe suggested that Kajsa turn around and share the bed's only pillow with her. Kajsa crept up along her side shyly, never having slept so close to an adult, let alone share a pillow. Neither of them said a word. Kajsa fell asleep immediately, surrounded by a never-before-experienced sense of warmth and security. Signe, on the other hand, lay awake for a long time, watching the light from the fire on the open hearth flicker across Kajsa's face. She, too, was aware of feelings she had hitherto never known; a desire to hold the child in her arms

---

63. Head to foot.

and protect her from the outside world. She brushed a stray lock of hair from Kajsa's forehead, then pulled her closer. In response, a small hand sought, then grasped, her own and they slept. From that night onward they slept close together, often with Kajsa encircled in Signe's embrace. Kajsa had found the mother she had lost with Raoul's birth, then lost again with Ester's death. And Signe had found the child she had always longed for but could never have. Neither spoke of the bond between them, each assuming she was alone in her feelings for the other.

"Why does Signe never come downstairs?" Kajsa asked her one night while they lay in bed waiting for sleep.

Signe was silent for a moment, not knowing what to say.

" 'Tis because of Arvidsson," she replied finally, hoping her answer would satisfy the child.

"What does Signe mean?" Kajsa persisted.

"He's not nice to me."

"Not nice?"

Signe took a deep breath.

"He calls me bad names and tries to touch me in places where a man shouldn't touch a woman."

Kajsa wondered where those places might be, but was afraid to ask.

"What kind of bad names?" she asked instead.

"Hor unge,[64] for example," she answered simply.

Kajsa thought for a moment.

"I've heard that myself," she said knowingly, reluctant to admit that she didn't know what it meant.

Suddenly their conversation was interrupted by a commotion downstairs, which quickly turned to shouting and then the sound of breaking dishes.

"What's happening?" Kajsa wondered nervously.

" 'Tis just Arvidsson," Signe told her. "He's drunk. Stay away from him when he's like that. He beats whoever crosses his path. 'Tis usually Mamma. He always finds something he thinks she has done wrong or not done at all. He also beats me if I am downstairs, even when he hasn't been drinking. Because I'm not his. He says I'm only good for one thing and often tries to come up to my room. That's why Mamma keeps the door to the stairway locked."

She spoke as if it were the most natural thing in the world, and indeed, for her it was. It was the only life she had ever known since

---

64. Whore child.

coming to Stenstorp as a baby nearly thirty years earlier. That tiny attic room had been the extent of Signe's world all those years. Hildur had done her best to care for her daughter, spending what free time she had with her, teaching her to card and spin, as well as to knit and sew. When Arvidsson was away from home she used to bring Signe downstairs and, if the weather was fair, take her outside. But as Signe grew older and her legs grew weaker, it became more and more difficult to get her down the stairs and back up again, then finally impossible.

As the commotion escalated, Kajsa crept closer to her.

"Not to worry, child," Signe soothed. "One gets used to such things. One has no choice."

Downstairs she could hear *Moster* Hildur crying.

"Let me be, Husband," she begged. "She's my dead sister's granddaughter."

Arvidsson's non-verbal reply was a heavy thud, followed by silence.

"Moster Hildur?" Kajsa ventured finally.

"She's used to it. Her father treated her mother in the same way."

Kajsa lay awake long after Signe had fallen asleep. As a small child she had understood that men could be violent when they smelled of alcohol, yet her father had only shown such violence towards her and Raoul, for they were but children. Although he could speak harshly to her mother, he had never hit her.

Little did Kajsa suspect the extent to which she had stepped into a new and alien world. The life she had known at Björkdalen had always played itself out behind a well-polished façade. Roland Sjöström was regarded by his fellow villagers as an honest and upright man, a reputation he went out of his way to uphold. That which took place behind his closed door or on his property, while at times experienced as cruel by those involved, was, in fact, nothing unusual. Such was accepted behavior of those who had money, and thus, power. Life at Stenstorp, on the other hand, was much more raw and out in the open, with no misleading façade behind which to hide. Arvidsson made no attempt to curb his behavior, for he had no social position to protect. Nor was he much different than many other men of his class, exercising power and control where he could find it.

The next morning when Kajsa opened the door at the bottom of the stairs she expected to see broken dishes lying about, but the room looked orderly as always. To her relief, Arvidsson was nowhere to be seen. But when Hildur came in with the morning milk her face was puffy almost beyond recognition, with a large still-open cut at her hairline and one eye ringed in shades of purple and swollen shut.

"Be not alarmed," Hildur told her. "That is how men are when they drink too much. Kajsa might just as well learn that sooner than later."

Kajsa had already learned that men could be that way toward children when they had been drinking. But that they could beat their wives black and blue, and that the women accepted it as part of life, was too much for her to comprehend. She knew one thing for sure: she was never going to get married.

Kajsa had looked forward to starting in a new school where no one knew her. Most of all, she longed to have a friend amongst the girls. This time she would not know the alphabet, and certainly not be able to read. But she worried about her clothes, for she remembered the way Anna and her friends had looked at her dress, and she suspected that it had as much to do with the way they treated her as did her reciting of the alphabet. She also understood that a maid at Stenstorp would not wear either of the two dresses she had taken with her from Björkdalen. More than anything, she wanted to be like the other pupils; to be accepted as one of them.

After brooding nervously over her situation for several days she finally got up her courage to approach *Moster* Hildur.

"I've no school dress," she said apprehensively.

Hildur looked her up and down.

"What's wrong with what Kajsa has on?" she asked.

Kajsa looked down at her dress and shook her head slightly.

"It's too...." she began.

Sizing up the situation at once, Hildur told her simply, "I shall find Signe's old dress for Kajsa."

The next morning she handed Kajsa a well-worn dark green dress with several patches on the skirt and a safety pin replacing a missing button. A smile crept over Kajsa's face when she saw it.

"*Tack* [65] *Moster,*" she said softly.

Much to Kajsa's disappointment, because there were only five children in that part of the parish, there was no school house with its tile stove

---

65. Thanks.

and rows of desks facing the teacher's platform and blackboard. Instead, there was an ambulatory school, whereby the teacher rotated between families that had school-aged children, receiving a week's room and board in each home in exchange for his teaching. And thus the children also rotated from *torp* to *torp* along with their magister. To sit on a cold floor, with only a box of sand in which to practice writing and her fingers on which to count, while the mother of the house went about her daily tasks and the younger children played amongst them, didn't feel like school to Kajsa. And she hadn't needed to worry about her dress; the other four pupils were boys. Likewise, it was unnecessary to pretend not to know the answer when called upon, for she quickly became too apathetic to care.

Instead, Kajsa's real education was about to take place within the four walls of the cottage at Stenstorp.

Up until now Arvidsson hadn't been aware of Kajsa's whereabouts during the day, since he spent his time working on the landlord's estate to pay the rent. But when Hildur informed him one evening that it was Stenstorp's turn to host Magister Ekdahl, he suddenly understood that Kajsa had been going to school. He put his foot down. Hard.

"I won't hear of it! Girls got no business goin' ta school!" he declared. "All a girl needs ta learn is to obey her father and then her husband. They'll do her thinkin' for her. If Hildur lets that schoolmaster with his newfangled ideas lift his foot over my doorstep I'll cast both her and him outa my house bodily. That child's here to work. Hildur fooled me once already with her worthless daughter. I am not feeding another child so she can piss away her time learnin' things she don't need ta know. Book-learnin' will jest make her think she's better an other folks. She's nothin' more than a parentless burden and it's well that she understands that. And if I find out she's goin' ta school 'hind my back, I'll beat her within an inch of her life!"

Neither Hildur nor Kajsa dared to challenge him, for he was known for living up to his threats. Thus Kajsa's education was reduced to what Hildur was able to pass on to her from her own scanty schooling, for her father, too, had believed that ignorance was the best way of keeping a woman in line. By the time education had become mandatory in 1842 it was too late for Hildur; she was already a mother. And even now, in the 1870s, the law overlooked girls who were poor and would never amount to anything. It was considered best for them to get used to working as early as possible.

Without school work to occupy her, time passed slowly at Stenstorp. Kajsa did her best to avoid Arvidsson, even when he hadn't been drinking. Either way she feared him. At night she could hear him trying to force Hildur to lie with him; sometimes begging, other times demanding, threatening to beat her if she refused. Her answer was always the same: "I would rather lie with a billy goat. He wouldn't smell any worse and at least he wouldn't be drunk." Although she did not yet know what it meant to lie with someone, she knew that it was something disgusting. It wasn't until her breasts started to bud a few years later that, thanks to Arvidsson, it began to become clear to her.

The day was warm, one of the first real spring days after a long hard winter. Kajsa was in the shed fetching an armload of firewood when Arvidsson appeared in the doorway, blocking the light. Immediately she clutched the wood to her chest and looked for a way to escape.

"Come, Little Missy, *Farbror* [66] Arvidsson wants Kajsa to do something for him," he said.

For once his voice was friendly, his words clear and unslurred. As he came nearer she realized that he only smelled of sweat and tobacco, without the added stink of alcohol.

"I's been feedin' an' clothin' Kajsa these past few years and now she owes me somethin' in return," he said.

"But I have worked hard to pay my way," she protested.

"Yeah, I know. Kajsa's helped Hildur lots. But she's done nothin' for me."

"What does *Farbror* wish me to do?" she asked innocently.

Putting his arm around her shoulders in a fatherly manner, he pulled her against his side, cupping his hand over her breast.

"Put down the wood she is holdin' and hold onto this instead," he told her, while reaching into the front of his britches and pulling out his man's limb.

Instinctively she started to back away, but his arm tightened around her shoulders, stopping her. Grabbing her hand, he wrapped her fingers around his quickly growing organ.

"Pump it back an' forth an' feel how it gets big an' hard," he instructed, his hand tight over hers.

She was too frightened to scream, nor could she break free from his

---

66, Uncle. Literally "father's brother," used for older men in the same way as "tant" is used for women.

grip. His breathing became heavy and panting, accompanied by inhuman groans, as he forced her hand to pump faster and faster until his limb was so huge that her fingers could barely encircle it. Then suddenly he pulled up her skirt and tried to jam it into her child's body. But he had waited too long. She felt something warm gush between her thighs with small jerks. Thinking he had peed on her, she ran past him out the door, holding her skirt away from her body. Once outside, she touched her legs gingerly, shocked to find that it wasn't pee. It was slippery and smelled disgusting. Gagging, she cast up her breakfast into the nettles in front of the shed.

"This is our little secret," Arvidsson hissed warningly from behind her. "Next time *Farbror* will show her how it's really done. But mark my words: If Kajsa tells anyone, they'll find her at the bottom of the well."

She tried to run, but her legs buckled and she fainted, falling to the ground. Scooping her up, Arvidsson carried her to the cottage.

"I found her lyin' on the ground outside the woodshed," he told Hildur, laying Kajsa on the seat of the *utdragssoffa*.

After he had gone out again Hildur went to have a good look at the child. Half way across the room the smell told her all she needed to know. Lifting Kajsa's skirt she saw to her relief that her upper thighs were dry. Only her skirt and knees were stained. Enraged, she went out in search of her husband. In vain, for he was nowhere to be found.

"What did Arvidsson do to thee?" she asked gently when Kajsa opened her eyes.

Frowning, Kajsa thought for a few moments.

"Nothing, *Moster* Hildur," she replied finally.

"What does she mean by nothing?"

Kajsa tried to shrug her shoulders nonchalantly, too frightened by the vision of the well to tell *Moster* Hildur what Arvidsson had done, nor had she the words to describe such an act. But Hildur had already guessed.

Several days later, not knowing what else to do, Hildur went to Reverend Holmgren.

"Tell me," he said after she had related what had taken place, "how often does Hildur perform her marital duty?"

She looked at him, wondering what that had to do with Arvidsson's molesting of Kajsa.

"This concerns my sister's granddaughter, not myself," she said.

"How often does Hildur perform her marital duty with her

husband?" he repeated, ignoring her remark.

"As often as he forces himself on me," she answered.

"So she does not do so willingly. And why not?"

"Because he's dirty and smells bad and is almost always drunk, as well as often violent."

"If Hildur accepted her husband more willingly, he would not have to look elsewhere."

Hildur could hardly believe what she was hearing.

"Look elsewhere? The child is but twelve years old!" she declared.

"Age is of no consequence. She probably tempts him in some manner, as is often the case with maids toward their masters."

"Tempts him? She's deathly afraid of him!" Hildur almost shouted.

"My advice to Hildur is that she go home and show her husband the love he deserves; that she willingly and lovingly gives herself to him when he so desires. Come back in a few weeks and bring the child along so I can speak with her."

And with those words he bid her adieu and ushered her to the door.

When Arvidsson returned, drunk, after several days, he claimed he had never touched Kajsa, that he had simply found her lying in a daze outside the woodshed and had carried her into the house.

"Ask her thyself if thee don't believe me," he declared.

"I've asked her. Many times. I imagine Arvidsson has threatened her, for she says nothing," Hildur told him.

Each night after that she forced herself to "willingly" lie with her husband, but in the days that followed his lust after Kajsa was all too obvious.

When Hildur returned to Reverend Holmgren with Kajsa in tow, all she could report was that, despite her "willingness" to lie with her husband, his eyes were constantly on her sister's granddaughter.

"Let me speak alone with the child," he said. "Hildur can wait out in the vestibule," whereupon he showed her to the door and closed it behind her.

"Now," he said, sitting down opposite Kajsa and putting his hands on her knees, "tell me, what has happened between Kajsa and Arvidsson that has upset *Tant* Hildur?"

Kajsa shrugged her shoulders silently while squirming out from under his hands. She didn't like Reverend Holmgren. He was big and fat, with his priest's collar sticking straight out angerly from below his jowls and double chin. His beady eyes looked as though someone had pushed them into his fleshy face with their thumbs.

"What has happened between Kajsa and Arvidsson?" he repeated.

"Nothing," she finally managed to say.

"Has she tempted him with her eyes?" he repeated. "She must tell the truth to her parish priest."

"Tempted? I don't know what Reverend Holmgren means."

"Kajsa knows well what I mean," he told her roughly. "It's a sin to tell a lie," he warned. "God punishes sinners."

Although she truly did not know what he meant, she held her tongue, more afraid of the well than the threat of God's punishment.

As a last resort, Arvidsson was called to the parish office. Although reluctant to oblige, he had no choice. The priest was the right hand of God and one did not refuse to obey.

Reverend Holmgren questioned him thoroughly, but Arvidsson was firm in his denial.

"I've not laid with the maid Kajsa," he said over and over, for he truly had not completed that which he had set out to do.

"Is Arvidsson prepared to swear to that on the Bible?" Holmgren asked finally.

He nodded.

"Does Arvidsson understand the seriousness of swearing on the Bible? If he lies with his hand on the Bible he is doomed to hellfire and damnation."

"I understand," he replied.

Reverend Holmgren called in one of the parish sexmen, along with the churchwarden, as witnesses.

"Place one hand on the Bible and raise thy other hand," the priest said once they were all assembled.

Arvidsson did as he was told, repeating that he had not lain with the maid Kajsa. But even though the statement in itself was true, his hands shook in anger. He knew Kajsa had told someone. As soon as he left the church he downed the bottle of *brännvin* he had in his pocket and set off to find the girl.

"Where's the child?" Arvidsson yelled when he staggered through the kitchen door, barely able to keep himself upright.

Luckily Hildur had seen him winding his way along the path toward the cottage and had sent Kajsa up to Signe's room. Not only did she lock the door to the stairs; she also removed the key from around her neck and hid it in the back of the cupboard.

"And what does my husband want with Kajsa?" she asked.

"I've unfinished business with 'er," he answered.

"Well, she's not here. And if Arvidsson goes anywhere near her I shall set the police on him."

Arvidsson burst into a gulping, drunken laugh.

" 'Tis that so, *din djävla satkäring!*[67] he grinned. "Long as she's livin' in my house she's my property. 'Sides, Holmgren he knows I didn't do nothin' to her; I swared an oath for him, with my hand on that big church Bible. So whatever she teld Hildur's a lie."

"She's told me nothing," Hildur retorted.

"Then she's teld someun else. Wait'll I git me hands on 'er!"

By now his alcohol-powered energy was ebbing and before he had a chance to elaborate, he collapsed onto the seat of the *utdragssoffa* and was soon bent over the table snoring.

Those summer months were anxious ones for Kajsa. She never left Hildur's side unless it was unavoidable, and only then when Arvidsson was not at home. Although she knew little of what men did with women, her female psyche could not miss the lust in Arvidsson's eyes when he gazed upon her. It made her feel naked and uncomfortable. At those times it was as if she were once again pumping his organ, the thin outer skin sliding back and forth over its hardness. It made her feel sick to her stomach. Nor could she find any escape in sleep, for he entered her dreams, always forcing her to pump as he panted and jerked. Many times her crying and thrashing woke Signe who, without knowing what lay behind her nightmares, pulled her close and hummed softly until she slept once more.

As usual, Arvidsson looked forward to the end of September, when the harvest was in and farm laborers had several days free to attend the annual *Mikelsmässmarknad,*[68] the largest market of the year, on St. Michael's Day. Although commerce was no longer limited solely to the cities, permitting small shops to spring up here and there in the countryside, it was at the open market that most country people made their

---

67. you damn bitch.

68. St. Michael's Day market, 29 September.

purchases for winter: staples such salt, sugar, flour, coffee, and salted herring. It also coincided with the one week in the year that all maids and farmhands were free. Consequently, it served as a meeting place, where widespread friends and families could get together and relax after months of continuous hard work. And for many men, it was a time of undeterred drinking.

On the day of the market Hildur was up earlier than usual. Carefully she packed the butter she had churned and salted during the summer, her major source of household money in the autumn.

"Take this to Herr Cederlund ," she told her husband. "He pays more for butter than anyone else. Lord knows what he sells it for in town."

Then, taking down a tin from the mantel, she counted out the coins she had managed to save since the previous spring market and handed them to him.

"This, together with what Arvidsson gets for the butter, should be enough for a keg of salted herring, a sack of flour, and a few coffee beans to roast and grind with the rye to give the coffee a bit of flavor. The herring is most important, because we only have enough left of two or three more meals."

He pocketed the coins and set the package of butter in the wagon, then climbed up onto the box.

"See that the butter doesn't stand in the sun," she called after him as he set off.

He smiled and waved.

Think how easy life would be if he never drank, she thought with a sigh.

The next day when he returned he was so drunk that, had it not been for his old horse who knew the way, he would never have gotten home. A sense of foreboding fell over Hildur when he came in empty-handed. Without asking, she went out to the barn, hoping that in his drunkeness he had forgotten to bring in his purchases. But the wagon was empty.

"Where's the keg of herring?" she screamed at him. "And the flour?"

"What herring?" he drawled.

"What has Arvidsson done with all the money? Empty thy pockets!" she commanded.

"They's already empty," he laughed, turning them inside out.

"Thy filthy swine!" she shouted, picking up the axe from the chopping block beside the hearth. "Get out of here!"

" 'Tis my house," he retorted. "Get out thyself!"

She raised the axe, but he grabbed it before it could strike him. Seeing her chance, she lunged at him with all her weight, throwing him off balance. He hit the floor with a thud and lay motionless.

"Come," she said to Kajsa, who was huddling in the corner. "He can sleep it off where he is." She tried to sound nonchalant, but her voice was shaking with anger. Together they went upstairs, locking the attic door behind them.

As usual after such a drunken episode, Arvidsson was gone in the morning.

"He'll be back in a few days," Hildur assured Kajsa. "In the meantime, we can relax."

Kajsa could no longer resist asking the question that had long been on the tip of her tongue.

"Why did *Moster* marry Arvidsson?" she asked.

"At times like this I ask myself the same question," Hildur answered, "but I didn't have much choice. I was an unmarried mother with a small child and he agreed to take us. Little did I know...."

SIGNE

1840

It was high summer. The sun beat down relentlessly from the cloudless sky, forcing the dew out of the newly-cut grass. A group of village women were pulling it into piles with their brightly painted wooden rakes, while the men planted the poles around which the haystacks would be built. The air was completely still, without a breath of wind to cool the sweat dampening the back of every shirt and blouse. Although the work was exhausting in such heat, no one complained, neither aloud nor inwardly. Rather, each of them silently thanked God for having given them such perfect haying weather. If it held just a little longer their livestock would be assured of making it through the coming winter. And if God continued to bless them until it was time to harvest their rye and then their potatoes, well, no one dared to speak openly along such lines, yet the thought played in everyone's mind. Too many famines had made people superstitious, careful about their thoughts and words.

Once again, Hildur packed her few blongings into the satchel in which her own mother had carried her as a baby, then laid her swaddled girl-child on top of the load, carefully tucked out of sight, and hoisted it over her shoulder. For many days she had lived at the mercy of the old woman who had befriended her, saving both her life and that of little Signe. But now it was time to move on, before the child's existence was discovered by the woman's neighbors. To put her at the mercy of their tongues was hardly a way to thank her for her kindness. They both knew that Hildur had no future in the countryside, where everyone knew everyone else's business. In the city she would be anonymous. Also there were paying jobs to be had, rather than occasional farm work that paid in kind. And surely she could find someone to look after Signe during the day. But it was with sadness, and even a few tears, that she bid the old woman good-bye and set out. In the short time she had lived in the woman's hut—for it was too poor to be seen as a cottage—they had been like mother and daughter, each filling an empty place in the other. But, as with all mothers and their children, there comes a time when every mother must let go and every child must leave home and make its own way in life. Both knew and accepted this reality, although it didn't make their parting any easier. To once again follow the road to

Stockholm would be easiest now during the summer months, when Hildur could sleep out of doors. There was always the possibility of earning a meal along the way by working in the fields weeding turnips and carrots and hoeing potatoes. And country women invariably needed help beating the winter's dirt out of their sheets and clothes on a lakeside dock during the semi-annual "big washing" that took place in every household during the summer. Yet, even though many extra hands were needed for such work, the hands of an unmarried mother were not welcome. Such girls were looked upon as dangerous outlaws, spreading sickness and evil wherever they went. Small children were hurried indoors at the approach of any unfamiliar young girl carrying a child. Pregnant women fled from the sight of them, afraid their presence would, in any number of ways, damage their unborn child. Hildur was aware of these reactions; all girl-children grew up with the fear of such treatment hanging over their heads. In many cases, it was enough to keep them safe until they married; in other cases a girl's desire and naïveté or hope of marriage proved greater than her fear. And then there were those girls who never had a choice. These were far more numerous than one might imagine; more often than not the victims of a step-father or an employer. But no matter under what circumstances a girl became an unwed mother, the burden was laid entirely on her. For the father of her child, life went on as usual. In some cases, he swore his innocence before the priest; in other cases he paid a one-time pittance towards the child's upkeep. Often he disappeared or simply remained unknown. Whatever the case might be, society placed no burden of guilt upon him. He could continue to live his life as a free man. For the girl, she became a mother for life. Even if she gave up the child or took its life, it remained a part of her, whether she wished it to or not.

Hildur was only fourteen and not yet confirmed, and thus had not officially entered adulthood, when she took her leave of the old woman. However, the bearing of responsibility for her child made her feel like a grown woman. She was fully aware of her position within society—or so she thought—and was prepared to stand against it when need be. But the news of that which was hidden in her satchel had traveled ahead of her.

"What is it she's carrying in her sack?" a woman too old to fear for her children, born or unborn, wondered the first time Hildur stopped to ask were she might find field work.

"A few clothes and possessions from my family home," she answered confidently.

"Twi!" the woman declared and spit three times. "Clothes in deed! Take thy bastard child and be gone from here! We've no need for such help in this village. We're God-fearing people."

She bent down and picked up several egg-sized stones from the path.

Hildur began to run, her satchel banging against her side, waking Signe. A stone hit the back of her head, another struck her shoulder.

"Git outa here with thy whore child!" the woman yelled after her.

Hildur ran until lack of breath finally stopped her.

It was only the first of many such episodes she encountered as she made her way through the countryside. Almost everywhere she stopped and asked for work she met with the same unfriendly, often hostile, refusal, despite the fact that she always left Signe hidden out of sight. A young girl going from house to house seeking work could only mean one thing.

Now and then the road took her through a larger town where she was unknown and she was able to buy a bit of dry bread and perhaps a half a sausage or a piece of cheese with a few of the coins that still lay safely wrapped in the bottom of her sack. Silently she thanked the old woman who had cared for her for refusing to take them as thanks when they parted.

"I've made it this far in life and now I've only meself to look out for," she had said. "Hildur must keep them. She's gonna' need 'em on her journey."

One day, after having been turned away at countless doors, she heard the familiar sound of hoof beats coming up behind her. There was no place to hide; only open fields in all directions. Before she had time to think, two mounted police had pulled up, one on each side of her, and demanded to see the pass that allowed her to travel outside the bounds of her home parish. In the process of digging into her sack after it Signe awoke and began to cry.

"It's been brought to our attention that Hildur Unosdotter has been beggin' at every farm and cottage along this road," one of them said, the sun dancing threateningly off his spiked helmet.

"I've not been begging, Sir. I've been seeking work," she answered respectfully.

"Seeking work!" he snorted sarcastically. " 'Tis not what peoples sayin'."

"I've not been begging," she repeated politely.

"And where does Hildur Unosdotter live?" the other policeman wanted to know.

She hesitated, not knowing what to say. The last place she had been officially registered had been the *spinnhuset* in Stockholm, when she had been arrested as a vagrant while searching for her sister.

"Don't go tellin' us she lives in Uno's shack," he continued, "'cause that was torn down last summer. Or more rightly, it fell down of its own and folk pushed the remains inta the river. So Hildur Unosdotter obviously has no place ta live, so well as no work. That makes her a vagrant. Surely she knows what that means."

Yes, she knew. But before she could say a word, they grabbed her by her arms and rode on with her squeezed between their horses, her bare feet swinging above the ground.

"Be careful of my child!" she screamed, but they paid her no heed, ignoring Signe's crying as she bounced against Hildur's back.

Upon reaching the parish office, they literally dropped her off at the door, her dress torn and her sweaty limbs covered in horse hair. One of them dismounted and escorted her into the building.

"Here's Hildur Unosdotter," he announced triumphantly. She was obviously expected.

The man behind the desk looked her up and down with disgust.

"We're a righteous and God-fearing people in this parish. Girls such as Hildur may not wander freely, spreading evil amongst us," he told her. "They are best confined to the poor house."

To be placed in the poor house meant forfeiting all of one's worldly possessions to the parish, along with any money or land one might have, as well as losing all of one's rights. But as a fourteen year old, Hildur had no rights anyway. Nor had she any possessions beyond her satchel containing a few rags and a couple of copper coins. What she didn't know was that Signe was also considered to be a possession.

Hildur stood in front of the man's desk, shifting nervously from one foot to the other while clutching Signe. Eventually a woman was called into the room and instructed to collect Hildur's possessions. Without a word she removed the satchel from Hildur's shoulder, then reached for Signe.

"No!" she cried. "Madam cannot take her!"

"All of her possessions," the woman said coldly.

"She is my child!"

"The child belongs to the parish now," she was told. "It will be placed in a foster home."

"No!" screamed Hildur. "She is my child and 'tis I who cares for her!"

When she refused to relinquish the child, Signe was wrenched from her arms and whisked out of the room. In her place, she was given a paper to sign, relinquishing the child and the right to any further contact with her. By now Hildur was exhausted and starving, without the strength to fight back. She knew one had no chance of winning over "them." Reluctantly she gave in and signed the paper in exchange for a bed and something to eat.

Later that afternoon Hildur Unosdotter was escorted to the poor house, a building outside the village that was as impoverished as the people it sheltered. She was stopped outside the door by the matron.

"Can Hildur read?" she was asked.

"Yes," she answered.

"Yes, Matron," she was corrected.

"Yes, Matron," she repeated dully. It was not the first time she had been forced to show respect where she felt none.

"These are the rules that must be followed when living here," Matron informed her, pointing to a paper tacked on the door. "Read them aloud so that we know Hildur has read and understood them."

Hildur squinted her eyes and began to read haltingly. Many of the words were beyond her understanding.

"Number one," she read. "All residents of the poor house must obey and treat with the utmost respect those in charge, in the same manner as they obeyed and respected their former employers."

She paused, reflecting. Although she had never had an employer, she had grown up witnessing how simple working men were forced to doff their caps respectfully when their employer or another person of rank appeared, and similarly, how women had to stop their work, grasp both sides of their skirts, and curtsey before their betters. It reminded her of the *spinnhuset*.

"Keep reading!" Matron snapped.

Hildur read mechanically, sounding out the words as if they belonged to a foreign language that had no meaning for her.

Further down the list she came to a rule that caught her attention.

"No resident is allowed to leave the premises, no matter for how short a time, without permission from the matron."

With the last rule came a threat: "He who speaks ill of the poor house or those in charge of it, or criticizes the clothes, food, or rules or spreads rumors about such, shall be punished as follows: 1) the offender will be given a reduced ration of food for 1 to 8 days, 2) for a period of 5 days he or she will receive no "sovlet" (food aside from the everyday bread, potatoes, porridge, *välling*,[69] such as meat or cheese), 3) the offender will not be granted permission to leave the premises for an undefined time, 4) minors will be physically punished."

Further, Matron made it clear to Hildur that failure to conform to the rules meant being cast out of the poor house, with nowhere to go but the *spinnhuset*.

By now Hildur was beyond caring. She fell into the bed assigned to her and immediately disappeared into an uneasy sleep, filled with nightmares of being squeezed between galloping horses and losing Signe along the way. Several times during the night she reached for the child, only to awaken with a jolt when she failed to find her, followed by a feeling of emptiness.

The days were long in the poor house. Most of the occupants were old and sick, unable to work or even care for themselves. Consequently, Hildur was kept busy day and night tending and feeding them, cleaning, and carrying out the myriad of other necessary jobs. She moved through each day mechanically, longing for Signe and wondering what had happened to her. She had never imagined that she could become so attached to what people referred to as a bastard child. Having heard adults talking while she was growing up, she had imagined that such children were deformed in some manner, perhaps having three arms or no legs or two heads or another skin color. Regardless, they were all regarded as being evil. But Signe had none of those traits. She was perfectly formed and anything but evil. Having to care for her had been the one thing that had given meaning to Hildur's life. Not knowing who the child's father was had never mattered; in fact, she had been glad she didn't know. That had made Signe hers and hers alone. But now? Matron had made it clear that Signe no longer belonged to her. Nor was she able to ask outsiders what had happened to the child, for no villagers, aside from the priest and parish welfare authorities, came near the poor house, if they could avoid it. The only other outsider was Old Man Arvidsson, the delivery man. But the way his eyes followed her when he brought provisions each week made her uneasy and she went out of her way to avoid him. She dared not approach him about Signe.

---

69. thin gruel.

The days and weeks passed. Hildur had become a slave imprisoned in the poor house, on call day and night. She was exhausted by overwork and the conditions under which the people were forced to live often made her physically sick to her stomach. Several times she had tried to run away in the hope of finding Signe, but each time she was brought back by the mounted police and given a sharp warning by Matron. Finally she was threatened with the *spinnhuset* if she left the premises again.

One sunny day in late autumn, while hanging up the sheets she had spent hours scrubbing in the stream behind the building, Arvidsson unexpectedly appeared behind her.

"I'm needin' Hildur ta come an' be my housekeeper," he said simply. "My wife died and I've no one ta do the women's work. I have seen that Hildur is a hard worker..."

" 'Tis the parish what owns me, not myself," she interrupted, hoping to discourage him. He was surely even older than her father.

"Then I'll speak with the matron," he answered, without inquiring as to whether she was willing to work for him.

Several days later she was called into Matron's office. Standing before her desk was Arvidsson, staring at his feet, cap in hand.

"I understand that this man Arvidsson has asked Hildur to work for him as a housekeeper, but I have had to inform him that the poor house cannot get along without her help. I shan't allow her to leave. So the matter is closed."

But for Arvidsson the matter was far from closed. The next day he went to Reverend Holmgren and explained his need of a housekeeper.

"The only possible way for Arvidsson to take her from the poor house is by marrying her," the priest told him.

"Then I'll marry her," he declared.

Hildur was sent for. But when she learned of Arvidsson's resolve she was horrified. How could she marry such an old man! Then suddenly she saw her chance.

"I will only marry him if I can have my child back," she said determinedly.

"A child?" Arvidsson queried.

"Yes, she has a child," Holmgren told him. "Will Arvidsson take the child also?"

"Of course," he replied, without a moment's hesitation. Four hands were even better than two.

"Then so be it," he said. "But Arvidsson must marry her first, before he can take her from the poor house."

"How soon can it be?" Arvidsson asked. "I'm badly in need of a woman at home."

"As before all marriages, both parties must prove that they are able to read and that they have adequate knowledge of *Luthers lilla katekes.* Then it must be determined that neither of them has any condition, such as epilepsy or mental illness, that would prevent them from marrying. In the meantime, Hildur must remain in the poor house and continue working."

Unbeknownst to Hildur, it had been difficult to find a foster home for Signe, for no one wanted to take a bastard child. As a result, she had been placed in an orphanage, which was a burden on the parish treasury. Thus it was a blessing that Arvidsson agreed to take her. As for Hildur, although she was a hard worker, her presence as an unmarried mother was not particularly welcomed among the parishioners. And so it was that Reverend Holmgren was glad to take care of the matter as quickly as possible and relieve the parish of all responsibility for Hildur Unosdotter and her bastard child.

Since Arvidsson had been married previously, and neither he nor Hildur had any family or relatives in the parish, there was no need for an elaborate wedding ceremony.

Several days later Hildur was interrupted by Matron while on her hands and knees scrubbing the wooden floor where an old man had vomited beside his bed.

"Follow me," she was told.

Hildur got to her feet slowly, dropping the scrub brush into the pail beside her.

"Come along now. She mustn't keep him waiting."

"Keep who waiting?" Hildur asked.

"Reverend Holmgren."

"Reverend Holmgren?"

"Yes. He's going to marry Hildur and Arvidsson."

"Marry us? Now?" She looked down at her tattered dress. It was filthy and wet in the front from where she had knelt on the hem.

"Yes."

"But where's my child?"

"Hildur shall have her once she is wed, not before," Matron said, taking her by the arm.

A parish *sexman* was waiting outside the door nervously. Like most villagers, he was reluctant to enter the poor house. Not only was the all-invasive smell repelling, but even more so was the reality of perhaps having to end one's days in such a place. His relief was obvious when Matron appeared leading Hildur by the arm. He grasped her other arm, as if they expected her to run away, and together they escorted her to the church. Reverend Holmgren was waiting in the vestry, along with Arvidsson, who was also still dressed in his work clothes.

As every girl, Hildur had dreamed of the day she would marry a young man whom she herself fancied. Following tradition, she would wear a long black dress and have flowers in her hair. And like all young girls, she wanted to wear the parish crown that was reserved for virgins. That she was no longer a virgin was beyond her control, but still she had hoped for a husband she could love, and a new dress. But her wedding contained neither of these attributes. On the other hand, at least it was taking her away from the poor house and giving her back her child.

The marriage ceremony was short, with Matron and Sexman Lind as witnesses. Afterwards she and Arvidsson were told to wait in the parish house and Signe would be brought to them. After what seemed like an eternity, a woman came in bearing an infant in her arms. Hildur rushed to her, clasping the child to her breast. Arvidsson stood silently, as if thunder-struck, his face red with rage.

Once on the road to his cottage, out of sight of the church, he exploded.

"Hildur has lied to me!" he yelled, striking her in the face with the flat of his hand.

"What does he mean?" she cried. "I've not lied to anyone."

"Hildur never told me the child is a baby and not old enough to work to pay its way. She has tricked me into marrying her just so she could leave the poor house and get her child back."

"I have not tricked Arvidsson. He never asked about the child," she retorted. "And it was Arvidsson who wanted to get married. He never even asked me if I wished to marry him. If he had, I'd 've said no."

"And that is how our marriage began and that is how it has continued to this day," *Moster* Hildur concluded. "First, he made me pay for the fact that Signe was only a baby and later for the fact that she was unable to work. When he's drunk, he still claims I tricked him into marriage. All his misfortunes in life are my fault, as Kajsa has heard and seen."

131

"But why does *Moster* Hildur stay with him?"

"What else can I do?" Hildur replied. "I've no money and no place to live. I can no longer take to the road with Signe, as I did when she was a baby. And when he is sober, Arvidsson supports us as well as any other husband. One gets used to it and manages as best one can. Men beat their wives. That's just how life is."

As Kajsa listened to *Moster* Hildur talking about her life she felt as though she had walked through a previously closed door into another world. Hildur's words made their way into a dark place inside her, awakening scenes that had lain hidden since she had left Björkdalen. Suddenly she could hear Raoul's helpless cries as her father beat him for having wet the bed, followed by the sensation of herself being beaten when he was bitten by a snake. And once again she felt the sting of the whipping she received the day she had muddied her dress. Now that the door was open, the scenes tumbled out one after the other. The day her father forced Raoul to drink *brännvin* at the haying fest, his anger towards her mother when Hilda Maria wasn't a boy. Worst was her fear of him when he smelled of alcohol, for then she never knew what to expect.

But it wasn't only her father who could be cruel and violent. She could still see little Axel lying over Magistern's knee, helpless, while being beaten for not knowing the alphabet. Even Reverend Holmgren, who preached about loving one's neighbor, treated people cruelly.

"I'm never going to get married," Kajsa said after some thought.

"Of course Kajsa will get married," Hildur replied. "What'll she otherwise do? It is almost impossible for an unmarried woman to support herself. Does Kajsa want to be a governess, living in someone else's house and caring for other people's children instead of her own, until she is an old woman? Wait and see what life has in store for her."

But Kajsa had made up her mind, her resolve strengthened by Arvidsson's never-ending attempts to come upon her alone, especially when he was drunk. She was tired of living in the shadow of the constant fear he cast over her life. The day he surprised her at the well when he was should have been at work was the turning point.

"*Moster* Hildur," she announced when she returned to the cottage with a pail of water, "I've decided to go and 'read for the priest.' "[70]

Hildur didn't need to ask what lay behind her sudden decision.

"Has Kajsa reached confirmation age already?" she asked instead. "It

---

70. An expression meaning that one was going to confirmation classes to study "Luther's Little Catechism" in preparation to be confirmed and thus enter adulthood.

seems not long ago that she came here as a child of eight."

"I'm thirteen," Kajsa told her.

"Time goes quickly," Hildur mused. "I shall ask Reverend Holmgren to try to find a position as a housemaid for Kajsa in one of the families in the village, so she can pay her way."

A week later Hildur came with the news that Holmgren had secured a place for Kajsa in the next parish at Lersätters Gård, with Squire and Fru Gröndal, one of the more prominent farm families in the area.

The confirmation class didn't begin till spring, but as they were short of help, they agreed to take Kajsa immediately.

Kajsa hadn't expected arrangements to be completed so quickly. While she had wished to get away from Arvidsson as soon as possible, she had no desire to leave *Moster* Hildur and Signe. Hildur saw her hesitation.

" 'Tis better so," she said. "It's time to leave before the situation with Arvidsson comes to a bad end."

"But *Moster* and Signe..." she began.

"We're used to this way of life. I'm thankful for the years Kajsa has been with us and I know Signe feels the same. Remember, we're all family and always connected. Besides, the village is not far away. 'Tis not as if Kajsa was going to America."

In spite of Hildur's seeming casualness, when it came time for her leave-taking none of them was able to hide her feelings. Especially not Signe, who clung to her, unable to utter a word. Kajsa had no way of knowing the extent of her loss.

FRU GRÖNDAL

Lersätter 1882

Although Kajsa had been reluctant to leave *Moster* Hildur and Signe, the further she got from Stenstorp and Arvidsson, the lighter became her step. It was as if a heavy mantle was slipping from her shoulders. It felt like a warm summer day even though it was late autumn. Yet the sharpness of the past was transformed into a new anxiety: the future. She knew nothing of the family to which she was going; only that they were rich and lived in a large house. It was common knowledge that such people were not necessarily generous. Nor did she know how to behave in such circumstances. But she had an even greater concern.

"Dear God," she mumbled half aloud, "don't let there be a man like Arvidsson there."

"Dear God," she mumbled half aloud, "don't let there be a man like Arvidsson there."

She approached the village late in the afternoon, just as the top edge of the sun was dropping behind the trees. Rounding a curve in the road, the house at Lersätter appeared suddenly, both majestic and frightening, like a castle out of one of Grimm's fairy tales. An avenue of trees lined either side of the gravel driveway leading to the front door, the round pebbles raked in even furrows along its length. She dared not walk on it, keeping to where it edged the lawn as she made her way to the side door. Getting no response after having knocked several times, she let herself into the kitchen. In the middle of the room stood a large, well-dressed woman, obviously Fru Gröndal, issuing orders to several maids. Hearing the door close, she turned around facing Kajsa.

"Get out of here!" she yelled. "We allow no beggars into this house!"

"I'm no beggar, Ma'am. I'm Kajsa, who has come to work here," she replied politely.

"Not in such clothes!" the woman declared. "We cannot have someone here looking like a pauper. Change thy clothes immediately. We're expecting guests."

"I've no better clothes, Ma'am."

She turned to the kitchen maids.

"Astrid, show her up to the room in the attic where she can sleep. And Berta, see if some decent clothes can be found for her. She's a disgrace to Lersätters Gård dressed as she is."

And with that, Fru Gröndal left the room, without so much as a welcoming greeting.

Taking a candle, Astrid and Berta led Kajsa up the back stairs to a tiny room under the eaves. Built onto one wall was a box bed containing a mattress bag half-filled with straw, with a horse blanket folded on top of it. A low cupboard leaned against the opposite wall, and between them, under the single window, stood a table and chair. There was no hearth. The draft from the window threatened to blow out the candle when Astrid set it on the table.

"Pay Fru Gröndal no mind. Just try to stay out of her way," Berta remarked. "Let's see if we can find Kajsa some better clothes."

She looked Kajsa up and down.

"I guess we are about the same size," she concluded. "She can borrow my old dress. It's not very fine, but it's better than what she has on."

While she went to get it, Kajsa took her few possessions from her bundle and placed them in the cupboard. She shivered in the damp chill of the room. Hopefully, come winter, the entire household would move into the warmth of the kitchen at night, as they had at Björkdalen.

Kajsa was put to work immediately, her first job being to keep the kitchen floor swept and clean from all the muddy footprints after those who came and went: the boy who brought in wood for the kitchen stove and the tile stoves found in every room, the kitchen maids who made numerous trips to the earth cellar to get potatoes and other vegetables, or to the storage house for dried meat that hung from the ceiling, or salted herring and lingonberries stored in great wooden barrels. And three times a day Lovisa, the milkmaid, tramped in to the pantry with fresh milk for one of the kitchen maids to pour into shallow wooden troughs and place in the separating cupboard. And of course there was food spilled while cooking, as well as dishwater splashed from the dishpan on the wood stove. Kajsa had never been so busy. By the end of each day she was so exhausted that she fell into bed fully dressed and slept until Astrid woke her at 4:00 A.M. to help start the fires in the tile stoves. The house was to be warm and the coffee ready when the family got up several hours later.

In time her duties varied, but not the long hours. Nor the fact that she was constantly reminded that she was a servant and of little worth beyond the work she performed. Sometimes after a full day's work she was instructed to sit in the front hall and await the return of her master and mistress from a party, in order to help them off with their coats.

That they often came home long after midnight didn't alter the fact that she must begin her regular duties at four in the morning. Should her head droop sleepily while she waited, poised on the hard straight-backed wooden chair, she was woken by a stinging slap on the face when her master and mistress returned.

"These peasant girls are like animals," she once overheard Fru Gröndal remark. "The're made for work and hardly need any sleep."

Thankfully, unlike Arvidsson, the master of the house ignored her, bidding her only a disinterested "good morning" when she set his breakfast before him.

That winter Kajsa was left to sleep in her attic room. The never-ending wind whistled in through the gaps around the window, often together with rain that soaked anything left on the table. In December the rain was replaced by snow forcing its way into the room, as well as the icy wind. Kajsa froze. She longed for *Moster* Hildur and Signe and the friendly warmth they radiated. She would have liked to spend her monthly free Sunday with them, but half the day was taken up attending the compulsory church service, leaving too little time for the long walk to Stenstorp and back in the deep snow. Instead, she looked forward to being with them at Christmas, innocent of the fact that the holiday season in such a large household was busy beyond anything she could imagine. Not only was there no chance to go to Stenstorp, but she was not even given her free Sunday.

The season began with Advent, the fourth Sunday before Christmas, and continued until St. Knut's Day, January 13th, when the holiday festivities officially ended.

First came the most unpleasant aspect of the Christmas preparations. Early one morning, when the sky was still covered with stars, the Christmas pig was dragged, screaming, from its shed out into the snow and slaughtered. As always, the youngest of the maids, in this case Kajsa, was made to stand at its side during the thrust of the knife and catch the blood in a bowl as it drained from the dying animal. This would later be mixed with a little rye flour, baked, and given the fancy name of black pudding. Next the men set about scraping the bristles from the still-warm hide while the women had the distasteful task of cleaning the intestines before stuffing them with chopped sausage meat. These would then be hung in the storage house to cure. The rest of the meat, aside from that to be consumed during the holidays, was salted and stored in huge wooden barrels. Lastly, the head had to be picked clean and head cheese made. This job also fell to Kajsa. The pig's head was split down the middle and presented to her with one half lying cut side up and the other half with cut side down, leaving one eye with its long lashes looking up at her. It was with trembling hands that she managed to pick out the meat before her stomach cast up its contents, accompanied by much laughter from the other maids and farm hands.

In the baking house great amounts of dough were set for various kinds of bread; white bread to be eaten fresh with the Christmas meal[71] and an assortment of rye breads to be dried and stored in bins for the coming months, or formed into donut-shaped "hole breads" and hung on poles from the ceiling to dry. Early on baking day a fire must be started in the brick oven built into the chimney. Hours later, when the bread had risen and the oven was finally hot, the remains of the fire were scraped out of the oven and the bread slid inside with a long-handled paddle to bake.

There were other foods that had to be prepared ahead of time as well: *lutfisk*[72] was put to soak, beer brewed, butter churned, crisp bread made, cakes and cookies baked.

But the Christmas season was not only about food; it was also the time of the big semi-annual washing. All the dirty laundry from the past half year was carted out to the wash house and put to soak for a few days in the huge wooden wash tub filled with lye water. Next it was scrubbed by hand, then taken down to the lake and rinsed in a hole cut through the ice, wrung out, and finally hung up to dry, leaving many red and half-frozen hands. And, of course, in the days that followed, all the sheets and towels and table cloths had to be mangled and the clothes ironed.

While the wash house was still relatively warm, all the members of the household, from the master of the house down to the youngest housemaid, took their twice-yearly baths in the wash tub, one at a time, all in the same water, according to rank. Although Kajsa was not the youngest, she was forced to bathe last because she was new. By the time it was her turn the water was cold, with a thick skum covering its surface. She emerged feeling dirtier than before she had bathed.

As Christmas Eve crept nearer, Fru Gröndal's orders increased daily: every corner of the house must be cleaned thoroughly, floors scrubbed and covered with straw, silverware polished, the best china taken out

---

71. Midsummer was the only other time fresh bread was eaten.

72. Dried fish softened by soaking in lye made from birch ashes.

and washed, Christmas decorations put up. Guest rooms needed to be opened and aired, their beds made up with clean bedding. All of which she supervised, demanding perfection, without lifting a finger herself. And finally, enormous amounts of food must be prepared according to her instructions and then the many guests served. After the meal, hosts and guests moved into the main room, leaving the maids to clear the table and wash the piles of dishes and pans filling the kitchen. The housemaids were at their superiors' beck and call day and night, being woken for more blankets, bed-warmers, wood to be put on fires, chamber pots to be emptied after use so as not to be offensive to sleepers. Kajsa was so exhausted by the end of the holidays that she felt sick to her stomach. She longed for Stenstorp, in spite of Arvidsson.

The week after Christmas Stenstorp was hit by a storm, followed by an intense cold spell. Outside the temperature dropped steadily, coupled with icy winds howling from Siberia. Nor was it much warmer inside. To Hildur's relief, Arvidsson stayed at the inn drinking with his companions in the evenings after work, finding a hard bench by the open fire preferable to the drafty cottage with ice covering the insides of the windows and lying thick over the water pail.

Upstairs in Signe's attic room the fire on the little hearth failed to overpower the wind forcing its way through every crack in the timbered walls. As often during the winter, Signe was bed-ridden with a chill. But this time it had quickly moved down into her chest, hampering her breathing. Hildur nursed her daughter as best she could, for there was no doctor in the countryside to summon, nor any money to pay him, had there been one. But each day Signe grew worse. At night Hildur crept into bed with her, getting up every few hours to lay wood on the fire. But even huddled together, with both her own and Signe's hides and well-worn blankets over them, it was impossible to shut out the cold. She watched helplessly as her daughter curled into herself lethargically and slowly slipped away into semi-consciousness. During her short waking moments Signe refused to eat or drink, or even speak. Often when her fever rose she became delirious, calling out Kajsa's name over and over.

One day a traveler stopped at the cottage to warm himself. When Hildur understood that he was passing Lersätter, she asked if he could deliver a message on his way. Grasping at straws, she sat down and wrote a note to Kajsa. Although she knew the child could not cure Signe, she hoped that she could at least rekindle her will to live. Without that,

138

Signe hadn't a chance.

Two days after Christmas a stranger knocked on Lersätter's kitchen door. Kajsa, who happened to be closest to the door, opened it.

"I seek a maid by the name of Kajsa Sjöström," he said.

" 'Tis I," she replied, puzzled.

"When I passed by Stenstorp I was asked to carry a message to her," he continued.

He fumbled in his pocket, pulling out a small bit of folded paper torn from the back of *Luthers lilla katekes,* and handed it to her. She unfolded it anxiously while he waited on the step.

"Signe is ill and refuses to eat or drink," it read in Hildur's unsteady handwriting. "She only calls Kajsa's name. Me thinks she is dying. Please come before it's too late. Hildur."

She read it through twice more, then looked up at the man.

"Did she say anything more?" she asked.

"Only that I must urge Kajsa to come as soon as possible. May I help in any way?"

"No, I don't think so," she told him. "Many thanks for bringing the message."

"It was the least I could do. Had I a horse and sled I would gladly turn about and drive the lass to Stenstorp, but I have only my two feet to carry me, and in the opposite direction at that." He turned to leave.

"Does he wish to come in and eat something before setting out again?" she asked.

" 'Tis not necessary. I've provisons with me. My thanks for the kind offer."

"God be with thee," she called after him as he hurried down the steps.

Gathering her courage, Kajsa sought out Fru Gröndal. She had had little to do with the woman thus far, having taken Astrid's advice and keeping out of her way. Now she was forced, by the urgency in Hildur's words, to approach her.

"Fru Gröndal," she began nervously, "I've just received a message from home saying that my foster mother is calling for me. She's dying. May I have permission to go to her?"

"Kajsa may go on her free Sunday at the end of January," she was told curtly.

"But Ma'am, that's almost a month away. It's urgent that I go home as soon as possible."

"Kajsa is under contract to serve as a housemaid here. She must obey the stipulations she agreed to."

"I've agreed to nothing," Kajsa blurted without thinking.

"Does Kajsa wish to see the signed agreement?" she asked.

"I have not signed anything. It must have been Reverend Holmgren who has agreed. He never told me of any rules."

"Of course not. He is Kajsa's guardian. It's he who makes the decisions in her life. He need not discuss them with her."

"But Ma'am, she's dying...."

"The answer is no!" Fru Gröndal snapped. "Now stop wasting my time and get back to work."

Kajsa was taken aback, unable to understand that the woman could be so unfeeling when someone so important to her was dying. At the same time, she suddenly realized that she was as important to Signe as Signe was to her. Without a second thought, she made up her mind to go to her, regardless of the consequences. It was too late in the day to set out immediately, but if she left just before dawn the next morning she would be home by afternoon.

That night she slept badly. Signe kept calling out to her in her dreams. When she couldn't stand it any longer, she got up and put on all her clothes on top of each other for warmth. Tip-toeing down the back stairs, she let herself out the side door, closing it silently.

The night was absolutely still. The three-quarter moon had washed all but the brightest stars from the cloudless sky. Long shadows lay across the avenue between the house and the road, rippling over the horse and sled tracks in the snow. She walked as fast as she could to keep warm, Signe's voice ringing as clear as the night sky in her head.

After several hours the moon sank behind the trees. Just as she began to fear the darkness it left behind, the sky lightened in the opposite direction, bringing with it the sun from where it had lain in waiting behind the forest.

She had almost reached Stenstorp when she heard voices behind her. Turning around, she saw two men in a horse-drawn sleigh approaching at a gallop. Hoping they might stop and give her a ride, she waited.

"Kajsa Sjöström!" one of he men shouted. "Take not another step! Thou art under arrest."

When the sleigh caught up with her she saw that the two men were the local policemen who, in the summertime, patrolled the countryside on horseback. "Arrest? I've done nothing wrong," she replied, perplexed.

"Kajsa has left her employer without permission," she was told.

"Fru Gröndal does not own me," she declared, ignoring the social protocol forbidding a person of her age and social standing to speak in such a manner to her superiors. "My foster mother is dying and I must go to her."

" 'Tis against the law to leave one's place of employment without permission."

Without further discussion, one of the men leaned down and dragged her into the sleigh, squeezing her between them. At first she feared they were taking her to the village or even to town. To be under arrest meant police and other authorities and perhaps even jail. She had heard tales of people in jail being given only bread and water for days on end. Suddenly she was frightened. But to her relief, the driver turned the sleigh around as soon as they reached a wide place in the road.

As expected, Fru Gröndal was in a rage when Kajsa was delivered to Lersätter. Not only was she given extra work to make up for the hours she had missed, but her free Sundays were taken away for January and February. The experience so unnerved Kajsa that she dared not try to leave again.

Hildur waited, praying that Kajsa would come before it was too late, while Signe's condition continued to worsen. Several days after the New Year, Signe opened her eyes and looked at her mother sitting by her bedside.

"I have no way to thank Mamma for all the years she has sacrificed her own life for my sake," she said smiling. "Jesus is calling me and I long to rest in his arms." She paused. "Kajsa can't come back."

Those were the last words she spoke. She closed her eyes and several hours later her breathing slowed, then ceased.

After Arvidsson had gone to work the following morning Hildur pulled on all the warm clothes she owned and set out for the village several miles away, hunched against the wind and swirling snow.

Her nearest neighbor, Margit, a widow who lived on the edge of the village, was just readying herself to go after an armload of firewood when she spotted Hildur plowing her way through the snow towards her house. Quickly she moved the three-footed coffee pot over onto the fire, then opened the door before Hildur had a chance to knock.

"I dare say I needn't ask what brings Hildur to my door in such weather," she said, hustling her inside and brushing the snow from her shawl. "I'm so sorry."

"Margit has guessed right. 'Tis Signe," she replied, struggling to keep her voice even. She paused, wiping her face with the back of her snow-covered mitten. "Would it be too much to ask Margit to come and lay her out? I know it's permissible for a family member to do it if there's no one else available, but I don't think I can manage it."

"Nor do I think Hildur should do it," Margit told her. "That is to expect too much of her. I shall hear if my cousin Ylva can help me."

She handed Hildur a cup and nodded toward the coffee pot.

"It's nearly hot," she said, then added the usual, "I apologize for having nothing better to offer than coffee boiled on the grounds, although I did put a *klarskinn*[73] in it," a meaningless remark, for everyone drank coffee boiled on the left-over grounds. "Sit here by the hearth and warm thyself while I go over to speak with Ylva."

Margit soon returned with Ylva and the three of them set out for Stenstorp together. But by the time they reached the cottage the fire had gone out and the water in the wooden pail was frozen solid.

"It is far too cold to wash Signe and lay her out here," Margit remarked. "Me thinks 'tis better to take her to the village. Has Hildur a sled?"

"Of course. I'll bring it to the door."

She had not been in the shed since they had been forced to slaughter their starving cow before Christmas and she had to struggle to clear away the snow and open the door. Once she managed to get the sled outside she filled it with left-over straw.

"If only we had a horse," she mumbled into the wind, "or a decent man who could pull the sled." She wondered how many times she had cursed Arvidsson over the years. She would have fared better in the poor house.

When she returned to the cottage Margit and Ylva had brought Signe downstairs wrapped in a blanket. Hildur watched as they bedded her down in the straw. Then the three of them took turns pulling and pushing the sled through the snow. It was dark long before they reached the village and already the wolves were beginning to howl.

"If only they don't pick up the scent of death," went through all their minds, although no one dared to speak the words for fear of bringing them on.

Upon unwrapping Signe's now frozen body the women were shocked to see how emaciated she had become. She had the appearance of a China doll rather than a woman of twenty-seven. Looking at her naked body, Hildur saw the child who had appeared from between her legs

---

73. Klarskinn: a piece of dried fish skin often put in the coffee pot to clear the cloudiness of the coffee that has been standing a while. It was supposed to improve the flavor, as well as pull the grounds to the bottom of the pot.

that long ago day in the forest; the child that had given meaning to her life, who had kept her from giving up. Whose was the greater sacrifice? Neither of them had had any choice. They had been imprisoned together, needing each other in order to survive. And now they were both free, each to go her own way alone. Strangely, it was not sorrow Hildur felt, but simply a sense of loss. Signe had never had the chance to live, yet she was never bitter. There was almost a holiness about her. She gave as much as she was given.

When Signe was washed, Margit took a package wrapped in brown paper from her bridal chest. Untying the string, she folded back the paper to a simple white dress with long sleeves and a lace collar. It had been her wedding dress and, like most women, she had put it away to be worn at her funeral. She held it up, comparingly.

"I'm afraid it's a bit large, but we can sew it in around her," she reckoned.

"No," Hildur protested. "Margit must keep it for herself."

"I wish Signe to wear it when she meets God," Margit said.

Together they pulled the dress over Signe's head and tucked the excess material underneath her.

"She looks like an angel," Ylva remarked.

"She was an angel," Hildur added tenderly.

It was late by the time they had finished and drunk coffee. Ylva had already gone home.

"Tomorrow we must have *Spik-Anders*[74] make a coffin," Margit said. "In the meantime, it's time for bed. Hildur can have the *utdragssoffa* nearest the fire, for she shan't go home at this hour. There's no moon and the wolves are hungry in such weather. Besides, 'tis nice with company at night."

"I appreciate all the help Margit has given me," Hildur told her. "I could never 've managed it myself."

"I am glad I could help. I was very fond of Signe. I never knew her to complain about the life God bestowed upon her."

"Yes, she was my only real joy in life, in spite of her dark beginning. And now at last she's released from the prison of her body."

They fell silent, each cradling her own memories of Signe before falling asleep.

---

74. Nail-Anders, the carpenter. A person was often nick-named according to his job.

By morning the wind had abated and suddenly the sun, which had not been seen for days, appeared in a clear blue sky.

" 'Tis a special blessing from Signe," *Spik-Anders* remarked, nodding towards the sky when he came to take the measurements. He stood back, regarding her reverently. " 'Tis but a child's coffin she'll be needing," he concluded. "I shall have it finished before nightfall."

The news of Signe's passing spread quickly through the village and to the outlying farms. As was customary, the open casket was set by the roadside during the day, giving friends and neighbors the opportunity to say farewell. All the women who had known Signe, and even some who had never met her, paraded past, wrapped in their warmest clothes and shawls, to pay their respects. A number of them brought their children along. Like birth, death was part of everyday life. Many a child had witnessed the departure of a grandparent or an old aunt or uncle who had been as much a part of the family as were their parents. Any sadness was overshadowed by the expectation of meeting again in heaven.

At Lersätter the holiday season had finally came to an end with the Thirteenth Day of Christmas on the 6th of January. The Christmas tree was taken out, along with the removal of all the Christmas decorations, and life had returned to normal. It was as if the house itself let out a great sigh.

The following day another messenger appeared at Lersätter. This time it was Herr Sandqvist, one of the sexmen from Stenstorp's parish. He came not on foot, but in a little horse-drawn sled. He was dressed in black. Once again, it was Kajsa who opened the door. She recognized him immediately.

"No!" she cried before he even had time to speak. "No! No! No!"

"I am afraid 'tis so, Kajsa," he told her.

"Oh, it can't be! Signe, I didn't mean to...."

Kajsa's legs gave way and she sank to the floor. Two of the house-maids, who had heard her cry, came running. Between them they carried her into the kitchen and laid her on the *utdragssoffa*. Fru Gröndal, having also heard her cry, appeared in the doorway.

"What's all the commotion about in here?" she demanded. "And who might this be?" she continued, glaring at the visitor.

"Sexman Sandqvist," he said, bowing politely.

"And why doth he enter my house uninvited?"

"I come with a message of sorrow for Kajsa Sjöström."

"And what might that be?" she inquired.

"Signe Hildursdotter has passed away. 'Tis said that she lost her will to live after Kajsa left Stenstorp."

"Humph!" Fru Gröndal snorted. "Bastards both of them."

"Signe's mother, Hildur Unosdotter, asked me to deliver the message and to inform Kajsa that the funeral will be on the next-coming Sunday," he continued, ignoring her comments.

"Kajsa lost her free Sunday when she left here without permission recently. Besides, I fail to see why she should attend the funeral. She was not related to the woman. In fact, she is not even related to Sjöström or his wife. That's why he sent her away."

"But it's said that Signe has been like a mother for Kajsa," Sandqvist offered weakly. He was far below Fru Gröndal on the social ladder and he knew he was overstepping his position by speaking so.

" 'Like a mother' has no bearing on the matter," Fru Gröndal informed him. "The answer is still no. Kajsa may not be free on Sunday to attend a funeral. She has work to do here," she concluded, ending the conversation.

Although Kajsa had been dimly aware of the words that passed between Fru Gröndal and Sexman Sandqvist, she had paid them no heed. The information they conveyed was absorbed unnoticed and stored deep within the folds of her mind, forgotten for years to come. In the days that followed, it was the guilt for Signe's death that obsessed her. She could never forgive herself for having left Stenstorp. It was as if she had killed Signe outright. In vain she beseeched God to turn back time, to un-do that which was irrevocable. But He turned a deaf ear to her prayers.

On the morning of the third day Hildur returned to Stenstorp to await Kajsa's arrival and prepare for the funeral on Sunday. The cottage was cold and lifeless, although she could see by the things strewn around the room that Arvidsson had been there. She went upstairs to put Signe's few possessions in order, but the task seemed overwhelming. The place reminded her of the prison cell she herself had once occupied and, ironically, the place where Signe had been conceived. To think that she had been sentenced to life imprisonment within that room for almost thirty years! She could understand that Signe longed to rest in the arms of Jesus.

Arvidsson came home that evening reeking of alcohol.

"Where'n all hell has Hildur been?" he yelled.

"In the village," she replied simply.

"And what business has she there?"

"I was making arrangements for Signe's funeral."

"Signe's funeral?"

"Yes. She died."

" 'Tis about time! Now at last my wife'll have time ta perform her wifely duties towards me, her husband, instead of constantly runnin' up and down stairs ta serve her bastard child." He looked at the empty table. "Gimme my supper!" he demanded, pounding his fist on the table.

" 'Tis best that Arvidsson returns to the inn. There's not a morsel in the house to eat, since he spends all his pay on *brännvin.*"

"I work for my pay and I'll spend it as I please," he told her roughly. "B'sides, 'tis almost thirty years that I've been supportin' thy bastard child and not a lick of work have I gotten outa her. For nearly thirty years I've been trapped by the lie Hildur used against me so she could get out of the poor house. Nor has the bastard's father paid one penny towards her keep! Who was he?"

"I have told Arvidsson hundreds of times, I do not know the name of her father. He was a prison guard who strapped me down and raped me."

"And I've heard that story hundreds of times, but even if I hear it a thousand times I shan't believe it. Me thinks 'tis time that Hildur comes forth with the truth!"

"How many times have we gone through this? I cannot tell Arvidsson something I do not know."

"Do I gotta beat it outa my wife?" he raged, slapping her across the face.

Hildur wondered how many times the same scene had taken place in that little room. And every time she had come out of it with a black eye, numerous bruises, and occasionally even broken bones. But now, without Signe to care for, nothing held her captive in Stenstorp any longer. Come what may, this was the last time she was going to be at the mercy of Arvidsson's drunken rage. When the funeral was over, so was her life under his thumb. Where she would go or what she would do was of no concern.

On Sunday Hildur waited as long as she could, but Kajsa failed to show up. Resigned, she dressed in her church clothes and set out alone.

The service had already begun when she arrived. Rather than cause a disturbance by going to her rightful seat in the front row, she slipped quietly into the last pew. From there she looked around her to see if perhaps Kajsa had come directly to the church, but instead, the simple white casket in front of the alter caught her eye. Quickly she looked away, struggling to keep her composure. High above it, Reverend Holmgren was leaning out of the pulpit, hands grasping its sides so hard that his snow-white hair fell over his forehead as he glared at his congregation, harangueing them about the sins of the fathers. Hildur was too taken up with holding herself together to pay attention.

After the final amen he placed himself beside the casket and cleared his throat loudly to get everyone's attention.

"Today we have come to bury Signe Hildursdotter. It is a pity that this innocent young woman is going to hell because of her mother's sins..." he began.

Hildur's composure snapped.

"How dare you say such a thing!" she shrieked, leaping to her feet.

Every head turned to look at her, shocked not only by her outburst, but even more so by her lack of respect in addressing a priest, of all people, with the familiar "you". Nor was she finished.

" 'Tis you who is going to hell, you fat pig, for the evil way you have treated people all these years!" she screamed at the top of her lungs. *"Tvi! Tvi! Tvi!"* She spit three times, as one did in the face of the devil, then turned to leave the church. Halfway to the door something exploded inside her and the world turned black.

For a few seconds the congregation reacted as a single body, paralyzed by shock. It was Margit who was first to move, rushing to where Hildur lay on the floor. Turning her over gently, she saw that it was too late. By now a crowd of women had gathered, most silently sharing the sentiments Hildur had dared to express towards Reverend Holmgren. She had spoken for them all, but the price had been too high.

Thus it was that Margit had another body to prepare. This time she had no dress to offer, nor had Hildur a wedding dress of her own, due to her sudden wedding years ago. Instead, one of the other women offered her newly woven sheet on which, ironically, she had just finished embroidering an "H". They wrapped Hildur in it as one would wrap a precious gift, with the "H" under her chin like a brooch.

In the meantime, Signe's funeral was put off until the following Sunday, when mother and daughter could be laid to rest together in the same grave. Everyone agreed that it was fitting, for they had given meaning to each other's lives.

As Hildur's closest friend, Margit took it upon herself to replace Sexman Sandqvist as the bearer of the tragic news to Kajsa. She was very fond of the child and dreaded having to tell her what had happened. But better her than a man on an official errand.

"She couldn't have lived without Signe," Kajsa said when told, then added barely above a whisper, "I wonder if I can live without them."

She looked down at her feet, her lower lip trembling.

"Margit shall have thanks for coming all this way to tell me," she said with a slight curtsey.

Without another word, she ran upstairs to her room, leaving the other kitchen maids to give her message-bearer coffee and a bite to eat before she set out for home.

The day after the funeral Margit took her sled and plowed through the new-fallen snow to Stenstorp. Arvidsson had not shown up to pay his respects during the week, nor had he been at the funeral service on Sunday. Word had it that he had barely stirred from his bench at the inn. By Monday he was most likely suffering a severe hang-over and, she hoped, had not gone home. However, Margit had no qualms about entering his cottage uninvited. Through the years she had often visited both Hildur and Signe and was familiar with the place. And she knew that she had Hildur's unspoken blessing when it came to removing their personal belongings before Arvidsson could get rid of them. What he didn't see he would never miss.

To her relief, she could see by the unmarred snow on the doorstep that he was not at home. Although he had always been civil towards her, she was aware of his temper when he had been drinking and the violence he had inflicted upon Hildur. She didn't trust him and felt the need to hurry. She did not wish to meet him.

Lifting the latch, she pushed the door open. A rat scuttled across the earthen floor towards her and out the open door. Hildur would have been horrified. She had prided herself on keeping all sorts of vermin—mice, rats, wall lice and the like—at bay, despite the poor condition of the cottage.

The room was almost completely dark, the insides of its two tiny windows coated with a thick layer of ice, refusing entry to the weak winter light. Taking a key from her apron pocket, she opened the door to the attic, thankful that Hildur had continued to wear it around her neck instead of hiding it somewhere. She felt her way up the stairs and lit the candle that always stood on the table by the window. Signe's few possessions lay on the bed, with Hildur's own personal belongings beside them: her worn out and patched clothes, a quilt she had made years ago, a small Bible as well as a copy of *Luthers lilla katekes,* and the satchel that her mother had carried her in as a baby and in which she herself had carried Signe. Such was the extent of her possessions after forty years. Likewise, Signe's possessions were few: a small Bible, *Luthers lilla katekes,* two changes of clothes, the quilt that she and Hildur had made together, and her sewing and knitting needles, threads and yarns. Several unfinished orders lay neatly folded at the foot of the bed. It was obvious that Hildur had been prepared to take what was rightfully hers and leave as soon as the opportunity presented itself after the funeral. Margit carried the things downstairs and tied them onto the sled. Lastly she locked the door to the attic and replaced the key in her pocket. Whether or not there would be the required inventory that followed all deaths didn't matter. Neither Hildur nor Signe had owned anything of value, nor had they any relatives who could inherit them. Arvidsson could take care of any official business, should there be any.

Satisfied, she turned the sled around and started towards home. Just as she rounded the bend out of sight she heard Arvidsson approaching the cottage from the opposite direction, singing loudly and drunkenly off-key. A shiver went down her spine and she hurried as fast as her legs could carry her, not resting until she reached the village.

The remainder of the winter passed unnoticed for Kajsa. She carried out her work as if in a trance, doing her best to avoid Fru Gröndal's dissatisfaction. Hildur's death had left her numb. It was incomprehensible. How could both Hildur and Signe be gone forever? Perhaps it would have been easier to fathom had she seen them laid out in their coffins and attended their joint funeral. Without any leave-taking it was easy for her to deny their deaths, for she had no proof. Often she entertained daydreams of going home to Stenstorp, of being welcomed by them. And then she would suddenly remember and a great emptiness filled her. Not only were they gone, but her mother and Svea were also gone. Everyone had left her. She made up her mind to never again depend on anyone. She would take care of herself. Hildur, too, had been alone and had managed to take care of herself, as well as a baby, at least until she was married to Arvidsson. Kajsa would go one step further. There would be no Arvidsson in her life.

HANS

Lersätter 1883

The sun streamed in the little window above Kajsa's bed, invading her sleep. Mechanically she pushed back the covers and, placing her feet on the cold floor, went to the window. Drops of melting snow fell from the eaves above, landing on the tin roof over the kitchen door with little plinking sounds. Much of the snow had melted during the night, leaving puddles of water in the path from the house to the barn. Could it actually be spring? It had been a long time since she had even noticed the weather. Each morning she had awakened to what she regarded as simply another dull gray day, hardly worthy getting up for. And many a time she wouldn't have gotten up, had it not been for her fear of Fru Gröndal's reprisals. But this day was different. She felt more awake than she had since the news of Signe's and then Hildur's deaths.

When she came down to the kitchen she was informed that Fru Gröndal wanted to speak with her. The sunshine evaporated from her day. What had she done wrong now? Nervously she sought out her employer.

"As I told Kajsa last week, the confirmation class begins this afternoon," Fru Gröndal informed her.

Kajsa looked at her blankly, having no recollection of having heard such news.

"It's time for Kajsa to stop pining over the past and using it as an excuse for ignoring everything else," she snapped. "Report to the parish hall after the noon meal. And see that she is dressed appropriately. Now get back to work!"

Kajsa wondered what being dressed appropriately entailed, but didn't dare ask. She had but one dress, aside from her two maid's uniforms. She chose the dress.

A dozen or so youths were already gathered around a table chatting when she arrived at the parish hall. She knew none of them, nor was there an empty chair available. She stood in the doorway awkwardly, wishing she hadn't come.

Suddenly Reverend Holmgren appeared. He looked older than when she had last seen him, and somewhat bent over. He no longer possessed his usual frightening aura. Kajsa experienced an intense dislike toward the man. She could hear Hildur telling about how he had tried to rape her when she had asked for a pass to go to Stockholm to search for Britta, as well as the way he had treated Ester when Britta died. And she remembered how she herself had been belittled by him in front of the whole congregation at her mother's funeral. Then, more recently, how he had accused her of having tempted Arvidsson, believing his denial, and maintaining that it was she who was lying. How could such a man be God's mouthpiece? No, she could not find it in her heart to worship Holmgren's God, who had taken her mother and Svea, and then Signe and even Hildur. All of them good Christian people. She didn't want any part of Holmgren and his God.

As usual, Reverend Holmgren cleared his throat loudly to get everyone's attention before speaking. When the room was quiet he pulled out his pocket watch, flipped open the cover and glanced at it, then snapped it shut.

"Well, I see that our little missy has finally blessed us with her company," he said, looking at Kajsa.

His words sealed her resolve. She turned around in the doorway and walked out. She was not going to be confirmed. Cost what it may.

Fru Gröndal eyed her sharply when she returned to Lersätter.

"Kajsa's back early," she remarked. "What about the confirmation class?"

"I am not going to be confirmed," she answered simply. Without further comment, she went up to her room to change into her maid's uniform.

"Kajsa will regret it," Fru Gröndal called after her.

The following morning a messenger arrived to inform Kajsa that she was to appear at Holmgren's office the same afternoon.

"Tell him I must work," she replied without thinking.

Something had changed in her since Hildur's death. Now that there was no longer anyone who stood behind her, she began to take command of her own life; or at least as much as it was possible to do so as a woman. It was not a conscious decision; it was simply a natural reaction.

After several more refusals to go to Holmgren's office, she finally acquiesced and presented herself at his door one afternoon. Sitting behind his desk, he looked small and tired.

"Why has Kajsa not attended confirmation classes?" he wanted to know.

"I do not wish to be confirmed," she replied.

"It is not something one 'wishes' to do; it's required by the church," he informed her.

"I do not wish to belong to the church. I do not believe what it says in *Luthers lilla katekes,* nor can I worship Holmgren's unjust and cruel God." The words had flowed from her mouth on their own, yet she knew it was true.

"Kajsa is too young to know what she believes," he told her. "Does she wish to sit in the stocks for her blasphemy?"

She sensed that he was grasping at straws, for there was no power behind his threat.

"As Holmgren wishes," she said. "But he cannot force me to believe something I do not believe."

"Kajsa may go," he said abruptly, waving her away with his hand.

Several days later the rumor reached Lersätter that Reverend Holmgren had had an attack and was poorly. A number of his parishioners paid their respects at the rectory; some to wish him a quick recovery and others to say good-bye. Because she had a few hours free one afternoon, Kajsa went to see him out of a morbid curiosity. She found him alone, sitting in a chair wrapped in blankets, when she came in. He seemed glad to see her.

"Has Kajsa come to apologize and ask for forgiveness?" he asked.

She was appalled by his arrogance. Once again her words came of their own accord.

" 'Tis Holmgren who should apologize—to many people—and ask their forgiveness," she said.

Holmgren opened his mouth to speak, but no sound emerged.

A week later he had a new attack, from which he did not survive.

Holmgren was replaced by a young priest, Reverend Petrus, who quickly proved to be the opposite of his predecessor. He treated the members of the congregation with respect and compassion, giving no one cause to fear him. But living under the shadow of Holmgren's heavy hand for so many years had turned people into victims of habit, making it hard for them to trust him. And Kajsa was no exception.

When Reverend Petrus took over the confirmation class, Kajsa decided to attend. Not because she had changed her mind about God, however. She still could not forgive Him for letting Holmgren act as his mouthpiece and for having taken the most important people in her life from her. Rather, the attraction was the chance to get away from Lersätter for a few hours once a week. But she made up her mind that, as soon as Reverend Petrus made a spectacle of her, she would walk out.

The first class began one afternoon after the noonday meal. Before she was free to go, Kajsa had to wait for the members of the household to finish eating so she could clear the table and wash the dishes before rushing up to her room to change out of her maid's uniform. Once outside, she set off at a near run. The village church was nearly an hour's walk away and she was sure to be late. Perhaps she had been stupid to decide to attend the class after all.

As before, everyone was already seated around the table when she arrived out of breath. But this time there was an empty chair beside a youth who looked somewhat older than the others. Just as she made her way toward it, Reverend Petrus appeared. She hesitated, ready to leave again.

"Hello," Petrus said, "and welcome. We have been waiting for Kajsa, hoping she would join us. I understand that she lives quite far away and must finish work before she is free to come, so I have suggested to the group that from now on we begin an hour later. That way, she can get here without having to run."

"Many kind thanks, Sir," she replied, hardly daring to believe what she had just heard. Perhaps not all priests were like Holmgren.

After the class the boy sitting next to her presented himself.

"I'm Hans Ängmark from Ellerbäcks Gård," he said, offering his hand.

Ellerbäcks Gård was Lersätter's nearest neighbor to the west, but because it lay off the main wagon road, Kajsa had never had cause to go there. She wondered if it was his family's home or whether he was just a farmhand there. But one didn't ask such things.

"Kajsa Sjöström from Lersätter," she said. She, too, was sparing with information.

Since they both took the same wagon road most of the way home, it was only natural that they walked together. Like Kajsa, Hans was not particularly talkative. When he did speak it was mostly about the crops or the weather. Surprisingly, Kajsa found herself enjoying his company. She had never had any real friends. The kitchenmaids at Lersätter were all older than she was and only interested in finding husbands. Kajsa was not looking for husband, but a friend would be nice.

The next week Hans was waiting for her when she got to where the road forked to Ellerbäcks Gård. From that day on, they walked to the village together every week. Bit by bit a familiarity grew up between them and Kajsa began to feel a brotherly kinship with him.

"Where does Kajsa come from?" he asked one day.

"I was born at Björkdalen, but when I was eight my mother died and I went to live with her aunt." She purposely omitted naming Stenstorp, which was well-known in the area for its poverty. "And what about Hans?" she reciprocated.

"I come from a *soldattorp*[75] that belongs to Ellerbäcks Gård" he told her.

"How does one get to live on a *soldattorp?*" she wondered. "I've never understood that."

"The big farms and estates are each responsible for providing the military with a certain number of soldiers. As part of their pay, these soldiers are given the use of a little cottage, a couple of out-buildings for a cow, a few hens and maybe a pig, as well as a tiny bit of land on which to grow potatoes, cabbages, and the like. In case of war or military exercises, the men must report to their units, leaving the running of the *torp* to their wives."

"So Hans's father is a soldier."

"He was a soldier, but the thing is, we're never in any wars. I think the last one was about 80 years ago, when we took over Norway, and he wasn't even born then. Finally he got tired of waiting for the excitement of a war which never happened, and a couple of years ago he just disappeared. Consequently, we were forced to move to let his replacement take over his job and the *torp*. I had to help my mother and sisters move and then support them. I was lucky to be able to get a job as a farmhand at Ellerbäcks Gård, but I had no time for confirmation classes, which is why I'm older than the others in the group."

"Did Hans ever find out what happened to his father?" she asked.

"It turns out that he had gone to America and gotten free farmland in Indian territory. There is something over there called The Homestead

75. A small soldier's cottage.

Act, where a man can stake out a claim and, if he builds a house and farms the land, after five years, it is his. I am saving money so that my mother and sisters can go over and then I will follow them when I can afford a ticket for myself. But what about Kajsa?"

"My life has been quite ordinary," she told him. "My father isn't a soldier. He has a farm that has been in the family for several hundred years."

"But why doesn't Kajsa live with him?"

"After my mother died he married a woman who did not like me, nor did I like her. That's why I moved."

Their walks continued in this vein throughout the spring, interspersed with observations of the flowers, trees, birds, and crops that they saw along the way. As Kajsa grew to know him better she told him about Hildur and Signe. Then one day she even told him about Arvidsson and why she didn't want to get married. There was a comfort about the fact that he would soon disappear from her life, not just when the confirmation classes ended, but when he finally emigrated to America. He would take her secrets with him and they would cease to exist.

But the events of that summer changed everything.

They were walking home after the last confirmation class when Kajsa suddenly realized it was the last time they would walk that road together. She had grown fond of his company.

"I'm going to miss thee," she told him. "And our walks."

He stopped and took her hand, pulling her to him.

"Marry me and come along to America," he said.

She stepped back and looked at him, surprised.

"Does Hans mean that?" she asked.

"Yes. Why not? Kajsa has no family to hold her here."

She didn't know what to say. He knew that she never wanted to get married and why.

"Give me a little time to think," was all she managed to say.

When they got to the fork in the wagon road, he took her hand again.

"Walk down my road with me a ways," he said, holding her hand so tightly that she had no choice but to follow him. "I want to show Kajsa one of my favorite places."

He led her into a little moss-covered glade surrounded by tall pines.

Although a gentle wind set their top-most branches swaying, causing the sunlight to flicker through the forest, there was not a breath of wind on the forest floor.

He pulled her against him, his arms surrounding her. Slowly he kissed her mouth, then pulled her tighter, slipping his hands down to her lower back and drawing her body tight against his hips. Feeling his hardness pressed against her caused her stomach to tighten.

"Marry me and come to America," he repeated, his breath heavy, as if he had been running.

"When I turn fifteen after Christmas," she answered.

He pulled her down beside him on the moss, tipping her onto her back, while his hand slid up along the inside of her thigh. When his fingers reached their goal he rolled on top of her, forcing her legs apart, and pushed his way into her. She arched in pain. Once he had jabbed in and out a few times, the initial pain subsided. And then it was over. While the act had frightened Kajsa, it had also excited her. So this was the great mysterious thing that happened between men and women; the act that was so sinful. It was not at all as horrible as she had been led to believe.

She didn't see Hans again during the nearly two months leading up to Midsummer. It was a busy time of year, leaving no free time for visiting nor time free for longing. But on Midsummer's Eve all work ceased and everyone celebrated the summer solstice with food, music, and dancing. In the evening young people from the surrounding farms congregated in the village, away from the scrutiny of parents and relatives, to meet friends, dance and look for possible partners. And to drink, of course: *brännvin* for the men and boys and coffee for the women and girls. Astrid and Berta had invited Kajsa to go with them and she looked forward to meeting Hans again.

The day before Midsummer's Eve, when the huge laundry from the past half year was at last finished, Kajsa took her semi-annual bath in the wash house tub along with the rest of the household members. Afterwards she brushed out her long hair, re-braided it, and covered her head with a freshly ironed kerchief. Lastly, she put on the hand-me-down dress Berta had lent her when she first came to Lersätter. How she wished she had a nice dress! It was one thing to wear such an old dress to church, where fine clothes were scorned as a sign of arrogance. But a

Midsummer celebration was different. There one must look one's best.

Folket's Park was alive with young people when they arrived. Astrid and Berta were met by their beaux and quickly disappeared, leaving Kajsa standing alone awkwardly. Finally she caught sight of Hans in a group of young men and women, standing with his back to her. Relieved, she made her way towards him through the crowd. One of the men in the group saw her and whispered something, whereupon Hans turned around. His face was filled with contempt. It was then that she saw he was holding one of the girls by the hand. Kajsa stopped short and stared at him.

"I-I-I thought..." she began.

"Kajsa lied to me about her background. I cannot marry a whore-child," he said simply, then turned back to his friends.

"Whore-child?" she said half aloud.

She had been called that as a school girl, but she never knew what it meant; only that it was something bad. She had been afraid to ask. A sense of shame crept over her. Quickly she made her way out of the park and ran towards Lersätter, unable to escape the sight of Hans holding another girl's hand.

The rest of the summer passed unnoticed for Kajsa. She performed the tasks given her, but found no joy in the life around her: not even in the early morning birdsong that she had always loved. Sometimes she felt physically sick to her stomach at the very thought of having to drag herself through another day. She missed Hans, but more than that, she was hurt by the fact that he had left her for someone else. That he had called her a whore-child she put out of her mind, for she dared not ask anyone what it meant.

Come August she could not bring herself to continue going to the confirmation classes. The thought of meeting Hans was too painful. She also understood that something was wrong with her. The last time she had had her monthly bleeding had been at the beginning of April. She remembered the day perfectly. She had started to bleed during the confirmation class and was concerned that Hans would see the blood on the back of her skirt during their walk home and be disgusted. But apparently he had not noticed it, for the next week they had walked together as usual, as if nothing had happened. And the week after that they lay in moss. But she was only fourteen; she couldn't be with child. She pressed the thought out of her mind. She wished there were someone she could confide in. Hildur would have known what to do.

Old Klara would know also, but she was probably dead by now. Besides, she was too far away. She tried to convince herself that it wasn't true, but by September it was obvious to her, and would soon be obvious to everyone. She had but one choice; to go to Ellerbäcks Gård on her free Sunday and tell Hans. She prayed his new girl would not be with him.

She found him splitting firewood behind the woodshed. Alone. He looked up as she approached, letting his glance fall on her belly, which she had made no effort to hide. His expression was not welcoming.

"What's Kajsa doing here?" he wanted to know, his voice cold.

"Hans can see why I've come," she replied.

He laughed. "Is she blaming that on me?"

" 'Tis no one else's."

"Kajsa can't prove it."

"I've lain with but one person. 'Twas with thee, that day on the moss."

"Does she actually expect me to believe she has lain with but one person?" he mocked.

"There has never been another. I'm asking Hans to help me. I cannot support a child alone."

" 'Tis thy problem. I've no desire to pay for another man's brat."

"There is no other man."

"With her background, anything's possible."

Suddenly he became angry.

"Be gone now before someone sees Kajsa here!"

He grabbed the axe and split the piece of wood standing on the chopping block so violently that one of the pieces nearly hit her.

Several days later Kajsa was summoned to Reverend Petrus's office. She wondered what she had done wrong to warrant such a meeting. Reluctantly she made her way to the church. Having to face a priest always made her nervous.

"Come in and sit down," Petrus said, smiling, when he opened his door to her knock.

Kajsa lowered herself cautiously onto the chair in front of his desk. Her nervousness increased as he looked at her over his clasped hands. After a long minute he cleared his throat noisily, a habit that Holmgren had had to indicate something unpleasant was coming. Kajsa tensed.

"I have asked Kajsa to come here for two reasons," he began. "First of all, I wish to inform her that I am not just her parish priest. I have also taken over Reverend Holmgren's roll as Kajsa's guardian. From what

I understand, she has no family in the parish."

"No, no family anywhere," she corrected.

"Secondly, I was wondering why Kajsa has not participated in the confirmation classes this autumn," he said, his voice curious.

Kajsa looked down in ther lap, not knowing what to say. He waited patiently.

"Has something happened to cause her to stay away?"

She nodded slightly.

He waited.

"Does it have to do with me or is it one of the class members?"

" 'Tis not Reverend Petrus."

"Is it one of the young men?"

She nodded again.

"Can Kajsa stand up for a moment?" he asked. His voice was kind.

She hesitated, then got to her feet slowly.

He regarded her closely.

"So that's it," he concluded. "Kajsa may sit down again. Is it someone in the class?"

She nodded.

"Someone who denies it?"

If she spoke now she knew she would begin to cry.

"If Kajsa tells me what happened I shall do my best to help her. Can you tell me who it was?"

She was silent, unsure as to whether she could trust him or whether he would turn against her if she told him the truth, as Holmgren would have done. But Reverend Petrus seemed kind and trustworthy.

" 'Twas Hans," she said finally, barely above a whisper.

"Tell me exactly what happened," he urged.

Her lower lip quivered and suddenly her tears, along with the events of the past spring, came flooding out together.

"From what I understand," he said when she had finished, "Kajsa has no one she can turn to for help."

"No, no one."

"I shall ask Hans to stay after the next conformation class so we can discuss the situation. I would like Kajsa to be here also," he concluded. "In the meantime, Kajsa is not to take matters into her own hands. I assume that, like every girl, she knows what I am talking about. We shall help Kajsa get through this."

Hans was angry when he realized why he had been asked to meet with Reverend Petrus. When confronted with the events in the mossy glade, he denied that he had ever had anything to do with Kajsa.

"It must'a been someone else what took her there," he retorted. "She has ta' be dreamin' if she thinks I'd marry her an' take her to America. Or even pay for the brat."

The only thing he would admit to was that they had walked together a couple of times after the class, simply because they happened to be going in the same direction.

Kajsa stared at him in disbelief.

"How can Hans lie in my face like that? And to a priest, also!" she cried.

"How can Kajsa make up such a story?" he retorted. "What does she want from me? Let the guy who gave her the big belly pay for it. 'Tis not my responsibility!"

"Is Hans prepared to swear on the Bible that he is telling the truth, that he has never had relations with Kajsa?" Petrus asked him.

Hans hesitated a few seconds before agreeing.

"As a confirmand who will soon join the Lutheran Church, I hope Hans realizes the significance of swearing an oath before God," Petrus told him sternly.

"Of course," he answered almost haughtily.

The big church Bible was placed before him and, with his right hand on it, Hans swore that he had never had sexual relations with Kajsa Sjöström and that he was not the father of the child she was carrying.

"That's the honest truth," he concluded. "Can I go now? I have other more important things to attend to."

Without waiting for an answer, he left the room, closing the door loudly.

"He's lying!" Kajsa cried.

"Yes, I know," Petrus said. "But there is nothing we can do about it right now. The important thing for the time being is to find a solution for Kajsa's situation. Even if he had admitted his guilt and perhaps even given her some money, her situation would be the same. The question now is, does she wish to keep the baby?"

"I've no possibility to care for it, nor do I wish to be reminded of Hans every time I look at it," she said without a moment's hesitation.

"Then, as Kajsa's guardian, I suggest that she consider the Public Maternity Hospital in Stockholm. There unmarried mothers can give birth anonymously, with no questions asked, and afterwards the child will be placed in the Public Children's Home for a certain fee. If the mother is unable to pay, she can live in the home with her baby for at least eight months. During that time she must nurse and care for the child herself, as well as for a baby that some mother has simply paid the home to take. When her own child is weened it will be placed in a foster home, whereupon she must sign an agreement stating that she will have no further contact with it. After that she will be free to go on with her life, as if nothing ever happened."

"But Stockholm...." Kajsa protested. Hildur's experience came immediately to mind and she shook her head.

"It's not to worry. I can arrange for people to help Kajsa and give her a place to stay when she arrives there. Then it is just to go to the hospital in good time. She will be well cared for and no one will know her identity. God forbids her to go into the lake or even contemplate giving birth alone and getting rid of the child in some way. And it is a sin to try to abort the child, a sin that can lead to Kajsa's death. Does she understand that?"

"Yes, Sir. I promise I shan't do any of those things. But how would I get to Stockholm?"

"I shall take care of that."

Once again Kajsa wept.

"I'm deeply indebted to Reverend Petrus," was all she managed to say.

Like all maids, Kajsa's contract at Lersätter ended at the beginning of "free week," the 24th of October.[76] Thus her departure would be natural, without causing suspicion or speculation as to why she was leaving. She counted the days. When the day of her leave-taking finally arrived, she rose earlier than usual, eager to be on her way. Hurriedly she pulled on the dress she had received as her wages for the past year and placed the bundle of her meager possessions in her satchel. Hanging it over her shoulder, she tip-toed quietly down the back stairs, opened the outside door, and stepped out into the chill of the October morning, letting Lersätter's door close behind her for the last time. The click of the latch gave her an unexpected feeling of freedom. However, by going without saying good-bye, she had not received the letter of recommendation from her employer that she would need when seeking her next employ-

---

76. Maids' and farmhands' contracts ended at the beginning of the last week in October, whereby they were free to seek employment elsewhere. They were also free from work that week, the only vacation they had during the entire year.

ment. On the other hand, such a letter would probably have been a detriment anyway. It was clear that she and Fru Gröndal shared a mutual dislike for each other.

Had she been truly free, she would have skipped joyfully down the road. But an uncertain future lay ahead of her; one she tried to put out of her mind. As soon as Lersätter was out of sight behind her, she slowed her pace. No need to hurry; she had several hours before her meeting with Reverend Petrus.

As always, he greeted her warmly when she knocked on his door.

"Come in, come in!" he welcomed. "Sit down, please."

He gave her a searching look.

"Kajsa looks happier than she has in a long time," he remarked.

"Yes, Sir, I am happy to leave Lersätter at last. In fact, I left early this morning before anyone was up. I didn't even say good-bye."

"Did Kajsa receive a letter of recommendation from Fru Gröndal?"

"No. But I don't think she would have had much positive to say about me anyway," she admitted.

"One day Kajsa is going to need such a letter," he told her. "But perhaps she is right about Fru Gröndal. However, I can write a letter of reference instead. Eventually Kajsa will need proof that she has not been in prison or worse during this past year."

"That is very kind of Reverend Petrus," she said.

He took out an envelope and slid it across his desk to her.

"Take a look at this while I write a few words," he told her.

Opening it she found two tickets: one for the horse-drawn postal carriage that twice a week passed through a town a half day's wagon journey from the village. The other appeared to be for a train. Meanwhile he wrote a few lines on a paper, folded it, and put it in a separate envelope.

"Now," he said, "Kajsa shall go to to town this afternoon with the ordinary wagon from the inn.[77] She shall be accompanied by *Tant* Greta Jansdotter, from Revsjö Parish, who is going to visit her daughter and grandchildren, so Kajsa won't be alone. If all goes well, the wagon should reach the inn on the edge of town by nightfall. Kajsa and *Tant* Greta will most likely have to share a bed for the night, but at least ye will be acquaintances by then. The postal carriage passes through town at ten o'clock the next morning. *Tant* Greta is taking it as far as the market

---

77. Local farmers were obliged to drive travelers from one inn to the next, or further, when necessary.

162

town, after which Kajsa will be on her own. From there it is not far to the train station, which she will reach on the evening of the second day. There she shall spend the night in the room reserved for women travelers, with benches where one may rest or sleep. The train for Stockholm leaves at half-past nine the following morning and arrives in the city that evening, a trip of about ten hours." He handed her a folded paper.

"Here is the address where Kajsa will stay in Stockholm, along with directions as to how to get there. It's not far from the station."

He returned everything to the envelope, then handed her a small coin purse.

"Here is money for two nights' lodgings and for meals. Has Kajsa brought along anything to eat on the journey?"

"No, Sir. I was in such a hurry to leave Lersätter that I thought of nothing else," she admitted, ashamed of her oversight.

"Never mind," he said. "I shall ask my housekeeper to fix her a basket of victuals for her journey. And by the way, has Kajsa ever ridden on a train?"

"Oh, no, Sir! I've heard about trains, but I've never even seen one. All I know is that they're very big and that they make a lot of noise and spew dirty smoke."

" 'Tis true," Petrus said, laughing. "But it's nothing to be afraid of, as long as one does not stand too near the tracks, that is. And if Kajsa needs help, she can ask one of the men in uniform. They are there to help people. But above all else, do not talk with any other men, even if they are friendly." He paused, seemingly embarrassed, then coughed lightly and continued. "One more thing: unlike a horse-drawn wagon or carriage, a train does not stop for passengers' needs, so one must take care of such things before going on board."

That afternoon Reverend Petrus helped Kajsa climb up onto the open two-wheeled cart beside Greta Jansdotter, a grandmotherly woman whose gray hair peeked out from under her scarf around a soft, friendly face. For once Kajsa was thankful for the chilly weather that called for all of her warm clothes under her winter shawl, hiding her now-rounded belly from prying eyes. She placed her satchel on the floor of the cart as a footrest and drew her shawl tightly around herself before waving farwell to Petrus.

"Tell Kajsa's new mistress that her guardian sends his greetings and thanks her for employing Kajsa at his recommendation," he called loudly, for the benefit of the curious by-standers who had nothing better to do than stand around hoping for some gossip.

163

"Many thanks, Sir," she called back spontaneously. Even though the future was uncertain, at least the past was behind her at last.

As the cart bumped along the rutted wagon road past Lersätter she looked straight ahead, vowing never to set eyes on the place again.

SIRI

Autumn 1883

By mid afternoon the once blue sky had slowly faded into light gray, with a veil of uncertain clouds drawing up from under the horizon. A dampish chill had taken over the day, mockingly pushing its way through sweaters and shawls. Kajsa shivered. The journey seemed to go on forever, interspersed with long waits at each inn while a new horse and cart were sent for, both of which were more often than not in poor condition. The wagon road itself wound around the edges of fields as well as up and down the many hills. Many a time they were forced to get out and walk beside the cart, now and then even pushing it from behind, to spare an old horse's energy. That the creature's ribs were clearly visible didn't deter the driver from beating it angerly, ignoring the fact that no amount of whipping was going to make the animal move any faster. Added to the numerous hills were a number of gates over the road, separating one farm's fields from the next. At each of them a gang of small boys vied for the chance to act as gate boy, opening and closing the gate for the passing cart, and thus earning the *öre* [78] tossed out by the driver. Should the lucky boy fail to catch the coin, a scuffle invariably broke out, resulting in bloody noses and torn clothes. If there were no boys at a gate, Kajsa was forced to get down and open and close it herself. Without pay. Although climbing on and off the cart was difficult in all her winter garb, it made the time pass more quickly and gave her a chance to stretch her legs. Even under normal conditions it would have been uncomfortable sitting on the hard seat being jostled to and fro hour after hour.

Kajsa and *Tant* Greta hardly exchanged a word throughout the journey, for the old woman was hard of hearing, complicated by the groaning of the cart's ungreased axle. Kajsa was thankful. She always found it difficult to lie. That Reverend Petrus's last remark pertaining to her employment was a lie didn't matter however; it was his lie, not hers. It had come as a complete surprise to her and, although she had responded without batting an eye, she was not at all sure she could elaborate on it convincingly if called upon to do so. She certainly did not wish to be asked where she was going and to whom.

---

78. The smallest coin.

It was dark by the time they reached the last inn, save for a huge harvest moon on its way up from behind the trees. Because it lay on a less well-traveled road, the building had been allowed to become run-down, its timbered walls showing signs of rot below the thinly thatched roof. Like most inns of its size, the interior was simple: one large room with beds built along the back wall, several tables and benches in the middle, and an open fireplace on one long wall. Likewise, the menu was simple: soup, salted herring, potatoes, dry bread, and of course, *brännvin*. As in most small villages, the inn was also the gathering place for the local population, which meant that it could be noisy late in the evening, with fist fights serving as the main form of entertainment.

Kajsa was glad for *Tant* Greta's companionship. Aside from the owner's wife, who cooked, served, and tried to keep the place relatively clean and orderly, they were the only women there. Kajsa had long ago had her fill of drunken men and would have been terrified had she been alone.

Later that evening, after the two of them had settled into their straw-filled bed together, there was a commotion outside. Suddenly two men burst into the inn, fighting and hurtling drunken curses at each other. Before Kajsa could pull the covers over her head, a knife flashed in the light from the oil lamps, followed by a schriek. *Tant* Greta propped herself up on one elbow to get a better look.

" 'Tis alright now, Child," she reassured Kajsa when the tumult had quieted down. " 'Tis over."

Kajsa struggled to sit up. On the dirt floor in front of the open fire lay a man in a swelling pool of blood. The man with the knife was nowhere to be seen.

"Is he...?" Kajsa began, her voice shaking.

"It appears so," *Tant* Greta answered.

There was a mumbling discussion amongst the others in the room. Kajsa and *Tant* Greta learned that the two were local men who had long been enemies. Recently one of them had defamed the other's honor by accusing him of being a rogue and a thief, traditionally a serious offense. That the accusations were false only made it worse, implying that the accused had the characteristics of a thief, as well as those of a rogue, for which he had the right to sue his accuser. But, rather than going to court, he had made up his mind to take care of the matter himself. Thus no one seemed surprised at the outcome; settling scores was the last act of a man with a boat ticket to America in his pocket.

Kajsa slept relatively well that night behind the security of the old woman's back. It brought back happy memories of nights with Signe, yet also served as a sad reminder of her aloneness.

The next morning Kajsa and *Tant* Greta were up and ready in good time. As ten o'clock neared, they went outside to enjoy the last fresh air before continuing their journey. Suddenly a horn sounded in the distance, announcing the approach of the mail carriage. Kajsa clutched her satchel tightly while squinting down the road against the sun. It wasn't only that she had never taken the mail carriage; she had never even seen it. Her excitement grew as soon as it came into sight; an enclosed carriage drawn by two white horses. On the driver's seat sat a fat man in a gold-trimmed uniform holding the reigns, while a man beside him blew loudly on a brass horn. She found an unexpected splendor in its arrival. If the mail carriage was so glorious, what was the train going to be like?

Although sitting inside the carriage on upholstered seats, protected from the weather, was a luxury compared to the previous day's open carts, that leg of the journey proved to be boring and uneventful. They were accompanied by several younger women, whose muted conversation, along with the swaying motion of the horse-drawn carriage, soon lulled Kajsa into a light sleep.

Later that afternoon *Tant* Greta tapped her lightly on the arm.

"I'll be getting off here," she said. "I hope all goes well," she added, glancing at Kajsa's stomach. "God be with thee, my Child."

Before Kajsa could respond, she was gone. Through the carriage window she saw a young woman with a flock of children gather around the old woman excitedly, relieving her of her scanty baggage. Then, with the small ones skipping at her side, she disappeared around a corner. It was a picture that was to remain with Kajsa for the rest of her life.

Kajsa arrived at the train station in a state of near exhaustion, having eaten sparingly of the food Reverend Petrus had sent with her in order to make it last the entire journey. But now she looked forward to stilling her hunger. She gathered her few belongings and followed the carriage's other passengers into the station house. Looking around, the enormity of the nearly empty waiting room, with its high ceiling and polished tile floor, left her breathless, as well as a little frightened. The voices and footsteps of the few people in the room bounced off the walls, echoing eerily. She had never imagined that such a huge building existed. Nervously, she looked for the women's waiting room. Seeing her plight, a young woman who had been in the carriage approached her. Kajsa saw that she was not much older than herself.

"Come. Let's go in here," she said, opening a door at one end of the room. "I must spend the night here before continuing to my relatives in Stockholm tomorrow morning. May I assume thou art traveling the same way?" she continued half questioningly.

"Yes, she has guessed right," Kajsa answered. "I'm going to my new position there," she added, amazed at how easily the lie slipped from between her lips.

The women's waiting room was poor by comparison to the village inn of the previous night, furnished only with a few wooden benches. It was obviously only for daytime use or for those women who could not afford a room in the station hotel across the square, of whose existence they were both unaware. Kajsa was too tired to care. They each chose a bench, ate a few morsels from their respective baskets, and curled up on the hard benches to sleep.

In the middle of the night Kajsa awoke with a start, needing very badly to relieve herself. She sat up and looked around. The only light in the room came from a single gas lamp in the far corner. Quietly, so as not to wake her companion, she stuffed her feet into her boots and tiptoed outside. The night air had taken on an autumn bite, frosting the grass in front of the station. There was not a sound, nor a breath of wind. The moon hung low in the sky, casting long shadows, but giving little light. Nowhere could she find an outhouse. When she could wait no longer, she pulled up her skirt, hunkered down on the side of the street, and urinated.

Relieved, she hurried back to the station house, grabbing the brass door handle to let herself in. But it stopped her short, refusing to budge, having locked behind her when she went out. Frantically she beat on it with her fists.

"Let me in!" she yelled over and over, until the words transformed themselves into hysterical screams. In vain. She began to shiver with cold, for she had come out without her shawl. Nor could she call out her companion's name, as they had never formally introduced themselves to each other.

After what seemed like an eternity, a mounted policeman approached, his pointed helmet flashing in the dim moonlight. Hildur's experiences with the police flashed through Kajsa's mind, coupled with tales of vagrancy, the *spinnhuset,* and the poor house. She glanced around, but there was no place to run in the unfamiliar town; no one to help her. She slid down in the corner of the doorway, huddling with both arms protecting her head, and wailed like a beaten dog.

"What seems to be the problem?" the policeman asked routinely, peering down at her from his horse.

Kajsa continued to wail.

"Is missy supposed to be spending the night in the women's waiting room?" he asked finally.

Kajsa nodded amidst her wailing.

"Come along, then," he told her, dismounting. Leading her to a side door, he lifted a ring of keys from his belt, picked out one, and unlocked the door.

"Get inside and stay there until dawn," he ordered, closing the door behind her.

Kajsa staggered into the women's waiting room, still sniffling, and collapsed onto her bench. Her companion was still sleeping, just as she had left her.

Kajsa slept fitfully. The bench was far from comfortable, the room unheated, and she was plagued by the thought of what would have become of her had the policeman not appeared. Most of all, however, she couldn't sleep for the fear of missing the train.

"Wake up," her fellow traveler called gently a few hours later. " 'Tis soon time for the train."

Kajsa sat up, rubbing the sleep from her eyes.

"I'm sorry about last night," she mumbled, embarrassed at the memory of her behavior.

"Last night?"

"Yes. I went out to relieve myself and the door locked behind me. I made a terrible racket trying to wake thee. Finally a policeman rode past on horseback and let me back in."

"I heard nothing at all. I'm a heavy sleeper."

She got to her feet and went to Kajsa, who was still struggling to wake up, and held out her hand.

"My name is Vendela."

"I am called Kajsa," she reciprocated.

" 'Tis best that we go outside," Vendela told her, as if she were accustomed to the ways of train travel. "We can eat something once we are on board."

A few people had gathered on the platform, shivering in the chill of the early morning. Suddenly the whistle of the approaching train cut the air like a glass-shattering explosion, relegating the memory of the mail carriage's horn to the insignificance of a bird call. Instinctively, Kajsa backed toward the shelter of the station house. The closer the train came, the more monstrous became the engine, shooing the waiting passengers from the edge of the platform with billows of stinking black smoke and the deafening screech of brakes. Vendela tried to stand firm, perhaps feeling the need to show that, as the elder of them, she was the braver. But she needn't have bothered, for Kajsa was more than willing to be guided by someone who was more experienced in the ways of the world.

A blue first class car glided slowly past behind the engine. Seen through the windows, it looked like the best room at Lersätter, with over-stuffed red sofas and cloth-covered tables, backed by wood panelled walls and curtains framing the windows. A couple of cigar-smoking men could be seen, relaxed, as if in the comfort of home, reading their newspapers, oblivious to the world around them.

Kajsa hadn't time to take much notice of the second class car, aside from the fact that it was green on the outside and empty on the inside, before several reddish-brown third class cars came to a halt in front of them. Quickly they climbed aboard the closest one lest the train should start to move again. The car consisted of a single room with unupholstered wooden benches. Everything was painted reddish-brown: walls, ceiling, floor, and benches. And it was packed with men, women, and children. Although some of them obviously belonged amongst the first class passengers, it was customary that they preferred to travel short distances in third class because it was much cheaper.

There was no place where the two of them could sit together, nor did anyone seem willing to move to accommodate them. On the other hand, the chattering conversations, as well as the constant rhythmic clattering of the train itself, made talking difficult. The closer they got to Stockholm, the more the confusion increased. At every station people got on and off, while local women tempted passengers with everything from buns and small cakes to traditional pretzel-shaped delicacies, held up to the train windows in baskets. If one had a few coins one need not go hungry.

When they finally reached Stockholm that evening Kajsa was so tired that even the grandeur of the central station failed to impress her. She was beginning to realize that the world was filled with endless wonderful things that she had never even begun to imagine. It was impossible to

170

take them all in.

She and Vendela stood in the gigantic waiting room awkwardly, not knowing where to look.

"I guess this is where our joint path ends," Vendela offered finally. 'Tis too bad we didn't have a chance to get to know each other," she continued, as if it were the right thing to say. She seemed anxious to be on her way.

"Maybe another time," Kajsa said, holding out her hand.

She, too, was anxious to go her own way before their situation became complicated.

They shook hands, said good-bye, and walked in opposite directions.

As soon as Vendela was out of sight, Kajsa dug in her pocket and pulled out the paper with the address and directions that Petrus had given her.

"Leave the station by the main door and go to the right...." it began. She memorized the street address, then folded the paper, returning it to the depths of her pocket.

Outside on the street she paused to look around. The sky was cloudy, hiding both moon and stars, leaving only the dim glow from the gas flames in the street lamps to help her find the way. She had never been in a town, let alone a city, at night. Nor even in the daytime, for that matter. The darkness was crammed with unfamiliar sounds: the sharpness of horse hooves and wagon wheels on the cobblestone streets, footsteps echoing off buildings, the drone of voices, yelling, brawling, cries of anger and fear. It unnerved her. She had assumed that the night would be accompanied by silence, as it was in the countryside. Her first reaction was to rush back to the security of the central station's gigantic hall, but instead she forced herself to begin walking. Once away from the station the street lamps stretched further apart, creating a black hole between them. Kajsa walked as fast as she could, without drawing attention to herself by running. On either side of her two and three storey high wooden buildings loomed threateningly, their heavy wooden doors closed against the night.

More than once well-dressed gentlemen emerged from the darkness in front of her. Invariably they hesitated, looking her up and down questioningly, then continued on their way when she failed to respond. Once a couple passed, the woman suddenly clinging to her escort's arm and giving Kajsa a wide berth, as if she had a contagious disease. One man even stopped in front of her, blocking her way.

"I thought the likes of *apelsinflickor*[79] carried baskets of oranges," he jeered.

Kajsa looked at him dumbly, ignorant of his intentions.

When she at last reached the address Reverend Petrus had given her, she found the door in to the courtyard barred against her. Nor did her knocking bring about a response. The thought of spending the night alone outdoors was more than she could bear, cancelling any inhibitions she might have had about causing a racket. She set about banging on the door with both fists. After what seemed like an eternity, it was opened by a young woman about Signe's age.

"Oh, is it Kajsa?" she exclaimed happily.

"Yes, Ma'am."

"Wonderful! Come."

Kajsa followed her into the courtyard, past empty pedlars' carts, piles of old building material, and other trash, as well as a row of stinking outhouses. The whole place smelled of urine.

"Sorry about the smell," the woman offered, as though she had read Kajsa's thoughts. "The men and boys can't be bothered to use the outhouse. 'Tis disgusting."

She pulled open a door on the opposite side of the courtyard and disappeared into the darkness.

"Be careful on the stairs," she called behind her. "They're uneven and the fourth one sits loose. Hold on to the hand rail."

She stopped when she reached a landing, her hand searching blindly for the latch, then a door opened on squeaking hinges. The weak light from a kerosene lamp greeted them.

"Come in," she invited. "It was getting so late that I feared she had missed the train or lost her way." She extended her hand. "I'm Siri, Hjalmar's sister. Welcome to our home."

"Hjalmar?"

"Yes. Reverend Petrus," she said. "Kajsa must be hungry after her long journey. Sit down. I saved some soup from supper for her."

The single room was crowded, with an *utdragssoffa* against the back wall and opposite it a wood stove and a low counter on which stood a copper dishpan, with a pail of water on a stool beside it. The rest of the room was taken up with a table, several chairs, cupboards, and a bureau that pulled out into a bed, like Svea's bed at Björkdalen. The room was

---

79. "Orange girls." Young prostitutes carried baskets of oranges, under the pretext of selling them (rather than selling themselves).

not quite as poor as that at Stenstorp, however, for it had a wooden floor rather than one of hard-packed earth, yet it was nothing like Björkdalen or Lersätter.

Presently there was the sound of footsteps on the stairs and the hall door opened.

"Has she arrived yet?" a man's voice called from the entranceway, accompanied by the sound of heavy boots thudding onto the floor. A tall man in work clothes appeared in the doorway.

Kajsa stood up politely.

"This is my husband Gustaf," Siri said.

"Welcome," he greeted as they shook hands.

His face was open and friendly. In spite of her mistrust of men, she liked him immediately.

She had assumed that Reverend Petrus had made arrangements for her to live with a well-to-do family where she would be required her pay her way by serving as a maid. But even if she worked for this couple, she could see that they barely had the means to feed her. But for the moment she was too tired to contemplate the situation.

" 'Tis late," Siri remarked. "Tomorrow is a new day."

She helped Kajsa pull out the bed hidden in the bureau.

"As she can see, we don't have much, but what we do have is hers, also. I hope she'll feel at home here," she remarked. "One more thing. If Kajsa hears any noise in the entranceway, be not concerned. It is just Arne, our lodger, who works in the harbor with Gustaf. He sleeps here. There is a huge housing shortage in Stockholm. Consequently, nearly everyone around here has one or more lodgers who sleep in empty corners. Some people even rent out their beds during the day. The few coppers one earns help pay the rent."

"Before retiring for the night," Gustaf said, "we always say a short prayer of thanks for what our maker has provided for us this day. It is not a church prayer; each of us simply expresses thanks in our own words. Kajsa is not obliged to join us, if she does not wish to. It is entirely up to her."

They bowed their heads where they sat around the table. Rather than listening to Gustaf's prayer, Kajsa thought about what she was thankful for. Siri thanked God for having brought Kajsa safely to them, and asked for guidance in helping her through that which was to come. When it was Kajsa's turn the words came easily and naturally.

"Dear God, bless Reverend Petrus for having helped me when I had nowhere to turn and bless these good people for taking me in. Amen."

That night Kajsa slept more peacefully than she had slept in months.

City life was completely foreign to Kajsa. She couldn't understand how people passed the time, for there was nothing to do. There were no cows to feed and milk and muck, no milk to skim and make into cheese, no Christmas pig to fatten with left-over scraps, no hens to lay eggs and now and then provide a meal, no berries to pick and save for winter, no sausages to stuff and smoke, nor meat to salt and save, no wood to split and carry, no storage buildings to fill with food for winter, no hay to cut and dry, no potatoes to plant and harvest, no oven in which to bake half a year's worth of bread to be dried and stored, no spinning wheel for spinning yarn, no loom for weaving cloth and rag rugs, no wash house with its huge wash tub for washing clothes and people twice a year. In the city people did not survive by creating what was necessary for their own lives. Instead, they were forced to work at jobs which had no connection to them aside from the money they gave. It was money, which one seldom saw in the countryside, that sustained life in the city.

Siri, at least, was able to use what she had learned as a child in the countryside. Her mother had taught her to sew when she was young, an ability she had continued to develop as an adult. Consequently, she had built up a core of customers, that grew like rings around a stone thrown into the water, until she was earning almost as much as Gustaf earned in the harbor as a stevedore. Not only did she alter and mend clothes for those more well-off than herself, but she was often called upon to design and sew fancy dresses for society women. Like Signe, she was known for the fine quality of her work. And happily, Kajsa was able to be of help by sewing simpler garments and embroidering monograms, an art that Signe had passed on to her during their long hours together.

It took some time to adjust to city life. At first Kajsa was afraid to venture beyond the courtyard on her own. Not only were the throngs of people and wagons overwhelming, but more than that, she was conscious of her protruding belly and the reactions it would have generated at home. She was surprised that no one cast stones or spat three times at the sight of her. More surprising still, no one seemed to notice her at all. She had never experienced anonymity, much less the freedom it offered. What a relief it was to move freely amongst strangers in the city, away from the specter of the judgmental village women. Soon she was doing the daily shopping, as well as running errands for Siri.

Several days after her arrival in Stockholm, November began to show its true face. Day after day rain fell in a continuous drizzle from a dark gray, overcast sky, forming streams of refuse and excrement between the cobblestones. It was impossible for women to walk anywhere without soiling the hems of their long skirts, as well as their shoes, and thus carrying the vile stink with them wherever one went. Although Kajsa was used to barnyard smells, the smell of human excrement mixed with rotting food and every other form of refuse imaginable made her sick to her stomach. It was well known that Stockholm was the dirtiest, most unhealthy city in Europe, but that it was so disgusting came as a shock. She was thankful that she could spend most of the day sitting indoors sewing with Siri. Like Signe, Siri became a surrogate mother for her, someone she trusted and who led her gently from childhood into adulthood.

One day when their conversation had become unusually personal, Kajsa's curiosity got the better of her.

"Have Siri and Gustaf taken in other girls in my situation?" she asked.

"No, Kajsa is the first."

"Why have thee taken me in?" She did not add that it had always seemed strange to her that they did so when they lived in such a small room and had so little.

" 'Tis very simple," Siri told her. "Hjalmar and I had a younger sister, Maja, who became pregnant not long ago. We never knew any of the details, only that she was so afraid to besmirching our family's reputation, and Hjalmar's in particular because he is a priest, that she tried to abort the child herself. Rather than going into the lake, as girls do in the country, she chose a way that is quite common here in Stockholm. She bought a box of matches. As Kajsa probably knows, matches contain phosphorus, which is very poisonous. She broke the heads off a handful of them, put them in milk, and drank it. Sometimes this causes the child to abort, but more often than not, it kills the poor girl. Anyway, one day she suddenly became ill, throwing up violently, accompanied by stomach pains so intense that they curled her into a ball. We all assumed she had caught some winter malady and didn't pay too much attention to her symptoms. The next day it seemed to have passed. But two days later, just as suddenly as before, she became nauseous, began vomiting, and had diarrhea. As the day wore on she became worse and worse, constantly crying out and knotted in pain, beseeching us to help her. But we were powerless. Nothing we did could relieve her pain. By the time the doctor arrived she had became delirious and was having convulsions. Finally she fell into a coma and died shortly afterwards. I have never seen anyone die such a horrible death! Afterwards the doctor discovered she had been with child and he understood from her symptoms that she had eaten phosphorus matches.

" 'I have seen it a number of times before,' he told us. 'One is fooled by the fact that the patient seems to be better the day after the first attack. But when the symptoms re-occur after a day or two and are much worse, it becomes obvious that it is due to phosphorus poisoning.'

"Both Hjalmar and I were witness to the torture she went through and we vowed that we would do everything in our power to prevent such a thing from happening to anyone else. So he contacted me when he learned of thy situation."

"I cannot express how thankful I am for the help I have received," Kajsa told her, at a loss to put her feelings into words.

" 'Tis God's will," Siri said, laying her hand on Kajsa's arm.

Before long Kajsa ceased to be anonymous at the stalls in the market place and in the small shops where she bought food. People greeted her with friendly smiles.

"I can't get used to the fact that strangers don't judge me, as they would have in the village," she remarked while she and Siri sat sewing one gray November day. "And I've seen other women with big bellies and no wedding rings."

"Unmarried mothers are quite common in Stockholm, especially amongst the poorer classes,"[80] Siri said. "Getting married here is not just a matter of having the banns read in church three Sundays in a row, like in the village. There everyone knows each other and the families have already agreed to the match. Also, it's the church laws which rule there, whereas here in Stockholm it is the government that rules and the church has much less power. Nor is the church the community's center, as in the country. Most of the young people who move to the city come on their own, without their families. Although a girl is under the guardianship of her father until she is 25, once she moves to the city he is too far away to have any say in her life. Yet she still must have his

---

80. In the 1880s every other birth in Stockholm was to an unwed mother.

permission, or that of her guardian, to marry if she is under 25. That is not always so easy. Some people lose contact with ther parents when they come to the city, or perhaps they come to get away from them for some reason. Also, often the parents back in the village cannot read or write, so a letter writer must be found—and paid—as well as other official papers obtained. Consequently, people find it simpler to just live together without going through all the time-consuming paperwork."

"It sounds much more complicated than it is at home," Kajsa concluded.

"It is. But there is another reason why many a woman in the lower classes chooses to live with a man without being legally married. As I said, an unmarried woman comes of age when she is 25. But when a woman marries, no matter how old she is, her husband becomes her legal guardian. She never comes of age; she is forever under her husband's control.[81] Everything she has belongs to him. She doesn't even have control over her own maney, be it inherited or earned by the sweat of her brow. Most young women come to Stockholm in search of a better life, with some degree of economic freedom, however small. Most are not willing to trade that freedom for another man's control over them. Also, many less fortunate working class men have a problem with alcohol, unfortunately. So it is to a woman's advantage to be able to keep whatever money she earns from small jobs, rather than being forced to turn it over to a husband who will often as not spend it on drink. Especially if she has children to care for."

Kajsa was silent when Siri had finished, trying to make sense out of what she had just heard.

"But Siri and Gustaf are married," she offered half questioningly.

"Yes, we got married for religious reasons. But at first we just lived together, because I wanted to be sure he was a hard worker and not a drinker, and that I could trust him. Before finally getting married we agreed that any money I earn is mine, as well as anything I might inherit."

Kajsa nodded in understanding.

"Keep that in mind before deciding to get married. One must be as sure as one can possibly be about the man one marries."

"I'm not ever going to get married," Kajsa told her.

"Kajsa is too young to make such big decisions yet. Not all men are like Kajsa's father or Hildur's Arvidsson. Nor like Hans Ängmark. Look at my Gustaf. Or Reverend Petrus. There are plenty of good men around."

"Perhaps," Kajsa admitted grudgingly. "But how do I judge the good

---

81. This was true up until 1920.

from the bad?"

"Patience. Kajsa is not even fifteen," Siri assured her. "One does not become an adult over night. She has already stepped into that world ahead of her time."

As November gave way to December, the rain ceased at last and the north wind took over with a vengeance, clearing away the heavy clouds and allowing the sun to make its existence remembered. Although the wind brought with it the usual cold nights, freezing the stinking streams between the cobblestones, it brought no snow, giving the air an almost spring-like feeling.

On one such a day, Kajsa set out for the open market with a basket over her arm, as usual. Once outside, the sun felt so good on her face, after days and weeks of gray cloudy weather, that she decided to walk a different way in order to enjoy it longer. Turning into a side street, she suddenly came upon a young woman gazing into a shop window. She recognized her immediately.

"Vendela!" she called as she got nearer.

The girl turned.

"Is it really Kajsa?" she gasped. "I'm so glad to see her again!"

They shook hands, each glancing down at the other's body, then burst into a chorus of laughter.

"Oh! This is the first time I have laughed since coming to Stockholm!" Vendela declared when she caught her breath.

The comment took Kajsa by surprise. In their short acquaintance she had seen the girl as being rather lighthearted.

"How has Vendela been since we parted at the station?" Kajsa questioned, sensing that all was not well.

"If I should tell the truth, I've not fared well."

"What's happened? Is Vendela not living with her relatives?"

"Yes, but they are not kind to me. Is Kajsa in a hurry?" she wondered.

"No, not really. Shall we walk together a ways?"

They walked arm in arm through the narrow streets in a part of town that was unfamiliar to Kajsa.

"How does Kajsa have it?" Vendela inquired.

"I am doing well. I am staying with a young couple, the sister of our parish priest. They are quite poor, living in one tiny room, but they are extremely generous and kind. I try to help out as much as I can, but they do not look upon me as a maid."

"Kajsa is lucky. Before coming here I had a position at a farm not far from home. Some of the village girls warned me about working there. The usual thing: watch out for the man of the house, Squire Svartholm. But I took the job because it was the only position available just then. At first Svartholm was very friendly and helpful, so I felt guilty about being on my guard. Then one evening he met me on my way back from closing in the hens for the night.

" 'Come around here,' he said. 'I want to show Vendela something.'

"He led me around to the back side of the barn, out of sight of the house. Suddenly he turned into another person. He pushed me up against the wall, put his hand over my mouth, and took me.

"By the time autumn came I could no longer hide the fact that I was with child. Fru Svartholm yelled at me when she saw my stomach, saying that she could not have such a sinful maid in her house.

" 'Tis *Fru'n's* own husband what has put the child in me,' I told her.

"At that, she became hysterical, calling her husband. When he heard what I had said, he slapped me so hard that I nearly fainted.

" 'Get out!' he roared. 'And if Vandela ever goes around telling people such a lie, I shall see to it that she lands in prison on bread and water for defaming my honor!'

"I had no choice but to pack my things and go. Actually, I wouldn't have wanted to stay there anyway. But when I asked him for my pay, since it was only a week or two until free week when I would be paid for the entire year I had worked there, he refused to give me a penny, saying I had broken my contract by leaving early.

"Not knowing what else to do, I went home to my parents. They were horrified, not because Svartholm had raped me, oh no. They accused me of having made that up, because they knew him and maintained that he would never do such a thing. No, they were horrified because I was with child! They had their honor within the community and I had tarnished it by my behavior. So it was not possible for me to live there. However, they contacted relatives in Stockholm. Meanwhile, I had to stay hidden, so no one in the village would see me. When the answer came from Stockholm it included a train ticket. Naturally I assumed they were thoughtful and kind people, having sent the ticket and all. Just as I had misjudged Svartholm, so I misjudged my relatives."

"In what way?"

"When I finally found my way to their home that night we parted company at the station, they flew into a rage because I was late. Then they informed me that I was to work for them in order to re-pay my train ticket. Fair enough. But it turned out that they are very religious.

179

They did not believe that I had been raped by Squire Svartholm.

" 'Svartholm is an honorable man. He would never do such a thing,' they claimed. So in their eyes I was not only immoral, but I was also a liar. Since that first night they have never ceased shaming me, calling me a whore and a sinner, saying I am possessed by the devil. They force me to get down on my knees and beg God's forgiveness, aloud, so they can hear me, before every meal. If my uncle doesn't think I sound repentant enough he whips me with a birch cane because, as he claims, he is now my guardian and has the right to punish me physically when necessary. Apparently they only took me in because they needed to re-pay some debt to my parents. They say that once I enter the Public Maternity Hospital they never want to lay eyes on me again, that, as far as they are concerned, I no longer belong to the family."

"Sometimes I think Christians can be more un-Christian than heathens."

"I agree," Vendela said.

"Does Vendela plan to keep her child?" Kajsa wondered.

"No. How can one keep the child of a man who raped her?"

"It can be left at the Public Children's Home."

"It costs too much money to leave it there."

"One can pay for it by nursing the child and acting as a wet nurse for another child. That is what I plan to do."

" I don't even want to nurse a rapist's child," Vendela replied. "By chance I met a girl who gave me the address of a woman who takes foster babies for next to nothing. Then it is done with once and for all."

By now they had reached a wider street lined with more prosperous looking houses.

"See that house across the street and up a ways? Number 16," Vendela pointed out. "That is where am living. We must say good-bye here. I'm not allowed to speak with anyone or have any friends. If my aunt sees us talking I shall be punished. Perhaps we shall meet another day. 'Tis not very often that I'm allowed to go out. It was only that my aunt needed something from the apothecary but was too lazy to go for it herself, so she sent me. Now I must go in. Please do not come here asking for me."

Kajsa walked away slowly, mulling over all that Vendela had told her. She knew all too well that people could be harshly cruel, especially towards children, often in the name of a religion that was apparently ignorant of Christ's teachings. But she could never get used to the injustice done to innocent victims. It seemed like children and women would always be at the mercy of those over them. Once again she silently thanked God for people like Reverend Petrus, and Siri and Gustaf, those who themselves hadn't known suffering at the hands of others, but who showed compassion towards those who had. They were the true Christians.

As her time approached, Kajsa grew anxious about giving birth, for she didn't know what to expect. It was not a subject that people spoke about. In the countryside, when a woman's time came, the men and children were simply sent away from home, often for hours on end. Only the midwife and the women assisting her were present, surrounding the event with a curtain of mystery. Nor had she been allowed to witness copulation or birth amongst the animals when she was a child at Björkdalen. Now her ignorance embarrassed her, preventing her from asking. What frightened her most was the thought of how the child in her stomach was going to get out. It was too big to come out between her legs, where Hans had pushed into her. Would she have to be cut open? She was becoming obsessed with the question. Nothing else held her attention, although she tried to hide her anxiety. Finally the day came when she was no longer able to pretend.

Siri had been aware of her growing anxiety, but such subjects were not something one talked about. The thought of doing so made Siri uncomfortable. Consequently, she had made up her mind to wait until Kajsa herself brought the subject up. But the subject was even more difficult for Kajsa to bring up. As her time drew nearer, it would be Mother Nature who rescued them both.

December remained unusually mild, with only an occasional thin, quickly-melting layer of snow covering the ground. Instead, the clouds offered a series of spectacular sunrises and sunsets nearly every day after Christmas. Kajsa remembered the blood-red sunrise she had awoken to on New Year's morning, the day of her seventh birthday. Old Svea had thought it was a good omen, but she had been wrong. According to what she had read in her father's *Bonde-practica,* a red sky on the first morning of the new year meant that great sorrow would follow. That was the year that her mother and Hilda Maria had died. Now on the eve of the new year, Kajsa prayed for thick clouds to cover the sky the next morning. She wanted no more great sorrows in her life.

She awoke to find her prayer had been answered. Low dark clouds hung heavily over Stockholm, nearly shutting out the daylight. She laughed to herself when she saw them, suspecting she was the only person in all of Stockholm who was thankful for such grayness.

Some days later the brilliant sunrises and sunsets began again, causing concern. People speculated as to their cause. Some feared with foreboding that the end of the world was nigh, while scientists claimed that the colors were due to dust from a volcanic eruption the previous August in a place called Java. Another more popular theory was that they were caused by a seemingly tailless comet which had recently been discovered[82] and could actually be seen with the naked eye. This latter supposition appealed to the general public. Several evenings Gustaf, Siri, and Kajsa joined the clusters of people gazing upwards from the streets hoping for a glimpse of it, one of the few public excitements offered during the Stockholm winter. But in vain. A fortnight later the excitement, as well as the spectacular sunrises and sunsets, faded and life returned to normal.

One day not long after the new year, Kajsa and Siri were huddled close to the wood stove sewing as usual. Kajsa was in the middle of embroidering a particularly complicated monogram decorating the top edge of a linen sheet, when she felt a strange pain in her stomach, causing here to gasp. Siri looked up knowingly.

"Have Kajsa's pains started?" she asked.

"I don't know," Kajsa replied.

All at once the door to the uncomfortable discussion was opened.

"Does Kajsa know how babies are born?" Siri asked.

Kajsa shook her head.

"What does Kajsa know about giving birth?"

"Not much," she replied, looking down at her lap shamefully.

Siri sighed and, focusing her eyes on her sewing, explained how her pains would increase in intensity and closeness, that her water would break, and that the hospital's midwife would help her after that.

"But one must remember that giving birth is natural. It's not an illness. And in some magical way, one forgets the pain afterwards. That's one of Nature's blessings bestowed upon women."

Kajsa looked at Siri questioningly, wondering how she knew so much about childbirth. As if reading her thoughts, Siri continued.

"I had a baby several years back. But as often happens, he didn't survive to his first birthday. Perhaps the safest time in a child's life is when it is inside its mother. After that anything can happen." She set down her sewing and put a couple of pieces of wood in the stove. "And now it's time for Kajsa to make her way to the hospital. It's not so far from here.

---

82. It was actually on a return visit, having been discovered in 1812 and named Pons after its French discoverer.

I'll write down the directions while she gathers her belongings. She must go alone in order to be admitted. And remember, even if she is asked, she need not give her name or her address. It's a place of complete secrecy, for the sake of those who do not want their situation known. By the way, is she still determined to stay and nurse the child for eight months and then leave it there?"

"Yes. It is the only thing I can do for the unlucky child. I can't start my adult life with a child to care for and no money, no job, no family, no place to live. That is no way for a child to begin life. There must be someone who can better care for it than I can."

They had never spoken much about Kajsa's decision to give up the child. That was what had brought her to Stockholm. It was simply something that had to be done. She felt no emotional connection to that which was growing inside her. It was as if it was something she were carrying around that didn't belong to her. She looked forward to being rid of it.

Once she was ready to go, Siri handed her a stamped and addressed envelope. Inside was a blank piece of paper.

"Please let me know how Kajsa is doing," she said.

"I don't know how to express my thanks," she began.

"This is not good-bye. We shall meet again," Siri told her. "In the meantime, may God be with thee."

"And may God bless Siri and her Gustaf." She threw her arms around Siri's neck and hugged her.

"Go now," Siri told her. "Kajsa doesn't have all the time in the world. If the pains come on the way, stop and breathe deeply. Do not be afraid. It's not far to walk."

Kajsa let her arms drop and took a step back from Siri. Both had tears in their eyes.

The fog, that had softened the harshness of poverty's reality all morning, had begun to lift, revealing the shabbiness of the neighborhood's wooden houses. Kajsa wondered if she could ever get used to city life. She hurried along, past the familiar small shops and the open market near the harbor, then into an unfamiliar and more prosperous part of town. Siri's directions were clear and easy to follow. Now and then she was gripped by a pain, but none were as strong as the one she had had while sitting and sewing. Walking seemed to help. Before long she saw the huge yellow hospital building before her. Her first reaction was to turn back, but when she felt something warm and wet running down her legs she realized there was no turning back. She pulled open the heavy door and went in.

The sister on duty took one look at her and called for help. No questions were asked. She was led to a large room containing a number of beds separated by curtains. From the bed assigned to her, she listened to the various degrees of moaning, whimpering, crying, and out-right screaming emerging from behind the curtains.

Not long after that she suffered her most powerful contraction yet. Without warning, a high-pitched scream escaped from within her. Suddenly she understood that the pain of childbirth was going to exceed even the most extreme pain her father had inflicted upon her as a child. Worst of all, she was caught in it, with no way to escape. Unable to control herself, she joined the chorus of moaning and crying.

Kajsa's labor was long and painful, as well as frightening. It went far beyond anything she could ever have imagined. In the midst of it she experienced an intense loathing for Hans, the boy she had trusted, who had put her in that situation and then abandoned her. She damned him, condemning him to the tortures of hell. And after that she prayed for relief through her own death.

After two days of exhausting labor she at last pushed a large boy-child from her body. Refusing to even look at him, she declared that she wanted nothing to do with the monster.

"*Fröken*[83] has three choices," she was told. "Either she takes her child and leaves here, or she pays to leave the child in the Children's Home, or she nurses him and another baby for eight months, as agreed upon before hand."

Kajsa realized that she had no choice but to stay and nurse the child. She also realized that it would give her a place to live and food during those months. The prospect pushed the reality of having to face the outside world on her own further into the future. On the other hand, she was so ashamed of her behavior while giving birth that she couldn't look any of the nurses in the face. She wished she could walk out of the place and never have to see them or her boy-child again. In the end, she was forced to swallow her pride and remain there.

The Monday after the child's birth a priest visited the maternity hospital on his weekly rounds.

"Are there any newborns to be baptized?" he inquired of the matron.

"Yes, there is one," she told him, nodding towards the bed where Kajsa

---

83. Miss.

lay. "She gave birth to a healthy boy-child several days ago. And there was one child who couldn't wait for Reverend's visit. We gave him an emergency baptism and he died two hours later. His mother departed from this earthly life the day after his birth due to childbed fever. They have both been moved to the mortuary to await burial."

"Is the mother's name known? Or where she came from?"

"No. We know nothing about her. She took full advantage of the anonymity law, nor did we find anything amongst her belongings that was of any help. However, it was obvious from her clothes that she was a country girl—a right young one at that—and that she had most likely been sleeping in the woods before coming here."

"Such a pity," the priest replied. "The law is good for those who wish to keep their condition secret, but there should be some means of identifying girls in cases like this. Such information could be placed in a sealed envelope, like when a mother leaves a child in the home, making it possible for mother and child to find each other at some future time, should they wish to. As it is now, some family is never going to know what has become of their daughter." He sighed. "Best we get on with today's baptism, at least."

Going over to Kajsa's bed, he introduced himself.

"Reverend Klingvall."

She took his hand.

"Ka...." she began.

"She need not give her name," he interrupted.

"It makes no matter," she told him. "I've no family from which to hide my condition."

"I'm sorry to hear that she has no family."

"Better than having one and being condemned by them. I've a few true friends who know of my situation and who have helped me, rather than judging me. One of them even shares Reverend's calling."

"A true blessing," he told her. "But what about her child? I shall baptize him, but first he needs a name."

"Bror,"[84] she answered decidedly, "to remind me of my little brother."

"How nice," came his reply. "We usually ask a couple of the nurses here to stand in as godmothers. I have been given to understand that he is going to be nursed before being left here."

"Yes. I've nothing to offer him as an unwed mother completely on my own. 'Tis better so."

And thus Bror was baptized. Kajsa had not chosen his name, in fact she had not even thought about a name prior to Reverend Klingvall's

---

84. "Brother" in Swedish.

appearance. The name Bror had simply popped out of her mouth of itself, as well as the reason for "choosing" it.

Suddenly she remembered Siri's envelope.

"Would it be possible for Reverend Klingvall to do me a favor?" she asked timidly.

"Yes, of course."

She took the paper from Siri's stamped envelope and wrote, "All is well. His name is Bror" and sealed it in the envelope.

"Many thanks," she said, handing it to him.

After Reverend Klingvall's departure, Kajsa suddenly began to wonder about Raoul, about whom she had not passed a thought since leaving Björkdalen. He must be thirteen by now, just about to leave home. How had he fared under *Tant* Agnes's hand? She felt guilty for having abandoned him to the whims of their father, who was determined to make a man out of him, yet she had had nothing to say in the matter. It was *Tant* Agnes who had decided her fate, and probably Raoul's as well. She promised herself that one day she would return to Björkdalen and find him. But for now, the best she could do was to keep him close in her thoughts.

A week later, once the risk of childbed fever, the much feared killer of newly delivered women, had safely passed, Kajsa and little Bror were moved to the public Children's Home. After registering her as *amma 7*[85] Matron showed her to the nursing room where she would live for the next eight months. Her eyes swept the room in dismay. A dozen girls in red checked dresses and stiff white aprons sat around the walls nursing infants, each flanked by two wooden cradles. The atmosphere was cheerless. No one talked or even smiled. Kajsa set her satchel on one of the chairs surrounding a table in the middle of the room, while still holding Bror. Matron indicated an empty cradle.

"Put the child there," she directed officiously, then pointed to a bed. *"Amma 7* shall have this bed and she shall keep her belongings in the cupboard beside it. While I look for a uniform for her she must read the rules for wet nurses so that, should she disobey any of them, she cannot claim ignorance." She pointed to a notice tacked up on the wall by the door, after which she looked Kajsa up and down quickly, judging her size, then disappeared in search of a uniform. While she was gone Kajsa read through the list of rules one must follow when living in the Children's Home, among them:

---

85. The 7th wet nurse of the new year.

1. One must be "God-fearing, obedient, respectful, and vigilant."

2. One must with attentiveness, tenderness, and love care for the children that have been placed with her.

3. One must never lie with an infant in one's own bed.

6. Not only must one keep the children neat and clean, but see to it that one is scrupulously clean oneself.

8. One must exercise the greatest care with the use of fire.[86]

9. One must carry out jobs ordered by the matron, as well as tending the fires in the nursing rooms and kitchen, carrying up wood, cleaning and scrubbing the floors in the rooms, corridors, and stairways, and other necessary jobs, such as mending and patching the children's clothes, as well as one's own.

10. One must not go outside the Children's Home without the matron's permission.

13. Should a wet nurse break any of the rules she shall be forced to leave, along with her child, who will lose its chance of being placed in a foster home.

Kajsa felt as though she had been placed in a prison, a feeling that increased when she was handed a uniform and instructed to put it on.

Lastly, another boy-child called Felix was brought in for her to nurse. His mother had not even paid to leave him at the Children's Home. He had been found wrapped in a tattered blanket on the front steps of the building one frosty morning. It was questionable if he would survive.

In spite of the rules about personal cleanliness and keeping the rooms, halls, and stairs scrubbed, there was the eternal problem of bedbugs.[87] To make matters worse, not only was the building over 200 years old, but, because it was to be replaced by a new building the following year, nothing was done towards its upkeep. It was impossible for the wet nurses to scour the cracks between the floor boards sufficiently to rid them of vermin. And in many areas the wallpaper had loosened, giving the bedbugs a perfect hiding place during the daytime, as well as easy access to the beds at night. Luckily, the infants were clothed and then swaddled, which served to protect all but their heads. But in spite of luring countless bedbugs into

---

86. Various kinds of oil lamps were used since there was no electricity in the old building.

87. Bedbugs, as well as lice, were a problem for both country and city folk, rich and poor alike.

vägglusbrädor,[88] Kajsa and the other girls were besieged nightly, leaving red bite marks on their bodies and blood flecks on their sheets. Although this was a common problem for nearly everyone in those days due to lack of sanitation, especially in the cities, it was made worse by so many people living in such close quarters. No matter what methods were tried in order to be rid of bedbugs, they were simply a fact of life and had to be accepted as such.

Before long Kajsa became aware of another problem: woodworms. The swaddled babies slept in wooden cradles and, because the unwinding and rewinding of the swaddling cloths was an arduous endeavor, they were only changed twice a day, rather than according to necessity. Consequently, the wooden cradle bottoms were almost constantly wet, creating a haven for woodworms. Slight improvements had been made by using removable bottoms, equipped with drain holes, that could be taken out and cleaned. But the problem would remain until the move into the new Children's Home with its metal cribs and the eventual end of swaddling. That the rooms smelled of urine was nothing uncommon in the days before indoor toilets. Nor was it helped by the fact that the wet nurses often simply hung the wet clothes and swaddling cloths up to dry, rather than bothering to wash them.

The days crept by slowly for Kajsa. She nursed Bror and Felix matter of factly at the assigned times and carried out her duties along with the others. Girls appeared and disappeared according to the onset of their individual eight month sentences. They were unknown to one another beyond an *amma* number. Bonds or friendships were seldom formed between them, leaving each closed in her own aloneness. No one was there of her own free will. In each case, an unpleasant event lay as a shadow in the background. Some were victims of rape, others the victim of false words or a broken promise. Whatever the cause, they were all there to rid themselves of the result; some of them willingly, others angrily, a few sadly. Once they left the Children's Home those months would became a closed chapter in their lives, hopefully disappearing into a fold in time. Were a friendship to follow one out into the ordinary world, it

---

88. Boards with many small holes drilled in them. The bugs liked to crawl into the holes during the daytime, whereby it was easy to get rid of them by shaking them out of the holes.

would most certainly serve as a reminder of a time one wished to forget.

With the coming of spring the atmosphere in the nursing rooms lightened considerably. But unlike the mothers, who had yet to experience spring in the Children's Home, the nurses regarded it as the quiet before the storm. Each year, almost without fail, the winds from the northeast brought about an epidemic of bronchitis both autumn and spring. And this year was no exception. Once an illness entered the gates of the Children's Home it quickly spread like wildfire, attacking infants as well as the older children waiting for foster homes. Only the strong survived. For the weaker, what began as bronchitis invariably moved down into the lungs to become pneumonia which, because there was no cure, in almost every case proved to be fatal.

Soon both Bror and Felix were coughing and crying with the others. Suddenly, and much to her surprise, Kajsa became anxious about both infants, to whom she previously had felt no emotional attachment. She slept fitfully, always with one ear on the alert for their cries and strained breathing. During the day, when other tasks weren't claiming her time, she held them, one in each arm, while rocking gently back and forth. Many a time she caught herself singing softly, encouraging them to fight for their lives. Bror seemed to heed her encouragement, but Felix, who had had such a poor start in life, fared worse. In spite of her round the clock care, Kajsa was unable to prevent his bronchitis from wending its way down into his lungs. One night his crying and coughing became unbearable.

"Put 'em out in the corridor so the rest of us can git some sleep," someone yelled. "He's gonna die anyway."

"Shut up, bitch!" she retorted, three words she had never in her life uttered, even though she had heard them many times. "He's a human being, too."

She unwound his swaddling cloths and held him against her body. He hadn't managed to nurse since the previous day and barely had the strength to cough. Instinctively she knew he was dying, but she could not give up her efforts to save him. Towards dawn his coughing ceased at last and he died in her arms. Kajsa was inconsolable.

"What's all the fuss about?" asked one of the nurses. "He wasn't even Seven's own child. He's not worth cryin' over. His mother never cared about him or else she wouldn't 'av left him on the doorstep in the dead of winter."

"I cared about him!" Kajsa declared, surprised by her words and the

190

feelings behind them.

"Well, a weakling like him's better off dead," concluded the nurse. "She'll get used to death in this place."

But for Kajsa, death was not something she could get used to. It had already taken too many people she cared about. And now she was even moved by the many infants who died that spring, even though she had not had any personal contact with them.

When the worst of the epidemic was over and most of last summer's conceptions were past, the number of new arrivals had lessened. They were distributed amongst the other wet nurses, leaving Kajsa to occasionally serve as a substitute when necessary. She was thankful to avoid close contact with any of the babies. It was enough to try to hold her emotions at bay while nursing Bror, knowing she was soon to lose him. She looked forward to the day when she could leave her life in the nursing room behind her, yet at the same time, dreading it.

As spring warmed the earth and the days grew longer, plants that had been hiding deep in the earth through the winter sent up tender shoots, followed by buds anxious to open. Buds also formed on the naked branches of the trees, swelling larger each day. Then, almost over night, they burst out of their confinement, letting tiny wrinkled leaves emerge and unfold in the warmth of the sun like butterfly wings.

Kajsa watched the rebirth of spring through the closed window of the nursing room. She tried to imagine the gentle wind in her face, filled with the familiar fragrance of spring: sap flowing upwards in the pines, the delicate aroma of mouse-ear sized birch leaves, the sweetness of bird cherry blossoms that she associated with spring. None of them existed in the city. Instead, she was surrounded by the eternal stink of urine, wet clothes, excrement, and sour milk vomit. Nor were the windows allowed to be opened to let in fresh air, for fear of the infants becoming ill once again. How she longed to go outside, away from the prison of the Children's Home. The pull of the outside world was even stronger than her repressed feelings for Bror, whom she held at a distance.

The beginning of August brought a lull in the flow of unwanted infants. And because Bror was healthy and gaining weight rapidly, he was put on solid food. Thus Kajsa was freed from the Children's Home earlier than planned.

While nursing Bror for the last time on her final morning, she found herself studying the little face she had avoided for so long, searching for something that set it apart from all the other baby faces she had seen pass through the Children's Home. But to her he looked like all the rest, save for a tiny star-shaped birth mark above his left eyebrow. His big blue eyes looked up at her hopefully. When she met his gaze, he smiled. It was as if he had waited months for her to see him. Instinctively she smiled back. It was more than she could bear.

"I must go now," she whispered in a shaking voice. His smile vanished.

Quickly she laid him in his cradle.

"Good-bye, my little Bror. May God bless thee with a better future than I could provide."

Grabbing her satchel, she hurried from the room without looking back. As she closed the door behind her she heard him start to cry. She was already crying herself.

Just as she started to pull the main door open, Matron called out to her.

"Wait, Seven! There is one last thing she must do before leaving."

Still weeping, she went into Matron's office.

"Seven shall write her real name on a paper and, together with her child's number and birth certificate, it will be sealed in this envelope. If at some future time either Seven or her child wishes to have information about the other or get in contact, the envelope can be opened and we can help them find each other."

She gave Kajsa the envelope to seal, then wrote "Seven" and Bror's number on the outside before filing it in a drawer.

"She is free to go now. And good luck in the future. Does she have some place to go for the time being?"

"Yes," Kajsa answered. She hoped she remembered the way back to Siri's and Gustaf's.

Matron held out her hand. Kajsa took it, and without saying good-bye, walked out the door into her new life.

VENDELA

Stockholm 1884

Once outside in the street, she looked around, not quite knowing in which direction to go. She realized she had not paid much attention to the way when she had come to the maternity hospital in the winter. Finally she turned to the right and began walking. Nothing looked familiar. Several women came towards her carrying full market baskets, giving her to understand that she was not far from the open marketplace. If she could just get there, then she would know how to get to Siri's and Gustaf's house. But once she passed the market square she became confused. The block where she was sure they lived was nothing but rubble.

"What's happened to the building that stood here?" she asked a passer-by.

"Oh, it burned down several months ago," she was told. "Thanks to God, nobody was hurt and it was put out before it could spread to other buildings. These old wooden houses flame up like a match lighting."

"Where've all the people gone who lived here?"

"Heaven only knows. First they was put in the old Cholera Hospital that's used for the homeless people. After that theys scattered to the four winds."

Bewildered, Kajsa went back to the market to ask for information. But the answer was always the same: no one knew where Siri and Gustaf had gone. But Fish-Maria, the old fishmonger, had other news for her.

"There was a girl here asking for Kajsa just a few days ago," she said, digging in her pocket. "She gave me this." She handed Kajsa a wrinkled scrap of paper.

Smoothing it out, the first word Kajsa saw was Vendela, followed by an address.

Quickly she thanked Fish-Maria and set off, asking for directions as she went. But when she found the right address, there was no house at the number written on the paper, only a tobacco shop. She went in to inquire. The girl behind the counter was bending over several cigar boxes, showing an older man two different brands of cigar, while he puffed on a third one, filling the room with thick smoke. Her stylish dress, painted nails, and up-swept hair-do concealed her identity, but nothing could conceal the identity of the voice beneath her laughter and flirtatious manner. Vendela! She waited by the door until the customer left with his purchase. As Vendela's eyes followed his departure she caught sight of Kajsa. They both burst into laughter.

"I see Vendela is doing alright for herself," Kajsa noted.

"That depends on how one looks at it," Vendela answered. "The fine clothes aren't mine and the woman who runs the place sends me out to have my hair fixed every morning. My job's not just selling cigars. I have to lure in customers with my looks and conversation, as well as remembering the regular customers' names and titles and favorite cigars."

"There're worse jobs than that," Kajsa offered.

"Perhaps, but I'm not so sure. I stand here from seven o'clock in the morning until ten or eleven at night. And even later on Fridays and Saturdays. The pay is so bad that I have to sleep in the back room, because I can't afford to pay rent anywhere. But that's not the worst of it."

She paused as the door opened. A middle-aged gentleman entered.

"Good day, Director Cedergren," she said in an unnaturally sweet voice. "I'll be right there. My cousin is just leaving." She turned to Kajsa. "Come back in an hour or so, Cousin," she whispered.

She followed Kajsa to the door, pulling down the shade over its window and hanging a "back soon" sign in the window.

When Kajsa returned an hour later, the shade was up, the sign gone, and Vendela's hair-do was a bit untidy. Kajsa gave her a questioning look.

"As I was saying, the hours and pay aren't the worst of it. There're certain regular customers who wish to have more than cigars. The competition amongst cigar shops is great, so owners try to out do each other with added services and attentions. If they had to perform them themselves, things would be different. But for now, it's a job and a roof over my head." She sighed, then perked up again. "By the way, where's Kajsa staying?"

"I don't know. I just left the Children's Home this morning. I had hoped to stay with Siri and Gustaf until I get on my feet again, but the place they lived has burned to the ground. No one around there knows where they have gone."

"Oh, yes, I heard about the fire."

"I knew nothing of it. We lived in isolation with a lot of squalling babies. That was the extent of our world."

"I don't think I could have stood it there," Vendela remarked.

"But what did Vendela do with her..."

Vendela's expression darkened.

"I shan't talk about it just now when I'm supposed to be cheerful in front of customers. Kajsa must stay with me for the time being. We can share my bed and talk then."

194

That night after the last customer had gone, leaving a trail of cigar smoke after him like a steam engine pulling out of the station, Vendela put up a "closed" sign, pulled down the shade, and they went behind the curtain into the back room.

"Phew! It's been a long day," Vendela remarked.

"Why's the cigar shop open so late?" Kajsa wondered while they prepared for bed.

"There're always men out at night, spending time and money in taverns and looking for women, rather than going home to a haggard wife and squalling kids. Many of them like to enjoy the luxury of being able to buy a cigar or tobacco—or a woman—when the fancy hits them, which often happens late at night while they are out drinking. Also, as Kajsa may have understood, a cigar shop serves another function, both day and night. If we close early, our customers will take themselves to another cigar shop. It is the competition for customers that regulates our hours."

"Why did Vendela get such a job in the first place?"

"It was due to Madame Bella. She saw me on the street and asked if I was looking for a job. I guess I looked lost. I had just gotten rid of the child and didn't know what to do or where to go. She said I had a pretty face and asked if I would like to work in a cigar shop. At that time I knew nothing of cigar shops and cigar girls' other duties. It was a while before that rude awakening occurred and by that time I was used to having a bed and a roof over my head and a few coins in my pocket. I couldn't see living on the streets again." She yawned. " 'Tis best that I get some sleep," she continued. "I have to go to the Inspection Bureau early in the morning."

"Inspection Bureau?"

"Yeah. I'll explain tomorrow on our way there."

Early the next morning they set out for the Inspection Bureau a mile away in the Old Town. The sun had been up for some hours, burning off the last of the fog that had lain on the water surrounding the little island that was the oldest part of Stockholm.

"To explain from where I left off last night," Vendela began, "one day after I had stood behind the counter in the cigar shop for a month or so, a man came in and waved away my question as to what brand of cigar he wanted.

" 'No cigars. Just the other,' he said.

" 'What other?' I asked innocently, not understanding. He pointed to the curtain over the door to the back room. 'In there,' he said. When I still did not understand, he came 'round the counter, took me by the hand, and pulled me into the back room. Before I realized what was happening, he had unbuttoned my blouse and was fondling me, then pulling off my skirt. He lay me on the bed and, pulling down his trousers, climbed on top of me. It wasn't like when I was raped. He was quite gentle. Afterwards he helped me on with my clothes and gave me some money. 'Don't give it all to Madame Bella,' he said. 'It's my little cigar girl who has served me, not her.' And with that he was gone.

"As I said, he was nice. But another time when a man came in asked for 'the other' it turned out that he was a policeman. He asked to see my Inspection Book, which prostitutes have instead of an identification paper from a priest, and of course I hadn't one. So he reported me to the authorities. Since then I have been registered in their files and am forced to present myself at the Inspection Bureau every Monday to be examined. All prostitutes are required to do so, but many are not registered and thus avoid it."

"Why must one be examined?"

"To make sure one doesn't have any diseases that can be spread to customers. But no one examines the men, which is unfair. They are the ones who give us the diseases in the first place. Men always go free. They can rape and spread disease and father children without giving a damn about the consequences. They can lie right and left and they are believed, whereas a girl who is raped is never believed. It's disgusting!"

By now they had reached the Inspection Bureau.

"Kajsa can come in and wait for me, if she wishes. It's not a very pleasant place, though."

The waiting room was filled with girls and women. Some were well-dressed, but others looked like they had spent their lives on the streets, sleeping in whatever shelter they could find. Several policemen stood by the door to the examining room and medical students passed in and out. The discussions between the doctor and the patients were audible to all.

"Take this one to the *curhuset*"[89] a man's voice ordered. A woman screamed as one of the policemen stepped into the examining room. A moment later he and a medical student emerged with the scantily dressed screaming woman between them.

"The *curhuset* is everyone's greatest fear," Vendela whispered. "I don't

89. Literally "cure house." A hospital for patients with venereal diseases.

know what happens there. No one talks about it; they just fear it."

Kajsa remained in the waiting room when Vendela's turn came.

"So it's Vendela again," the man's voice said. The tone was cold. "Mouth open," he commanded. "Stick out thy tongue....ears and nose now....Have they both seen that all these bodily openings are free from sores?" he continued, apparently addressing the medical students. "One must check the lymph nodes for any swelling....now kneed the belly in search of any abnormality such as a fetus....then check the insides of the thighs for any rashes. Now, up in the examining chair." All was carried out quickly, with military precision.

"Must I?" she heard Vendela say.

"Yes, she must! We must probe the sexual area where diseases hide."

"I have no diseases. I have been very careful," she pleaded.

"Lower class street walkers know nothing of such things. Now get up there, girl!"

"Doctor knows I am no lower class street walker."

"That's enough prattle now. Up!"

There was a creaking sound from the chair.

"Legs spread!" came the command. "Legs spread, I said!"

There was silence, but for the faint sound of sniffling.

"Help me spread her legs and strap them into the stirrups," came the next command, obviously aimed at the two medical students. Kajsa could hear the sounds of struggling.

"There now. Come and have a look, gentlemen. No sores around the anus. Take a careful look at the urethra. Does it look healthy?"

"Yes, Sir."

"Now for the vagina. Hand me the speculum."

"No!" yelled Vendela.

"Hush! A baby has already passed through there, and who knows what else. A speculum is nothing."

"Don't open it so wide," she begged.

"I am the one to decide how wide to open it," she was told. "Now have a look, men. What can be said about this one?"

"Ow!" Vendela cried.

"It looks healthy to me," she heard one of the medical students say.

"Alright, I guess this one is healthy enough to use," the doctor concluded.

"I should think so, since Herr Doctor uses me himself," Vendela retorted.

"Watch thy tongue!" he snapped.

197

A minute later there was the sound of a rubber stamp on paper and the scratching of a pen.

"Take thy Inspection Book and get out!" he concluded. "That mouth is going to get Vendela into trouble, if she's not careful."

"Let's go!" Vendela exclaimed when she returned to the waiting room.

By the time they reached the street she was raging.

"He does everything he can to publicly insult and degrade me, yet he comes to me almost as often as I am forced to go to him," she blurted.

They walked in silence for a few minutes. Suddenly Kajsa realized Vendela was crying.

"I have to get out of this way of life," she sobbed. "I haven't even told Kajsa what happened to my baby."

"No. I've been wondering."

Vendela took a deep breath.

"After he was born I had to nurse him while I was still in the hospital. When I finally left there I went to the woman I had heard about who takes foster babies. But by that time my feelings towards him had begun to change. Perhaps it was because he was all that I had in the world after having been thrown out of my parents' home. Yet at the same time, I knew I couldn't survive here as a vagrant with a child. So I left him with the women, paying her all the money I had for his care. I hoped to take him back when my situation had improved. Getting the job at the cigar shop meant that I could have him with me in the back room. But when I went to get him the woman told me he had died. I was shocked and asked to have the death certificate and to know where he was buried. She said she had to go and find the certificate, so I said I'd wait. She disappeared into another room and I stepped into the hall from the porch. I could hear a number of babies crying. When she didn't come back immediately my curiosity got the better of me and I opened a door at the far end of the hall. There lay six or seven babies in make-shift cribs. They looked more like skeletons than living infants. Their flesh was tight on their heads, their eyes seemed to fill their faces, and their bony arms jerked weakly as they cried. The smell in the room was enough to choke me. I understood that I had unknowingly left my child with a so-called angel-maker. I had heard about such people, but hadn't really believed that there existed women who were so evil that they let small babies starve to death for the sake of a little money. To be honest, I was also scared to death. I felt as if I were to be her next victim. I closed the door and hurried back to the front porch. Just then the woman returned to tell me she had been unable to find the death certificate at the moment.

I told her to never mind, that I would come back another day. Then I went straight to the police and told them what I had seen. They didn't seem too surprised or even particularly upset. They simply said they would look into it. Two months later I went back under the pretext of wanting the death certificate. Once again the woman disappeared, pretending to look, I suppose, giving me a chance to look into that room again. It was the same as the first time I had seen it, although I imagine the babies were different. No infant could have survived for two months under those conditions. This time I went to the child welfare office. They were very concerned and the woman was eventually arrested. But it was too late for who knows how many babies, mine included. I never thought I'd regret having given up my baby, but there was something about nursing him that tied him to me. It's as if a part of me has been cut off, killed."

"I know what you mean," Kajsa said. "Strangely, I didn't feel that connection with Felix. Not even when he died. It was as if my body knew that Bror was a part of me, but that Felix wasn't. I wonder how it would've been if the babies had been switched from the very beginning, without my knowing it."

They walked in silence for a while.

"I don't like Stockholm," Vendela remarked suddenly.

"Nor do I," Kajsa agreed. "I long for the countryside, like where I grew up."

"Shall we try to find work as house maids on a farm somewhere?" Vendela suggested.

"Yes! It's certainly worth a try."

"We can look at the want ads in the newspapers that we sell in the tobacco shop."

Suddenly they were filled with life and hope.

Upon returning to the tobacco shop, Kajsa took the day's *Dagens Nyheter, Aftonbladet,* and *Stockholms Dagblad* into the back room and began searching the ads, while Vendela waited on customers. Suddenly she burst out laughing.

"What's so funny?" Vendela called from the other side of the curtain.

"Listen to this: 'Urgent. A middle aged widower and confirmation-aged son need two maids who can share indoor and outdoor farm work. Reply to Roland Sjöström, Björkdalen....'

"What's so funny about that?" Vendela wondered.

"Roland Sjöström is my father. After my mother died he had a house-keeper. She and I did not get along. Finally she forced him to send me to live with my mother's Aunt Hildur. He had never liked me, mostly because I wasn't a boy, and was more than glad to be rid of me. Anyway, this is the only ad I found for two maids. For some reason, I think we should at least answer it. Just for fun. We can always change our minds."

"But if he doesn't like Kajsa, then he probably won't hire us."

"He will never recognize me. I left there when I was eight and I have changed a lot since then. Give me a paper and pen."

While Vendela waited on a customer Kajsa composed a letter.

"How does this sound?" she asked when she had finished. "Dear Sir, We are two country cousins, 15 and 16 years old, who have discovered we are not city people. We grew up on farms, and after working as maids here in Stockholm, we wish to return to the countryside. Sincerely, Stina Jakobsdotter and Vendela Jakobsdotter. And the address to the tobacco shop."

"Stina?" Vendela asked.

"My name is actually Stina-Kajsa, but I have always just been called Kajsa."

"But what if he wants references from previous employers?"

"I can give Siri and Gustaf and the address of the house that burned down. If a letter should reach them, they would surely give me a good recommendation. Otherwise the letter would be returned, saying that they had moved to an unknown address. Ask Madame Bella if she could write a recommendation, if necessary. But somehow I don't think references will be necessary. The add said urgent."

Ten days later they received an answer:

Dear Cousins,

Many thanks for the answer to my ad. Is it possible to start work by the end of August, rather than waiting until the free week in October? We need help as soon as possible.

Sincerely,

Roland Sjöström

On a separate sheet of paper were instructions as to how to get to Björkdalen.

Kajsa wrote back, assuring him that they could get there well before the end of August. Vendela gave her notice, saying that she had to go home immediately to tend her dying mother. Two days later they were on their way.

The first leg of the journey was by boat, through Mälaren with its many islands, then along the Hjälmare Kanal into the less interesting Hjälmaren, finally disembarking in Örebro. From there, since the weather was warm, they walked in order to save what little money they had. On the evening of the third day they reached Björkdalen.

"Remember to call me Stina," Kajsa reminded her companion.

"Not to worry, Stina," Vendela reassured her. She had been practicing ever since they had received Sjöström's letter. During their journey they had also created a joint past as cousins, so as not to give themselves away. So thoroughly had they re-made themselves that they actually became their fictitious selves.

They were met at the door by Sjöström. Kajsa was shocked to see how he had aged in the past seven years. His once black hair had turned completely gray and he walked slightly stooped forward. His eyes were tired.

"Welcome," he greeted, holding out his hand. "I'm Roland Sjöström."

"Stina Jakobsdotter," Kajsa said, shaking his hand, "and this is my cousin, Vendela Jakobsdotter."

"Our fathers are brothers," Vendela added.

"Come in, come in," Sjöström gestured. "This is Raoul," he said, pointing to a youth sitting at the kitchen table, "and this is my right hand, Henning," he added, indicating the sandy-haired man on the other side of the table.

Henning looked at her and smiled, his eyes twinkling, while Raoul continued to stare at the coffee cup in front of him. Kajsa saw that he was still the cowering child she remembered, just older. On the table between father and son stood a half-empty *brännvin* bottle.

"Fetch some coffee cups for our guests," Sjöström barked at him.

Reluctantly, Raoul dragged himself to his feet and staggered across the room, casting a hate-filled look at his father's back. It was then that Kajsa realized he was drunk.

"He's not even 'nough of a man ta hold his liquor," Sjöström muttered, as though reading her thoughts.

Having set the cups on the table none too gently, Raoul dropped heavily onto the bench beside his father.

Sjöström poured the coffee, stopping when Kajsa's cup was half full. *"Kaffe kask?"*[90] he asked, holding up the *brännvin* bottle questioningly.

"No, thanks," she replied.

He repeated the same gesture while pouring Vendela's coffee.

"No thanks, not me either," she answered.

---

90. Coffee laced with *brännvin*.

"Henning he also says no thanks," he informed them, " 'xcept now an' then on special occasions, when he consents ta take a drop. But only a drop. He's a good man. Pity he's not my son, so he could inherit this place when I'm gone. Raoul here's never gonna to be man enough ta take care of it properly. He's too lazy." He paused to pour himself the last of the coffee, carefully so as not to stir up the grounds hiding in the bottom of the pot. Barely filling a quarter of his cup, he topped it off the other three-quarters with *brännvin* before continuing.

"He's from a *tattare*[91] family on his mother's side. His grandmother was a *tattare* who passed herself off as a proper woman an' fooled my next door neighbor into marryin' her. But once a *tattare*, always a *tattare*. It's in the blood. *Tattare* they're lazy, afraid of work, a worthless buncha thugs."

He downed the rest of his *kaffe kask* and wiped his mouth the back of his hand.

"I've been tryin' fer years ta beat some sense into his thick head, but haven't succeeded. He's ta take over the farm when he turns five and twenty, but he don't show the least bit of in'trest in it."

All the while he talked as if Raoul was not present. And, in deed, Raoul was far away in his own world, oblivious to the words he had heard as long as he could remember.

"Stina and Vendela can take the room upstairs," Sjöström said, changing the subject. "My mother was confined ta that room for the las' fifteen years of 'er life. She finally died a few years back. 'Tis a relief not to have 'er up there, what with all her bitchin' and demandin'."

"So she didn't cook and take care of the house," Stina ventured, baiting him for information.

"No. There was a housekeeper who more or less moved in on 'er own after the wife died. Agnes. She was just as overbearin' as my mother. Worse, in fact, 'cause she was not confined to one room. She was everywhere, constantly givin' orders. She wanted me to marry 'er, hopin' ta git 'er hands on my money, but I refused. She was enough to drive man to drink."

It was hard for Kajsa to sit silently while listening to him. Although she agreed that tant Agnes certainly could have driven a man to drink, she was hardly the cause of his drinking habit. But worse was the manner in which he derided Raoul. Although many of her childhood memories in regards to Raoul were hazy due to her young age at the time, they had left a heavy feeling in her that she was unable to articulate, even for

---

91. Tinkers or people who went from place to place doing odd jobs. They were looked upon as even lower than gypsies.

herself. But with Bror's birth and her spontaneous choice of his name, such feelings had become clearer. And now, sitting in the very room where most of her memories were rooted, she began to relive the pain and terror of those years. Not only her own pain and terror, but Raoul's also. How had he managed to survive the last seven years at the hands of his father and tant Agnes? It was no wonder that he drank.

Suddenly Kajsa stood up.

"Can someone show us to our room?" she interrupted. "I'm exhausted from our journey and must lie down for a bit." She had begun to shake uncontrollably.

"Of course," Sjöström slurred. But rather than attempting to stand up, he pointed to the door on the far side of the room. "The stairs're in the hall, through th' door there."

"I can show our guests up to their room," Henning offered, getting to his feet.

"Guests!" Sjöström snorted. "They's come here ta work!"

Ignoring him, Henning led the way into the front hall and up the stairs to Mor Dagmar's old room.

"Pay him no mind," he told them. "He drinks too much sometimes."

"Does he become violent?" Stina asked.

"No. I've heard that he used to become violent when his wife was alive. Not toward her, but towards the children when they were small. Raoul and his wife's daughter Kajsa."

"His wife's daughter?" Kajsa asked innocently.

"Yes. I don't know the whole story, but apparently at one time there was talk that Kajsa was not his child. But no one seems to know whether she was his wife's child or someone else's, or whether it was just a rumor. He is very private and rarely talks about his past. Personally, I think he is carrying a great burden that has aged him and pulled him into the bottle. I've worked for him for seven years, yet I cannot say that I really know the man."

"But the way he talks about his son in front of him," Kajsa probed.

"It's ghastly!" Henning replied. "The boy is drunk most of the time, and quite honestly, I can understand him. But nothing I say to either one of them does any good. They seem to have long ago established a pattern of behavior between them that neither can break. Raoul is too young and lethargic to save himself, no matter how much I try to back him. The best I have been able to do is to stand between them when necessary, to see that things don't get out of control. But I find it difficult at times. Excuse me for talking this way about my employer, but I thought it best to warn Björkdalen's new maids."

"I am glad that Henning took it upon himself to explain the situation to us," Stina told him.

"I hope that I have not frightened thee away," he told her. "I have been looking forward to some womenly atmosphere around here at last."

"Not to worry," Stina told him, but Kajsa was not at all sure that she could manage the situation into which she had so blithely gotten herself.

On the one hand, she wished she could be honest and reveal herself to Henning; on the other hand, she wished he would take his leave of them quickly, before she broke down.

"I hope our new maids are good cooks," he added cheerfully. "I'm a pretty rotten cook, although I dare say I'm a good sight better than Sjöström, who can barely stir up a pot of porridge."

They all laughed and he disappeared down the stairs.

"Oh, Vendela, I don't think I can stand being here," Kajsa cried once she heard Henning close the hall door downstairs. "I don't know what I expected. I never really considered the situation between Raoul and my father. I certainly didn't expect to have become so bad...."

Vendela put her arms around her comfortingly, as Signe used to do when she was upset.

"I have a feeling that Henning is right," she said, "that what is between Raoul and his father has become something neither of them can change. But now that we are here, let us see how things go. We've not signed a contract, so we're free to leave when we want to."

Without Vendela, Kajsa could never have been able to survive in her childhood surroundings, with the endless stream of memories constantly confronting her. Many of them concerned her father's treatment of Raoul. She longed to take him aside, reveal herself, and talk openly with him, but she saw it was not possible. He was not the Raoul she had known as a child. He had become a stranger to her, but not simply because of the seven years they had not shared. He was closed to her and to everyone around him, like an empty shell. There was no light in his eyes. He spoke mechanically, as briefly as possible, and only when spoken to. Kajsa realized that their shared childhood must be as hazy for him as for her. Yet she had been lucky enough to escape from Björkdalen and its daily reminders, whereas he had been forced to remain in that world. It was obvious that the events of those years were deeply engraved in his character.

Although she went out of her way to be kind to him, she could see that nothing mattered to Raoul. Except for alcohol. She was thankful to Henning for standing between father and son, taking advantage of Sjöström's dependence on him to defend Raoul against his cruelty as much as possible. His presence at least made Raoul's life bearable.

Henning's kindness toward her brother was not the only thing that endeared him to her. He treated both her and Vendela with respect, never pawing at them or making inappropriate remarks, as was the male custom. He seemed older and more responsible than his six and twenty years. Often he accompanied them to local dances or other young people's events, watching out for them from a distance. He never took even "a drop" when they were with him. Without realizing it, he helped heal the wounds both Kajsa and Vendela had suffered at the hands of other men.

Time passed quickly at Björkdalen. There was much to be done and Stina and Vendela worked well together. They had become more like sisters than the cousins they pretended to be. With time a deep friendship grew between them. They had no secrets from each other and, unlike other women, considered no subject to be taboo. Their closeness sometimes puzzled them, causing them to wonder if they loved each other as men and women did. Even such a possibility was not taboo to them, although they concluded that their closeness was more likely due to the that fact that, without family, they only had each other. Rather than dwell on why, they simply reveled in their feelings for each other when out of sight of prying eyes.

But they need not have wondered.

The spring following their arrival to Björkdalen Vendela was loaned out to a neighboring farm to help with the big spring laundrying. Rather than walking back and forth, she had been asked to stay the two nights between the washing days. When she finally returned on the evening of the third day Kajsa immediately saw that she had changed.

"What has happened to Vendela?" she asked. "She is lit up like a lantern."

Vendela's light immediately dimmed.

"I don't know what to say," she answered.

"Whatever it is, Vendela can say it to me."

Vendela was silent.

For the first time, a little door had closed between them, scaring Kajsa.

"Please tell me," she persisted.

Vendela sat down on the edge of the bed and took Kajsa's hand.

"Herr and fru Asklund have a son..." she began.

"Does Vendela mean Johan, that good looking young man we saw in church?"

"Yes," Vendela admitted, looking down as if she had committed a sin.

"So Vendela's sweet on him!" she exclaimed, laughing.

Vendela nodded.

"There's nothing terrible about that. Oh, I'm so happy for her!" she exclaimed, clapping her hands.

Vendela looked up at her, surprised.

"I thought Stina might be hurt," she admitted.

"Why? Of course Vendela shall have a beau. And one day a husband. We'll still be friends. Friends and husbands are not the same."

"Does Stina mean that? I still want to be friends. And one day I hope she meets a man."

"As I have said many a time, I'm not going to get married. But that has nothing to do with Vendela. If our friendship were what we have sometimes feared, I would not be happy for thee. But I only feel joy in my heart."

On Midsummer's Eve Vendela and her Johan became engaged and after the festivities she followed him home, leaving Kajsa to walk home on her own. But no sooner had she started down the road than Henning caught up with her. He surprised her by taking her hand.

"Now I have Stina all to myself," he remarked.

"What does Henning mean?" she wondered.

"I mean that I have waited for this moment ever since Stina and Vendela came to Björkdalen. I felt it was unfair to come between two such close friends, chosing one and rejecting the other. Besides, I was in no hurry. I wanted to get to know Stina first, before jumping into anything."

Kajsa laughed.

"Me thinks perhaps it is time for me to be honest," she told him. "Henning does not know me at all."

"What does Stina mean?"

"To begin with, my name is not Stina Jakobsdotter and Vendela and I are not related in any way. My real name is Kajsa Sjöström. Roland Sjöström is my father and Raoul is my brother. Björkdalen was my home until I was eight."

Henning stopped short, pulling her around to face him.

"What is Stina saying!" he exclaimed.

"Just that. Vendela and I met in Stockholm. We both wanted to get out of the city. So when I saw Sjöström's ad seeking two maids, we decided to apply. But because I did not want to risk our chances by letting my father recognize me, I decided to use my other name and Vendela's last name. He never liked me when I was a child. Me thinks he likes me better now, when he doesn't know I am his daughter."

"Is Stina telling me that she isn't Stina, that she is Kajsa? I can't believe what I am hearing! Be so kind as to start from the beginning and tell me all that again."

"It's true what I've just said. But I'm the same person, regardless of my name and background."

Henning was silent a long while, then a smile crept over his face. He squeezed her hand gently.

"I guess it doesn't matter whether thou art Stina or Kajsa," he said, "The truth be known, I just want to make thee my wife." He paused. "That is, if she will have me for her husband," he added.

"Henning must hear all of my story first. He may want to change his mind," she warned.

"I shan't change my mind. I have been watching thee for almost a year now and my feelings just grow stronger as time goes by."

Henning was as good as his word. Nothing in her past changed his feelings for her. Not even Bror's existence.

"Hopefully we can find him," was his reply when she confessed to his existence.

It was Kajsa who changed her mind. She forgot her vow never to get married and said yes to Henning.

While Midsummer 1885 was a time of joy and hope for four young people, it was a time of tragedy—or perhaps release—for another. As was common amongst youths on Midsummer's Eve, Raoul and a friend drank themselves into a stupor. Towards dawn they decided to row out in the lake behind Björkdalen to watch the sun come up. When Raoul didn't appear for breakfast, Henning went to look for him. He found Raoul's friend passed out in the bottom of the row boat and Raoul's lifeless body floating face down nearby.

Kajsa went to pieces when she saw Henning carrying her brother up from the lake. Sjöström said nothing. He simply locked himself in the best room, where he remained for the better part of two days.

The news of Raoul's death spread quickly, thanks to his friend who told everyone he met that Raoul had jumped out of the boat to take a swim. Upon hearing the news, Vendela hurried to Björkdalen to comfort Kajsa, knowing how much she had cared about her brother.

When Sjöström finally emerged from his isolation, he was an old and broken man. He was so closed within himself that it was impossible to surmise his feelings. Had he seen the part he had played in Raoul's life? Or did he still condemn him for failing to become a man? Had he gone so far as to see himself and how he treated other people? Or was he still the man he had always been? Questions, but no answers. For months afterwards Roland Sjöström spoke not a word.

When at last he did speak, he voiced but one concern:

"I must find my daughter ta let her know that she'll inherit Björkdalen. I shall make a new will, stating that, should she not be found within a year after my death, everything I own shall go to Henning, for he has served both me and Björkdalen well."

Kajsa and Henning looked at each other. Finally Kajsa spoke.

"I have a confession to make. Father needn't try to find his daughter, for she is right here in front of him."

Sjöström suddenly awoke from his apathy.

"Kajsa?" he said hesitantly.

"Yes, Kajsa Sjöström. If Father wishes proof of my identity, I can tell him things about my childhood that only he and I know."

A horrified look crossed Sjöström's face.

"No, no, I don't need reminding!" he cried, shuddering.

No one uttered a word for a long while. Sjöström continued staring at Kajsa, his eyes big with fear.

"Sjöström needn't worry about the future of Björkdalen," Henning said finally. "Kajsa has agreed to be my wife, so it will be in good hands, both inside and out."

But his words went unheard for the moment, for Roland Sjöström had passed into another world from which he would never fully return. Although Sjöström's body was partially recovered, allowing him to live on, bedridden, for another year, his spirit was dead. What had taken place within him when Raoul died continued to remain within him, as did the effect of Kajsa's return. Had the combination of the two events suddenly brought to light the memories that all three of them had shared? Perhaps. It was impossible to know. His only interest in life seemed to be watching Kajsa's stomach grow larger and being able to address Henning as Son. Like all family members who had grown old at Björkdalen, he now lived in the upstairs room that his mother had occupied during her last years. Kajsa cared for him as he grew weaker, yet not simply out of duty. She felt an ambiguous sense of compassion for this man who had treated others so cruelly. She couldn't help seeing him as a newborn baby, innocent. What had gone wrong? It was clear that he was not at peace with himself nor with God.

By the time Kajsa gave birth to a boy-child, he was barely able to sit up in bed. The day after the birth, Henning placed the child in his arms. Sjöström smiled.

"What name shall we give him?" Kajsa asked her father.

He thought for a minute before answering.

"Can we name him after *Farfar*[92] Jonas? He didn't have a very happy life an' it would be nice to give his soul a new chance, as well as a kind father this time."

Kajsa had never heard of *Farfar* Jonas, for her father had seldom spoken of his family, and never to her, but she was moved by his words and the thought behind his choice.

"A fine name," Henning agreed.

"Welcome, Jonas," she said, reaching over and taking his little hand as he lay in Sjöström's arms. "I hope Father will tell us about *Farfar* Jonas sometime. I know nothing about him."

"Sometime," he said, closing his eyes while still gently hugging Jonas. Kajsa had never seen him look so peaceful.

That night Roland Sjöström died in his sleep. Whether he died in peace or filled with regret will never be known. Nor would they ever hear *Farfar* Jonas's story.

---

92. Father's father or a grandfather.

Kajsa

Björkdalen 1952

Flecks of sunlight danced in and out from between the rolls of gray stratocumulus clouds that were attempting to cover the sky. As so many times during the past two years, I walked the short distance to Björkdalen from the old fieldhand's cottage that had become my home. Kajsa was at the wood stove making coffee when I arrived, having already set the kitchen table with cups and saucers and a plate of cinnamon buns still warm from the oven. I laid my copy of our last conversation, along with a red pencil, beside her place as usual. She poured the coffee, then picked up the papers and, after a few quick corrections, returned them to me and took a bun. I waited for her comments. The purpose of our *kafferep* [93] was three-fold: to help me learn Swedish, to help Kajsa learn English, and most of all, to put the story of her life down on paper. This had become our weekly ritual, its only variation being whether we sat in the kitchen or out in the yard.

"I think we have come to the stopping point," she said simply, setting down her cup.

"Stopping point?" I asked, surprised.

"Yes. My life with Henning holds no secrets, but there is no one who knows the story of my childhood. That is why I wanted to tell about it."

"But why stop here, just when your life made a significant change for the better?"

She smiled and I could see she was counting something on her fingers.

"We can sum up the rest of my life in six words."

I looked at her, puzzled.

"Six words?"

She smiled, her eyes shining. I never ceased to be amazed at how much she looked like her mother, my great grandmother Elsa-Carolina.

"And they lived happily ever after," she said.

We both laughed.

"I admit that it sounds like a fairytale, but for me, it was like that. I could not have asked for more."

"But why not tell about it?"

"How? It is too hard to put into words without it sounding overly sweet. And it was too ordinary. We did the things everyone did, things that were hardly exciting. What made it special was the connection between

---

93. Coffee klatsch.

us. Everything is wonderful when experienced by two people who are on the same cloud. But there are no words for that feeling. Besides, people are not interested in the ordinary things in someone else's life. They want to hear about the unusual things, even if they are terrible. And I think that, in many ways, it is the negative things that form us into the people we become."

"Perhaps," I said. "But you were only 17 at this point. Your life had barely begun."

"But it was the turning point in my life. After Sjöström died, it was as if my past life died also," she continued. "There was little left to remind me of my first fifteen years. Even at the time of his death, almost everyone who had played an important part in my life was already gone, those I loved as well as those I feared. It seems strange that there were so many. But in those days, Death was always standing in the corner waiting to collect his next victim, be it from childbed fever, or an illness for which a cure was yet to be found, or one of the numerous accidents that could befall one. Not to mention starvation. Or even the loss of the will to live. Sadly, he even took Jonas's little sister Sara before she was a year old. Finally there were only two people who were connected to the past: Siri and Vendela. Yet neither of them were actually part of my past; they were simply bridges between my old and new lives.

"It's as if I have lived in two different worlds. As I was growing up, our world was small and quite isolated: home, family, the village. We were mostly self-sufficient and self-contained, largely concerned with our own private world, rather than with the world beyond us. Then things began to change. We became part of the larger world. We needed to earn money to buy the things we once had produced ourselves. And even though we were not directly involved in The Great War, like everyone else, we were forced into the joint struggle to survive its side effects. After that came the various fights for social change, particularly women's rights, which touched everyone, followed by the horror of Hitler's war. Never again would we live in an isolated world. Each person's personal story became but a tiny part in the much larger universal story that one can read about in history books.

"Marrying Henning gave my life a sense of security. At last I belonged somewhere, and to someone I could trust, who would not abandon me. Of course, he eventually abandoned me by dying, but by then we had had nearly sixty years together. Henning was a very special person, and I don't say that because he was my husband. I was honored that he chose me, because he could have had any girl he wanted. He was one of those

211

rare people whom everyone liked and respected, someone who was always there, ready to listen and help when needed, someone who was kind and generous and could be relied upon. And honest to the core. Not only that; he was fun and funny. Just being with him was a joy. I fell in love with him the first time we met, when he smiled at me as Sjöström introduced us. But I never in my wildest imagination dreamed he would one day become my husband." She paused and looked down, twisting her gold wedding band. "There are no words for how much I miss him."

It was clear that talking about Henning brought up emotions that, although happy, were edged with sorrow and longing. She shrugged, her voice becoming thick.

"Talking about our life together still makes me choke up, even after almost ten years. I suppose there are some things one never gets used to."

She got to her feet and slid the coffee pot over onto the hottest part of the wood stove.

"And I miss Vendela almost as much as I miss Henning, although in a different way. As a man, Henning could never fill the part of my life that Vendela filled. Men and women have one kind of closeness and two women have another kind. Equal but different. Vendela and I spent a lot of time together, helping each other with whatever needed to be done, for farm work was never a solitary occupation. And we talked about everything under the sun. The tragedy in Vendela's life was that she was never able to have more children. She always felt that such was the price she paid for letting the one child she did have be murdered. Yet her life was not without children. She and Johan were godparents to both Jonas and Lotti and played a big part in their lives.

"After I came to Björkdalen my life calmed down and the past seemed very unreal and far away, to the point where I sometimes wondered if those first fifteen years had actually existed. But now and then I got a reminder."

She got up and disappeared into another room, returning with a shoe box. Without needing to hunt through it, she pulled out a letter and handed it to me. I unfolded it curiously and began to read:

Stockholm, 5 May 1890

My Dear Kajsa,

Hopefully I have found Kajsa at last, thanks to my beloved brother Hjalmar. After the fire that destroyed our home, we were housed in the old Cholera Hospital that was used for such emergencies. From there we were moved to various temporary places, to the point where I hardly knew where I was living from day to day. Finally, we found something permanent. Nothing special, but at least it has a roof and we can call it home.

At the end of that August, after Kajsa had left the Children's Home, I went there seeking information about Bror, as well as thy whereabouts. They certainly live up to their reputation of protecting people's identities! I told them that we had agreed that I would take Kajsa's baby as a foster child (excuse me for taking such liberty, but I was convinced that she would not mind). But they said they didn't know of any Kajsa or Bror, that they used numbers instead of names. Once again I drew on my brother and his power as a priest and, after a long drawn-out process, we finally succeeded in finding Bror and becoming his foster parents. But they said they did not know what happened to his mother. Not even Hjalmar was able to find Kajsa Sjöström, in spite of all of his connections. Of course he tried Björkdalen, but only found two maids working there, Stina and Vendela Jakobsdotter. Finally we gave up our search, thankful to have Bror, at least. Then not long ago, quite by chance, Hjalmar came across Kajsa Sjöström and Henning Lindblom and their two children registered at Björkdalen. Kajsa can imagine my joy!

Now that I have found Kajsa at last, I can report that Little Bror is now six years old and in good health. He is out-going, curious and quick to learn, obedient, and already helpful. However, I am fully aware of the fact that we are only borrowing him and that Kajsa has the right to take him, should she wish to do so.

Enclosed is a photo taken on his sixth birthday.
Fond greetings from Siri and Gustaf

Fishing the photo out of the envelope, Kajsa found herself staring at a bright-eyed little boy with blond curly hair, dressed in short pants, a middy blouse, and high-topped leather boots, holding a little wooden horse.

"He's beautiful!" I said, "even if one doesn't use such a word to describe boys. You must have been overjoyed to get her letter."

"You simply can't imagine! I wrote back, saying that I was so happy that they had Bror and that I would never take him from them. I could never have done that to Siri and Gustaf. Never. No matter how much I wanted him. I knew they would have given him to me, but there was something between the lines of her letter. At the time I couldn't put my finger on it, but I later learned that they were unable to have more children after losing the first one. However, I had one request: that when he was old enough to understand, he must be told the truth and that we should meet. As you well remember, I was 79 when I met my mother for the first time, here in this very kitchen, and discovered that Sjöströms were not my real parents. I had always suspected that I didn't belong to them, but I'd never had any proof. My life, as well as my relationship with them, would have made much more sense to me had I known. I didn't want Bror to go through life with the same unanswered question lurking in the back of his mind, for sooner or later something would happen to make him suspect that they were not his real parents. I am eternally thankful that they took him. They loved him as their own and were wonderful parents."

"Did you ever meet him?"

"Oh, yes, of course."

"How did it feel to see him for the first time?"

A smile crossed her face, removing at least 20 years.

"Siri and I wrote to each other often. She loved writing about Bror and of course I loved reading about him. The more I got to know about him, the more I longed to see him. But it was not possible to just pack a bag and go to Stockholm. Not only did we have the farm to take care of, but by then we also had two small children. But the autumn before he turned eight, Henning, Vendela, and Johan gave me a wonderful gift. At the end of October, when the harvest was finished and life had slowed down to wait for winter, they informed me that it was time for me to take the traditional free week and go to visit Siri and Gustaf and meet Bror. Jonas and Lotti were six and two at the time. They had spent so much time with Vendela and Johan that their farm had become a second home for them. Consequently, they had nothing against staying with them while I was away. The only person who was not jumping for joy over my departure was Henning. He never said a word, but I could read his feelings. However, the whole plan had been his idea in the first place and it was he who had saved the money to pay for my journey, so I knew he was prepared to accept the consequences.

"I must admit to having been nervous about the meeting. I don't know why, for Bror had only been told that I was an old friend coming to visit his mother. Once in Stockholm, I stood outside their door for a long time, trying to get up my courage to knock. When I finally did, I could hear small feet running in my direction. The door was pulled open and suddenly there he stood! The first thing I saw was the tiny star-shaped birthmark above his left eyebrow.

"Mamma, 'tis *Tant* Kajsa!" Bror called over his shoulder.

"I am Bror." he said, turning back to Kajsa and offering his hand.

"And I am *Tant* Kajsa," she said, shaking hands with him. "I am so pleased to meet Bror. Mamma Siri has told me so much about thee."

Siri came up behind him. In the nearly eight years since Kajsa had seen her she seemed to have grown younger.

"Come in, my dear Kajsa!" she exclaimed. "At last!"

Immediately they began talking on top of each other. Bror's face fell.

When their conversation finally slowed down, Siri looked around. Bror was nowhere in sight.

"Bror?" she called. "Where has my Bror gone?" She put her head into to the little alcove that served as his room. "Oh, what is he doing in here?"

There was a faint sniffing sound.

"I thought *Tant* Kajsa was coming to visit me, too," he said.

Kajsa jumped to her feet.

"I am so sorry, Bror. I have come to visit thee, also! I just forgot my manners when I met Mamma Siri, because I have not seen her since before Bror was born. Mothers can be very silly and selfish at times."

"Is *Tant* Kajsa a mother?" he asked, surprised. When Siri had told him that a friend of hers was coming to visit, he had never considered that she might belong to other people besides his mother.

"Oh yes. I have two children, Jonas, who is six, and Lotti, who is two," she said, sitting down beside him on the edge of his bed.

"Where are they?"

"They stayed at home with their father and their godparents, *Tant* Vendela and *Farbror* Johan."

"Where do they live?" he wondered.

"Jonas and Lotti live with their father and me on a farm and Vendela and Johan live on another farm nearby. 'Tis quite far from Stockholm."

"How did *Tant* Kajsa get here?"

"First I traveled with a horse and wagon, then a train, and finally on a boat. It took two whole days."

His eyes grew bigger and bigger with each new means of transportation. "Was it exciting?"

"Quite!"

"What's a farm like?" he continued, in a hurry to hear more.

"Well, it's hard to explain in a simple way. We have some cows and pigs and sheep and chickens, as well as big horses that can pull wagons and farm machines." She waited to see if he could follow her.

"What does one do on a farm?"

"We grow food for ourselves and for our animals. Bror must come and visit us and see for himself."

"I'd like that," he said. "Mamma, can we go and visit *Tant* Kajsa's farm?"

"If she invites us," Siri said, winking at Kajsa over his head.

"Oh, do invite us!" he declared.

"Bror, remember your manners. One must not invite oneself."

"I don't think *Tant* Kajsa minds," he said. "She seems like family. I'd like to meet *Tant* Kajsa's children," Bror continued. "Maybe they could be my cousins. Everyone has cousins except for me."

"I am sure they would like to be your cousins," Kajsa assured him. "The only cousins they have live in America and we've never even met them."

"I'm glad I don't have brothers and sisters," he continued after some thought. "It's nice not to have to share my mother and father with anyone. If I had a brother maybe he wouldn't be nice to me, 'specially if he was older. My friend Tor has a brother who hits him all the time. They have to share the same bed and his brother kicks him in the back at night. Tor can't do anything about it because they are in the same family. And besides, there is no room for him to have his own bed. When he is older he is going to run away and go to sea. Cousins are better. One doesn't live with them. They just visit and if someone's not nice, it's just to go home."

Where Bror's pragmaticism came from was a mystery, but even as a child it served him well.

During the week that Kajsa was in Stockholm Bror showed her around eagerly, always making sure that Siri came along. Hand in hand between them, he acted as guide through the neighborhood, introducing them to his world. That the area where they now lived was poor beyond anything Kajsa had ever seen, consisting of wooden shack-like houses twisted with age, some barely standing, did not phase him. It was his home, what he knew, and it never occurred to him to apologize for it. To Siri's surprise, many people they passed greeted him by name. She knew that he earned a few coins doing small jobs for others in his free time, but she had never imagined the scope of his contacts.

At first Kajsa had had regrets about letting her son grow up in such surroundings. But she soon saw that he possessed a certain strength of character and compassion that put him at ease in every situation. How much of it had to do with Siri and Gustaf and how much of it was his natural temperament, was impossible to know. But certainly he was not suffering from his surroundings.

Before leaving, Kajsa invited him to come to Björkdalen the following summer.

"Then you can get to know your new cousins."

"I would like that very much, but I don't think I can. I have a lot of work to do in the summer," he answered a little sadly.

"What sort of work?"

"Well, I collect things that I can sell to junk dealers and I run errands for shopkeepers," he told her. "To do my part."

"Yes," Siri told her later, "he is proud to be able to help out, although we have not encouraged it. It makes him feel grown up, I think."

"But how much money can he make selling junk?" Kajsa wondered.

"It depends," Siri said. "One summer he earned enough to pay for a month's worth of fire wood; another year it was just enough for a bit of meat now and then. What is important to him is doing his part."

What she omitted telling Kajsa was that, although Gustaf worked long hours in the harbor, like most working class men, his pay was barely enough to survive on, let alone support a wife and child. Without Siri's sewing and other sporadic jobs, they would have been reduced to abject poverty. Sensing this, Bror had taken it upon himself to do his share.

When she returned home, Kajsa told Henning of Bror's reaction to her invitation to visit. He immediately wrote a letter addressed directly to him:

Dear Bror,

As the owner of Björkdalen Gård, I need young farm hands to help with the many outdoor jobs that must be done during the summer. I have already employed Bror's cousin Jonas and I wonder if Bror would be willing to join him. The pay is guaranteed (even if it rains), as well as three meals a day and a bed to sleep in. Jonas is looking forward to meeting his cousin Bror.

Sincerely,

Farbror Henning Lindblom

Bror was elated! He wrote back all by himself:

Dear Farbror Lindblom,

   I would like to work on Farbror's farm this summer. I can work hard and I shall not disappoint Farbror Lindblom. I am looking forward to meeting thee and my cousins. And Tant Kajsa too.

Sincerely,

Bror

When June came Bror could hardly contain his excitement. Several days before he was due to leave he took out his old clothes and looked at them, wishing he had something better to take with him. They were all right for collecting junk; everyone who hauled around old metal soon had their clothes torn to shreds and covered with oil and rust stains. But he suspected that farm work was dirty in a cleaner way. Siri patched things as best she could, but even her fine stitching failed to transform them. Having no alternative, he thanked her and stuffed them into a satchel. As for his boots, he had but one pair. Not only could he hardly get his feet into them, but they were badly in need of repair.

At last the long-awaited day arrived. Rising earlier than usual, he ate a hurried breakfast of fried herring and left-over potatoes, then donned his school clothes. Together he and Siri walked down to where the Örebro boat stood waiting, puffing a stream of black smoke into the stillness of the morning air. Because he was to be accompanied by an older couple whom the captain deemed worthy of looking after him, the journey cost nothing. Upon arrival in Örebro he would be met by Henning and Jonas, whereafter they would continue to Björkdalen by horse and wagon. He had never spent a night away from his parents, let alone ridden on a boat, and suddenly he was about to step beyond the bounds of his familiar world. He had no idea of what to expect. Yet he experienced no sense of apprehension; only the excitement of adventure.

Henning and Jonas were waiting on the quay when the boat docked. He walked straight toward them and held out his hand.

"I'm Bror," he said.

"I'm *Farbror* Henning and this is Jonas."

They shook hands.

Jonas and Bror looked each other up and down, as boys are wont to do. Although he was the younger of the two, Jonas was slightly bigger and his boots were newer. That he was bigger didn't matter; it was his boots. Envy was new to Bror. But the feeling passed quickly, lost in the chaos of so much else that was new to him. Before he could take it all in, Henning gave him a helping hand up onto the wagon, placing him between himself and Jonas, and they set off.

The journey was long, the narrow roads bumpy, and the groaning of the wagon made conversation nearly impossible. Bror was exhausted by the time they stopped at a village inn for the night. He barely ate of the cheese and smoked sausage that Henning placed in front of him before collapsing into the bed he was to share with Jonas. It had been a long day, filled to overflowing with wonders he had never imagined existed beyond the boundaries of his Stockholm neighborhood.

Bror fit into the life at Björkdalen as though he had always been a part of it. Although Lotti was too young to join them, he and Jonas became fast friends, both working and playing together. Henning gave them simple jobs to carry out: feeding the pigs and chickens, collecting eggs, bringing in firewood, hoeing potatoes, herding the sheep when they were in the outer pasture, tramping on the hay to pack it down as it was loaded onto the wagon. To his relief, Bror saw that Jonas always went barefoot, no matter what the job, and thus he gladly cast aside his own boots. As for his ragged clothes, in the face of all that was new and exciting, they no longer mattered.

Having Bror in her life gave Kajsa a sense of joy and fulfillment. The guilt of abandonment she had carried since his birth was lifted from her, for she realized that it had also been a gift. Otherwise he would not have had Siri and Gustaf. Their relationship to him was pure, unmarred by the trauma Hans Ängmark had perpetrated against both her and Bror. Although she rarely thought about it, the pain of Bror's creation had remained a part of her connection to him, like a tiny thorn from which she was never free. Now at last she began to see him not as hers, but simply as a person she cared about.

Because Jonas and Bror got along so well together, they were also able to share Kajsa and Henning equally between them. Likewise, Kajsa and Henning treated both of them them equally, never favoring one over the other. By the end of the summer it was agreed all around that Bror would return to Björkdalen as soon as school let out the following June.

The day before he left, Kajsa approached him on a subject she hoped would not hurt his pride.

"It occurred to me that Jonas has some clothes that he has outgrown," she told him, indicating a jacket, several shirts and pairs of britches, as well as a pair of boots, that she had taken from a chest. "I wonder if Bror would like to have them. It's a pity to cut them up for rag rugs."

His face betrayed his longing when he saw them. Especially for the boots. He looked at her questioningly.

"Does *Tant* Kajsa really wish to give them away?"

"Yes. Jonas can't wear any of them anymore and Lotti wears girls' clothes. They are just taking up space in the chest. One usually passes such things on to one's cousins."

"I would like that very much," he said, running his finger over the toe of one of the boots. Compared to his own they were almost like new.

"It looks as though Bror will be needing a bigger satchel," she remarked, gathering together the clothes.

"I can wear the boots," he said. "And maybe we could throw away my old work clothes. I don't think I'll be needing them."

Kajsa agreed with a laugh.

The day he was to leave he once again donned his school clothes, along with his new boots. Henning presented each of the boys with a small leather pouch containing their earnings for the summer. Before he had a chance to open his, Kajsa pinned it to the inside of his britches pocket.

"Don't open it until you are safely at home," she told him. "No one must know that he has any money with him. One's fellow travelers are not always as honest as they pretend to be."

The first thing he did when he reached home was to pull out the pouch and empty it onto the kitchen table. To his surprise, it contained more than twice as much as he had earned during his best summer in Stockholm. Also included was a short note:

"Many thanks for a job well done! I look forward to employing thee next summer. Henning."

And so it was that Bror came to spend his summers at Björkdalen.

Kajsa picked up the photo of six year old Bror, slipped it into the envelope with Siri's letter, and returned it to the shoe box.

"It was so long ago," she sighed, "yet at the same time it feels as though it was just yesterday. So much happened during those years. The summer he was twelve it was decided that he was old enough to be told about his background. I can tell you, I lost sleep worrying about how he would react to the fact that, rather than growing up in relatively well-off means as had Jonas, we had let him live in a working class home where poverty was constantly waiting just outside the door. At the same time, he was proud of the fact that, like other working class children his age, he was able to contribute to the family financially. He had a sense of responsibility that Jonas lacked.

"That spring Gustaf had been laid off in the harbor and thus I suggested that he and Siri follow Bror to Björkdalen for the summer. Although Henning had never met them, he immediately offered Gustaf a job. Summer was the busiest time of year and extra help was always needed, especially during haying. It was a nervous time, for only God had control over the weather. Consequently, everyone kept one eye on the sky, unable to relax until the last forkful was safely in. But even then I could not relax, for the thought of telling Bror the truth hung over my head. I had no idea how he would take it.

As usual, after church Kajsa and Henning, Siri and Gustaf, and Bror and Jonas gathered for Sunday dinner. Only six year old Lotti was missing, having stayed to eat with Vendela and Johan after inspecting their newborn kittens. Unable to finish eating, Kajsa set fork down on her plate with a little clink.

"Before everyone leaves the table, I have something to say," she began.

But before she could continue, she realized that the words that she had rehearsed her mind hundreds of times had suddenly disappeared, leaving her staring at her plate. Finally Siri came to her rescue.

"Perhaps it's better that I say it," she said, clearing her throat. "There is something that Bror should know, now that he's almost an adult."

He looked at her curiously.

"What's that, Mamma?" he asked.

"I am not Bror's real mother," she said simply.

"What does Mamma mean?" he asked, confused.

"I mean that sometimes a woman has a baby but is not able to take care of it. So the baby is raised by a foster mother. I'm Bror's foster mother."

"Because the baby has no father?"

"Well, yes. It is difficult for a mother to take care of a baby alone, when there is no father."

"Then who is my real mother?" he asked, his gaze turning slowly towards Kajsa.

She couldn't hold back a smile.

"Is it *Tant* Kajsa?" he declared, jumping up from his chair. "I have two mothers!" he shouted, hugging Siri and then Kajsa. "And I have two fathers! Papa Gustaf and *Farbror* Henning! Oh, that's much better than cousins!"

"No cousins, Bror, but a half brother and a half sister," Kajsa told him.

Jonas had sat silently all the while, dumbfounded.

"Is Bror my brother?" he asked when Bror had quieted down.

"Half brother," Kajsa told him. "Jonas and Lotti are my children with Papa Henning and Bror is also my child, but with a different father."

"Who is he?" Bror wanted to know.

"A young man named Hans Ängmark."

"What happened to him?"

"I don't know. When he found out I was going to have a baby he disappeared. Me thinks he went to America."

"I'm glad he disappeared. Otherwise I wouldn't have Mamma Siri and Papa Gustaf."

"I'm glad, too," Siri said tearfully.

"Me, too," Kajsa added. "Otherwise I wouldn't have Henning."

But clearly Bror was happiest of them all. Thereafter he never failed to refer to that day as the happiest day of his life.

Kajsa brushed a few crumbs on the table into her hand and dumped them into her empty coffee cup.

"At the end of the summer Henning offered Gustaf a permanent job at Björkdalen and he and Siri started a new life here with us. Bror lived with them in the little farmhand's cottage where you are living and we all worked together. Those were the happiest years of my life, surrounded by Henning, Vendela and Johan, Siri and Gustaf, and the three children. In spite of my childhood years, I must say that I've had a wonderful life, for which I am deeply thankful. However, as the youngest in my generation, I have had to watch the rest of them take their leave one after the other. Even Jonas and Bror, although they have only gone to America. But none of them have really left. I can feel their presence when I am alone here and often they come to me in my dreams, which is a great comfort. And then there was that unbelievable summer that I got to know my mother and learned about my background. Those few short months

222

tied a ribbon around the package that is my life. I want for nothing more."

Two days later, when Kajsa and I were drinking *elva kaffe* out of habit, Katja appeared. For the past year she had been teaching in a town two hours away and we hadn't seen much of each other.

"Mormor," she burst out excitedly, "I just came to say that the telling of your life story has not been in vain. Come winter shall present you with a great grandchild to pass it on to."

Kajsa's face lit up like the sun.

"Just when I thought my life was already complete!" Kajsa remarked with her big Elsa-Carolina smile.

BIBLIOGRAPHY

Bondeson, Lars, *Seder och bruk vid livets slut,* Verbum, 1987.

Dahlberg, Hans, *Vårt 1800-tal,* Bonniers förlag, Stockholm, 2003.

Ejdestam, Julius, *De fattigas Sverige,* Rabén & Sjögren, Stockholm, 1969.

Fredlund, Jane, *Stor Boken om Livet Förr,* ICA förlaget, Västerås, 1981.

Fredlund, Jane, *Så Levde Vi,* ICA förlaget, Västerås, 1971.

Frykman, Jonas, *Den kultiverade människan, Hel och ren,* Liber, Malmö, 1979.

Frykman, Jonas, *Horan i bondesamhället,* Lund, 1977.

Geijerstam, Gustaf, Fattigt folk, Wilhelm Bille, Stockholm, 1884.

Gosselin, R.E., Smith, Hodge, *Clinical Toxicology or Commercial Products,* Williams & Wilkins, Baltimore, 1984.

Grimberg, Carl, *Svenska Folkets Underbara Öden,* volume IX, 1844–1907, 1913.

Hansson, Hans, *Utflykter i den svenska kulturhistorien.*

Hansson, Ingrid, Spinnhuset vid svingeln, Göteborgs historia, online.

Högberg, Ulf, *Svagärens barn,* LiberFörlag, Stockholm, 1983.

Höjeberg, Pia, *Trollmor, sägner om moderskap,* Gidlunds, 1985.

Jakobsson, Svante & Sten W., *Orons och förtviflans gerningar,* Allmänna Förlaget, Stockholm, 1987.

Johansson, Levi, *Om renlighetsförhållande i Frostviken,* 1927, *Svenska landsmål and svenskt folkliv,* Jämtland.

Lennartsson, Rebecka, *Malaria urbana,* Brutus Östlings Bokförlag, Stockholm, 2001.

Levander, Lars, *Fattigfolk and Tiggare,* Gidlunds Förlag, 1934.

Levander, Lars, *Landsväg, Krog & Marknad,* Gidlunds Förlag,1935.

Lindström, Ulla, *Med barnets väl för ögonen,* I samhällets utkant, Tidens Förlag, 1989.

Ljung, Olof, *Ingevaldssläkten,* two volumes, Mellerud, 1962 & 1964.

Mansén, Elisbeth, *Sveriges Historia, 1721–1830,* Norstedts, Stockholm, 2011.

Marklund, Andreas, *I hans hus, svensk manlighet i historisk belysning,* Boréa bokförlag, Umeå, 2004.

Norlind, Tobias, *Svenska allmogens lif, folksed, folktro och folkdiktning,* Bohlin & Co., Stockholm, 1912.

Pettersson, B. & Svanberg, I., *Människan och Naturen Ethnobiologi i Sverige* Whalström & Widstrand, 2001

Rosengren, Annette, När resan var ett äventyr, Natur och Kultur, Stockholm, 1979.

SMHI, weather reports from 1883–84, SMHI, Norrköping.

Spinnhuset vid svingeln, www.alltidgot.com.

Svanström, Yvonne, *Offentliga kvinnor, Prostitution i Sverige 1812–1918,* Ordfront.

Sveriges järnvägsmuseum, online.

Takman, John, Föräldralösa spädbarn i Stockholm 1888, I *samhällets* utkant, 1989.

Taussi Sjöberg, Marja, *Durvans Fångar, Brottet, Straffet o Människan i 1800-talets Sverige,* Författarförlaget, 1986.

Taussi Sjöberg, Marja, *Skiljas, Trolovning, äktenskap och skilsmässa på 1800-talet,* Författarförlaget, 1988.

Taussi Sjöberg, Marja, information via e-mail.

Stolt, Jonas, *Forntida Minnen och Tidsskriften 1875–1878,* Oskarshamn, 1956.

Tillhagen, Carl-Herman, *Barnet i folktron,* LTs fölag, Stockholm, 1983.

Wrangel, Ewert, ed., *Svenska Folket Genom Tiderna,* volume 8, Tidskriftsförlaget, Malmö, 1939.

Wrangel, Ewert, ed., *Svenska Folket Genom Tiderna,* volume 9, tidskriftsförlaget, Malmö, 1939.

Åberg, Alf, *När byarna sprängdes,* LTs Förlag, Stockholm, 1953.

Örebro läns museum, *Från bergslag och bondebygd, Kvinnor i Örebro län,* 2003.

Made in the USA
Columbia, SC
11 July 2017